Bob Broeg's

REDBIRDS

A Century of Cardinals' Baseball

Introductions: Stan Musial
Jack Buck

RiverCity
Publishers
L I M I T E D

Saint Louis, Missouri

Other Books by Bob Broeg

Don't Bring That Up   *(A.S. Barnes 1946)*
Stan Musial: The Man's Own Story (*Doubleday* 1964)
Super Stars of Baseball (*The Sporting News* 1971)
Ol' Mizzou (*Strode* 1974)
We Saw Stars (*Bethany* 1976)
Football Greats (*Bethany* 1977)
The Man Stan: Musial...Then and Now (*Bethany* 1977)
The Pilot Light and the Gas House Gang (*Bethany* 1980)

Photographs Courtesy of:

St. Louis Post-Dispatch
The Sporting News
National Baseball Hall of Fame, Cooperstown, NY

First Printing May 1981
Second Printing June 1981
Third Printing November 1981
Fourth Printing April 1982
Fifth Printing November 1982 (1982 World Champions)
Sixth Printing April 1983

Published by River City Publishers, Limited, St. Louis, Missouri.

Printed in the United States of America

Library of Congress Catalog Card Number: 81-50102

ISBN: 0-933150-02-4

Statistical research by William J. Miller

Designed by Jerry Moore and Janet Moody

The Lineup

Dedicated To:
The Old Flash, Stan the Man and other heroes—yours and mine—in the Cardinals' march to a century's drums as one of baseball's most colorful, craziest, often best and occasionally worst ball clubs. Happy reading and rooting!

Infield Practice

Whether "Braig of St. Louis," as I'd pronounce it, or "Brogue of Boston," as Casey Stengel phrased it long after both of us left New England for even happier days, I've been lucky.

As a boy, I was fortunate enough to watch a leathery-looking pitching master, Pete Alexander, throw short-armed strikes as accurately as if home plate were a tin-cup target. I saw Rogers Hornsby hit line drives with a comet's tail on them. My boyhood favorite, Frank Frisch, made diving stops as his cap came off, proving you can't keep a round hat on a square head. And my baseball-writing favorite traveling companion, Stan Musial, would let out on the bases as if he were Lou Brock or Garry Templeton.

I could thrill to Dizzy Dean, who looked then as if he needed another meal even more than another victory, pitching the Gas House Gang to a pennant. Pepper Martin was a sight to behold—good and dirty. And I

delighted to watch Bob Gibson strike out seventeen men in the spotlight of a World Series. And to see "The Wiz," as I personally tab Templeton, prove to me that even if I enjoy the past, I'm not blind about the present or future.

I'm lucky, you see, because Erby Young, an imaginative, young idea man who now has prodded me into three books, face-guarded me into writing this book now rather than waiting until I retire. Heck, I might forget one day to inhale and exhale.

I always did want to write an informal history of the Cardinals, concentrating more on the people than the teams. I wanted to write about the spearcarriers as well as the stars. And I wanted to use plenty of pictures, because readers like them and they best describe the person about whom you're writing.

Erby liked that idea even more than I did. I'm grateful to him and to the man who designed this book

tastefully and with talent, Professor Jerry Moore, and his most able associate, Janet Moody. I appreciated, also, the editor's pencil of Irene Miller and, speaking of Ladies' Day, a bow to my wife, Lynne, who, as I said in a dedication to Bethany's book, *The Pilot Light and the Gas House Gang,* understands that a writer must write.

This is MY book. I hope my observations are right, not wrong. If, for instance, you think I'm not kind enough to Branch Rickey, certainly not so obsequious as his cult, I did feel that I admired his accomplishments even if I didn't respect him so much as others did.

Although I wasn't here or with Colonel George Custer when the Cardinals were playing ball the day the famous frontier fighter ran into too many Indians who weren't from Cleveland, I tried to be fair, "fair" as in "just," not as in "mediocre," I hope. That's about the best epitaph I think any newspaperman could want.

Batting Practice

Editor's Note: *STAN MUSIAL, seven times National League batting champion and three times its Most Valuable Player, held into the 1980's the league record for both base hits (3630) and doubles (725). En route to first-year eligible election to the Hall of Fame, he hit the most All-Star game home runs (six), played on four pennant winners and general-managed the Cardinals to the 1967 world championship. After years in the restaurant and hotel business, in 1980 he became president of the Steamers, St. Louis's indoor soccer team.*

Timing is important, timing even beyond trying to hit a baseball. As a player, I'd beat a coat hanger on a clubhouse chair or play a slide whistle to stay loose before a game. Timing can turn a tradition into a dynasty, which I'm sure Gussie Busch and the brewery would have done if Anheuser-Busch had bought the Cardinals about twenty-five years sooner.

When the brewery got into baseball, you couldn't beg, borrow or Lou Brock a player if you hadn't developed him, unless, that is, you were fortunate enough to deal talent for talent. If only the "Big Eagle" and his stockholders had controlled the ball club earlier. . .

Take, for instance, the 1940s. We won four pennants and never finished lower than a close second for nine years. What if the Cardinals' ownership hadn't traded Johnny Mize or sold Walker Cooper or Murry Dickson for cash?

With big John teeing off on that short right field at old Sportsman's Park, W. Cooper lending batting power and catching experience and Dickson winning often enough—or, at least, not beating us—I think we could have swept through the decade. That's right. Like the New York Yankees at their best.

The Cardinals DO have a rich, colorful tradition, as caught by Bob Broeg in *Redbirds*, a book that covers National League baseball as well as Terry Moore and Marty Marion used to cover center field and shortstop. As well, too, as Pepper Martin, Lou Brock and Garry Templeton covered the bases.

But the Cardinals would have won even more if their ownership had been more substantial or more possessive, willing to do anything to win.

In the peak period of Branch Rickey and Sam Breadon, aptly described by Broeg in one chapter as "The Odd Couple," the Cardinals began a farm system to compete with the rich. Instead, invariably, they wound up selling ball players to the competition. I would imagine a sportsman like Busch, who could get almost as angry at losing a gin-rummy set or a jumping-horse ribbon as at seeing a brewery threaten to out-produce his, would have hoarded his baseball blue ribbons. He would have established a trophy case of championships.

I played for Mr. Busch when he paid me even more than I asked. (I asked for $91,000 in 1958, and he decided to make me the first six-figure player—$100,000—in National League history.) Now, I'd like to play for Gussie in the era of free-agency. I'd probably have wound up with a small brewery or his sumptuous estate, Grant's Farm.

Seriously, I have no complaints. I had a couple of early holdouts, only one of which endured. From it, in 1947, I got from Sam Breadon my most significant raise, a post-war increase from $13,500 in 1946 to $31,000 a year. I'd had a big season in the outfield, moving to first base to solve a problem, and hit .365.

Actually, Mr. Breadon had his problems, as Broeg relates in the book. He had been a poor man who feared ever wanting again. They say he could be so tight at times that when electric clocks came in and traveling secretary Clarence Lloyd bought one, Mr. Breadon suggested he pull the electric plug at night. I don't know about that. I do know that even though St. Louis didn't draw before World War II as it has since, he could be generous if it counted. To illustrate, he told

Lloyd's successor, Leo Ward, never to question a player's signed meal ticket at a hotel if the tab was for food, not liquor.

Before I came aboard, he had had some really tough contract sessions, such as the historic salary fight with Rogers Hornsby mentioned in this book. Still, I found Breadon willing to sacrifice seats. When he wanted to know why we didn't hit too well on Sundays, I pointed out that Phil Wrigley had given his hitters a better batting background at Chicago's Wrigley Field, eliminating the problem of trying to pick up a white ball coming out of a white-shirted background. He then had the center-field section of bleacher seats at old Sportsman's Park roped off permanently.

Mr. Breadon could be cold, sometimes naive, but he was a straight-arrow guy. He was naive to think when good Cardinal teams weren't drawing well in the early 1930s that Detroit's American League franchise would let a colorful National League rival enter its territory. He was briskly cold, all right, when a Ponca City oil man named Lew Wentz sat in Breadon's office and haggled over the ball club's value. Breadon set a price. Wentz vacillated. Breadon said he'd give the visitor thirty minutes to make up his mind. A half-hour later, glancing at his watch, Breadon turned those blue eyes on a man who obviously thought this was poker-table bluffing and said coldly, "Sorry, Mr. Wentz, time's up."

The Man and the Flash: The author's two favorite players of a generation apart, Frank Frisch (right) and Stan Musial, both Baseball Hall of Fame members, get together for a laugh and a cold one.

In my holdout into March, 1947, after I had turned down big money to jump to Mexico the previous summer, the Cardinals' manager then, Eddie Dyer, finally effected a compromise between Mr. Breadon's original $21,000 offer and the $37,000 I'd asked for. After we had signed, my wife Lil and I were going in to dinner at the club's hotel in St. Petersburg, Florida. When Mr. Breadon walked into the room, we asked him to join us. He did and seemed to have a good time. But when I asked for our dinner checks, including his, he would not let me pay for his dinner. Yet, he wouldn't pay for ours, either! He's an unforgettable person in *Redbirds*.

When the Cardinals played the former St. Louis Browns of the American League in the city's one-and-only streetcar World Series (1944), Lil and I lived with young son Dick at the Fairground Hotel, located near the ballpark. Lil listened to the whoops and hollers, to neighborhood commotion and conversation. Surprised, she said, "Why, this is a Browns' town!"

It wasn't, really. By then, however, the Cardinals had made victory an old hat, having won eight of their twelve pennants. The Browns, pure underdogs, just had won their first American League flag after forty-three years. As Bob Broeg points out, the four straight pennants won back there in the late 1880s when the American Association was a major league were achieved by lineal antecedents of the National League. Still, the name "Browns" did have understandable allure to St. Louis graybeards. Confusing? Not if you read *Redbirds*.

Although in recent years the Cardinals haven't enjoyed the success St. Louis-area fans deserve, I'm glad Bob Broeg wrote the book. He has lived much of it and traveled the road. I sit in with him as a member of the National Baseball Hall of Fame's Veterans' Committee. So I know that when he analyzes players, he does it fairly, whether they were friends or strangers.

Broeg deserved the recognition when he was honored last summer at Cooperstown, New York, with the J.G. Taylor Spink award, the baseball writers' presentation for meritorious service as a writer. He won an amusing tribute from Ted Williams.

"Teddy Ball Game," who says what he thinks as firmly as he hit a baseball, shook Broeg's hand and said, "You're okay. You deserve the award, which I wouldn't say to many writers. Yep, you're okay—even if you are a 'Stan Musial man.' "

When it comes down to championship champagne cases, I like to think I can call 'em as I see 'em, too, if not quite so flamboyantly as Williams. I meant it when I said the year after the Cardinals won a pennant without me (1964) that they couldn't have won with me in left field. Lou Brock, after all, came to town like a whirling dervish. I mean it, too, when I say that I hope the spirit of this book—the success and tradition of the Cardinals—will rub off on players paid so well that they need extra incentives.

I'm not preaching. But even though I've seen baseball go from day to night, from regional to national in the majors, from trains to planes and from cabbage leaves under the helmet in hot weather to air-conditioned clubhouses and even dugouts, I've never seen any change as remarkable as the reserve-clause elimination. Free-agency option has created chaos.

Understand, please, that I'm more astonished by the expensive and expansive salaries given fringe players and marginal free-agent athletes than I am over the paychecks of the stars. I wonder most about the length of contracts.

Even though I believe I played with enthusiasm and consistency, still I remember a three-year contract signed with Sam Breadon. Even though I had a long way to go for security, I honestly found it hard to rely on pride to provide full concentration early in the contract. (Editor's Note: Poor Stan! All he did those three years was to bat .357, .347 and .365.)

Of the super-stars and others—and I enjoyed meeting or renewing acquaintance with many of the "others" in *Redbirds*—not many ever got multiple-year contracts in the so-called "good ol' days." Most of them, somehow, still had a lot of fun playing, as much fun as I hope you'll have reading about them.

Still, aware how tough it was to make a baseball buck for the big boss as well as the little one before the new stadium and different times turned around a town and shrank a dollar from the size of a manhole cover into a molecule, I can't help smiling, particularly when I think of how Sam Breadon would feel if he were involved in present-day baseball ownership. In the language of dear friend "Chilly" Doyle, a boyhood newspaper favorite I enjoyed in the old *Pittsburgh Sun-Telegraph* before I met him when I played ball, "If Sam Breadon were alive today, he'd turn over in his grave."

A Press-Booth View

Editor's Note: *JACK BUCK, sports director of St. Louis's Columbia Broadcasting System station, KMOX Radio, has aired Cardinals' ball games since a successful look-hear date in 1953. He's a CBS football network star who also has broadcast or televised main sports' All-Star games, World Series and Super Bowls. In addition, war-wounded John Francis Buck has appeared on all networks in all sports except one. He can't call horse races because he's color blind.*

If I live as long as some of the colorful old crocks about whom Bob Broeg writes in *Redbirds*, a history of a ball club as bright as the male beauty of its species, I'll never forget my first game as a broadcaster for the Cardinals.

Like a ball player, they called me up from the farms. I'd done American Association games in Columbus, where I'd gone to Ohio State and then at Rochester, home of St. Louis's long-time International League team. So I sat under the tin-roofed, cramped old pressbox of New York's historic Polo Grounds and broadcast an historic game.

Facing Sal Maglie, one of the top National League righthanders at the time, the Cardinals fell behind the New York Giants that day in 1953, 11-0. From that early-inning deficit, however, the Redbirds rallied, and, using two home runs by Solly Hemus and one by Enos Slaughter, they came from behind spectacularly,14-12.

I've covered some great games and some lousy ones since then, but never one to match it for ability to offset the most devastating deficit.

Sure, Bob Broeg mentions it and many others, too, but, really, he doesn't make this a game-by-game or play-by-play recall, but, rather, a one-man recollection of Cardinals from Alpha Omega to Alpha Brazle, from Chris Von der Ahe to Gussie Busch.

I wouldn't say Broeg has been around since Hernando DeSoto discovered more water than he or his troops could drink—the Mississippi—but I know why Bob missed George Washington Bradley's first National League no-hitter in 1876. It was BB's day off.

He covers the spearcarriers as well as the super-stars, and I'm glad. When I was a kid trying to rub two nickels together with odd jobs in Cleveland, the first Indians' player I met was Oscar Grimes. He was only a utility man, but he came into a drive-in, short-order joint where I was a carhop. I was thrilled.

So maybe here you'll come across a little-remembered Redbird to whom you had an attachment. Time does make even rich memories dusty, and the Cardinals' tradition was established even before I was a kid rooting for ball clubs that had two chances—little and none. I was born in Red Sox territory, Holyoke, Massachusetts, and grew up finally in Cleveland.

There, I still rooted for Jimmy Foxx, whose muscles even had muscles. I saw Foxxie hit a home run in the 1935 All-Star game at Cleveland Stadium when the left-field stands were as far back as Broeg's memory and recollections.

But I wasn't there the summer afternoon in 1936 when the Gas House Gang came to town to play Cleveland for charity and when eighteen-year-old Bob Feller made his professional debut in the exhibition game. That's the day Broeg's boyhood idol, Frank Frisch, watched Feller warm up with unbelievable velocity and absolutely no control.

The old Flash turned to a kid outfielder and asked him if he'd ever played the infield. No, the rookie hadn't. "Well, you are today," said Frisch, eager to live another day.

Broeg skipped that one here because he covered it in a recent book, *The Pilot Light and the Gas House Gang*. He also skips much of what he wrote with Stan Musial and me for Bethany Press in *We Saw Stars*.

This is a new book with new pictures, a story that proves a good picture IS worth 10,000 words. After all, not even a writer as windy as Broeg could tell all he knew about everyone who participated in the Cardinals' first century as the old Browns and the new Redbirds.

I'm glad he took time for the more obscure in the minds of the moment—obscure only because of time and not lack of talent—to write about (and to display) Austin McHenry. I thought I just didn't know enough early St. Louis

background to understand McHenry, but, then, I found that the Cardinals' veteran publicity director, Jim Toomey, didn't know about McHenry until Branch Rickey explained it himself.

Broeg, too, needed an interview with Rickey himself, when Bob was a hot-shot high school editor, to learn about McHenry, a right-handed-hitting left fielder who played for the Cardinals when Rickey was the club's manager. McHenry hit .350 in 1921 but suffered a brain tumor a year later and was dead at only twenty-seven.

That story is told succinctly, but well, I believe, in a book that doesn't gild the lily. Whether in triumph or tragedy, from rags to riches, from failure to success, the history bears one man's opinion, which is the way it should be.

BB and the Buckeye: "BB," as the guys with whom he works at the Post-Dispatch call Bob Broeg (left), is interviewed over the Cardinals' flagship station, KMOX Radio, by his friend, the Redbirds' nationally known play-by-play broadcaster, Jack Buck. Buck's "Jack the Buckeye" label is from his days at Ohio State.

For instance, Broeg respected Branch Rickey's baseball brilliance far more than some of the old man's methods. None, of course, is involved with Mr. Rickey's undeniable contributions in establishing baseball's first farm system and, particularly, in re-opening baseball's doors clanked prison-shut to blacks in the last century.

Like me, Broeg has great regard for Bob Gibson, hailed by many of us, including Musial, as the greatest competitor we ever saw. Despite the need to cover 100 years of baseball, both Gibson and exciting Lou Brock thread strongly through three of the last four chapters of the book.

Even though Broeg enjoys nostalgia, which is obvious from columns written for the *Post-Dispatch* and for *The Sporting News* and yarns spun on KMOX, he's not completely a four-eyed ostrich. He believes, for example, that, avoiding mishap, Garry Templeton well could be the best ball player the Cardinals ever developed.

Branch Rickey, who returned briefly to the ball club shortly before Bing Devine's "El Birdos" were so successful in the mid-1960s, came up with a noble idea one time. He wanted to fire Leo Ward as traveling secretary and to name me to the job!

It was nice of Mr. Rickey to think well of old JB, but, board member Mark Eagleton, Sr., said at a club directors' meeting, just what 'n blazes did the traveling secretary have to do with winning or losing a pennant? (Ward was an avowed "Sam Breadon man" when Breadon owned the Cardinals earlier and Rickey was general manager.)

As for me, I liked the flattery and confidence, but I wouldn't have liked the salary. The difference between front-office salary and players' pay was funny even before removal of the reserve clause made the sky the guys' financial moon.

I hope the players as well as the Cardinals' extremely loyal fans will read *Redbirds*. Bob Broeg might have timing as terrible as the trouble many people have in pronouncing his name, which rhymes with "plague." But having tasted with him at least the milk-and-honey of the Cardinals' more recent success, I hope that the Redbirds fly like fierce falcons to the top perch and stay and glare there, challenging anybody who dares to knock off a feather.

Winning never bores me.

1

Comiskey und der Poss Bresident

No, it's just simply not true that Lewis and Clark formed St. Louis's first baseball battery before Thomas Jefferson's doughty duo traveled up the Missouri River to determine whether the President had made the biggest steal at least until Lou Brock. The fact is, though, if someone proved that Meriwether Lewis and William Clark warmed up with a little levee-side pitch-and-catch at St. Louis or St. Charles before striking out for the vast unknown, it wouldn't surprise me.

I've never quite got over the wonder of realizing that a little more than a half-century later, St. Louis was so civilized that they were playing big league baseball here in 1876 on the windy, warm June date on which Colonel George Armstrong Custer and so many members of the famed Seventh Cavalry Regiment were wiped out by s-o-o many Sioux on the banks of the Montana Territory's Little Big Horn.

The frontier then was as far-flung as one of Babe Ruth's famous home-run blasts or Pepper Martin's wild throws from third base. But, then, baseball's own frontier also is obscured in the dim dust of distance and time. Nobody ever stopped playing a refined version of an old British game called rounders, stepped back and decided that he was inventing something new.

Although baseball obviously wasn't invented in 1839 at Cooperstown, New York, by Abner Doubleday, then a West Point plebe who would become a Civil War general, it should have originated there, if only because the Lake Otsego town, home of the National Baseball Hall of Fame and Museum, is a scenic setting. Most certainly the Johnny Appleseed of the game was Alexander Cartwright, an engineer who took the game from the Elysian Fields of Hoboken, New Jersey. There, in 1845, he devised permanent standards of nine men on a side, nine innings to a game and that agonizing ninety-foot race between man and ball to each base. Cartwright took baseball all the way to Hawaii.

When it first came to St. Louis is certainly as mystifying as where the game really began. For this essentially photographic history, accept the fact that baseball was played on the west Mississippi banks of the old French fur-trading post before the Civil War, in an era which saw the beginning of old Sportsman's Park at Grand and Dodier Streets that endured for a solid century.

The game was different then, painfully so, because even though the early baseball before the cork center (1910) was almost marshmallow-soft by comparison, it stung bare hands. Until late in the nineteenth century, pitchers delivered the ball underhanded, even for a time having to throw it where the hitter wanted it, and the catcher stood back, a safe and sane distance from the plate.

Pitching distances were shorter until the final increase in 1893 to the modern sixty-feet-six-inches. Errors outnumbered hits, which were frequent, and hits outnumbered runs, which also were so numerous that as "recently" as 1907—thirty years afterward—a nostalgic anniversary dinner was held to salute the recollection of a game played in 1877 in St. Louis.

In what now would be regarded as a good game, yet hardly historic, but considered in that bare-fingered, high-scoring era a masterpiece of baseball perfection, the old St. Louis Maroons and Syracuse Stars played a fifteen-inning scoreless game. No errors were recorded; St. Louis got only two hits and Syracuse six.

By that time, St. Louis already was in the year-old National League, conceived by an imaginative Chicagoan named William Hulbert. A St. Louis lawyer named C. Orrick Bishop, an enthusiastic boyhood right fielder, had drawn up the league's first constitution, binding reserve clause and contract form. Judge Bishop, son of a former Virginia slaveholder, lived until 1929. At a ripe old eighty-seven, he had survived to see St. Louis begin National League domination with pennants in 1926 and 1928.

The Brown Stockings, actual antecedents of the current Cardinals, gave St. Louis its first professional team in 1874, five years after Cincinnati's historic first all-pros, the unbeaten Red Stockings of '69, were organized.

The St. Louis team, made up of local amateurs, was kicked around so often pros were imported to form a team capitalized for $20,000. A prominent St. Louis real estate man, John R. C. Lucas, was most active financially as the Browns set up shop downtown at 406 North Fourth Street, a couple of blocks away from the cigar-and-sporting goods shop operated at 619 Olive Street by S. Mason Graffen.

Graffen managed the Browns when the National League began in 1876, a year after the rival Maroons, led by a home-town player named—no foolin'—Joe Blong, folded because of financial difficulties. St. Louis's co-founding National League cities included Chicago, Cincinnati, Philadelphia, Boston, Brooklyn, Louisville and Hartford.

A St. Louis pitcher named George Washington Bradley pitched the National League's first no-hitter that first season in which Custer lost his command and his life. Bradley no-hit Hartford in a most impressive

season, 45 and 19. Yeah, most impressive because the record by which St. Louis finished second to A. G. Spalding's Chicago Nationals was exactly the same—45-19!

So Spalding, a pitcher-manager who would make a larger name for himself in the sporting goods game, flashed $2000 in 1877 and St. Louis lost "Grin" Bradley, as they called him. The twenty-one-year-old kid from Reading, Pennsylvania, went from great to mediocre, but he lived long enough at Philadelphia to see the Cardinals beat the Athletics in the 1931 World Series.

The 1876 team captained by first baseman Harmon Dehlman, who faded faster than any Lewis-and-Clark era resistance to Jefferson's Louisiana Purchase, made a good showing. But St. Louis lost a chance to equal Chicago's stature as the only National League charter without a lapse in the league membership. Lucas and Bishop walked off in disgust a year later when they tried to improve a fourth-place finish behind Boston. They had obtained six talented players, but four of them from Louisville were exposed as having contrived to throw ball games.

So St. Louis was without big league ball until 1882, when two of the most colorful names in the city's early baseball annals led to the one moment of glory until the Cardinals achieved success nearly forty years later. Charley Comiskey came to town, and Chris Von der Ahe stuck his big red nose, his money and his opinionated Dutch accent into baseball.

First in Shoes: First to take his foot off first base, too, and to give the early-day "Cardinals" pennants when they were the American Association Browns, Charley Comiskey. They called him "Commy" when it wasn't a dirty word and, later, as he founded the Chicago White Sox, the Irishman became the "Old Roman."

In 1881 Al Spink, who founded *The Sporting News* with J. G. Taylor Spink's father, had spotted Comiskey, a tall first baseman-outfielder, with the Dubuque Rabbits, a semi-professional team. A new major league, the American Association, was coming, and Spink wanted Comiskey here. To help finance the franchise, Spink talked fast to Von der Ahe, who reasoned shrewdly that the beer business at his saloon near the Grand Avenue ball park would be better if organized baseball came back to town.

Von der Ahe was a character, Comiskey a clever baseball man. Credited generally as the first man to play first base with a foot off the bag, the Irishman knew talent. He put together four successive pennant winners for Von der Ahe, 1885 through '88. Ultimately, the "Old Roman," as Comiskey became known, helped build the American League as founder of the Chicago White Sox franchise.

"Commy" developed championship ball clubs, but he was inconsistent. At one point, as a player, he fought for the Players' League, which sought briefly to combat the financial pressures of the restrictive reserve clause. Later, when Von der Ahe needed help, Comiskey was generous. Yet, as a clubowner, he paid so poorly that members of his great 1917 world champions threw the 1919 World Series to Cincinnati. Eight of the so-called "Black Sox" were barred for life. The most brilliant, nine-season hitting star, "Shoeless Joe" Jackson, career average .356, was an illiterate who received only $6000.

In the early 1880s, however, Comiskey worked wonders with the old Browns, whose stars included a hard-hitting pitching ace, Bob Caruthers, and an early-day Rabbit Maranville as an infield pixy, third baseman Arlie Latham. The old Brownies even gave the Association its only pre-World Series championship with a seven-game victory in 1886 over Cap Anson's powerful National League champions, the White Stockings, now the Cubs.

In the final game played before a king-sized crowd, 10,000 at the old ball park here, Anson's athletes led by 3-0 into the eighth inning over Caruthers and the Browns. But St. Louis finally scored a run and had

A Mighty Mite: Bob Caruthers—"Parisian Bob"—was only 5-7, 138 pounds, but he had a 218-99 record for nine years through 1892. Two straight years, 1886-87, he batted .334 and .357.

two on when Latham stepped up to hit.

Latham, labeled "The Freshest Man on the Earth," proved that the nickname fit like the modern-day batting (or golfer's) glove they used in the field then. Little Arlie played it like a real-life Casey at the Bat with a happier ending. He stepped up, silenced the roaring crowd and announced:

"Don't get nervous, folks; I'll tie it up."

He did. Latham's two-run triple sent the game into extra innings. In St. Louis's tenth, Curt Welch, an outfielder, stuck a shoulder into a pitch and started to first base, but Mike "King" Kelly, Chicago's prominent "Slide, Kelly, Slide" catcher, beefed, and the umpire ordered Welch to bat over.

Angrily, Welch returned and singled. With one out, he had reached third. Clarkson uncorked a high-and-tight pitch that eluded Kelly. Happily, as the home audience applauded, Welch came in with what became known as the "$15,000 slide."

Anson had insisted on a winner-take-all series, and Comiskey, gulping for fear of Von der Ahe's wrath, had agreed. To his relief, Chris was as breezy as the open barouches pulled by horses draped with brightly colored blankets as he drove his uniformed team around town in 1887. The blankets read, "St. Louis Browns, Champions of the World."

"The Freshest Man on Earth": Arlie Latham, comically talented third baseman of the early championship St. Louis club, went to England with the Canadians in 1917 to teach the British that baseball wasn't cricket.

Ach, "Der Poss Bresident," as Von der Ahe liked to describe himself, was eating high on the head cheese then. He loved the limelight, and when Spalding sold Kelly to Boston in 1887 for $10,000, an astronomical sum then, Chris thought he could do the same. He began to sell his stars. Stubbornly, too, when Comiskey was offered a handsome $7500 in 1892 to manage Cincinnati, Von der Ahe refused to match the offer. Himmel, what did the Irishman know about the game that he didn't! When the Browns were running rampant, Von der Ahe could walk off dramatically after each game with a wheelbarrow loaded with money bags, flanked by armed guards.

"Too late schmart," as the old low-Dutch proverb puts it, Chris began to put on promotions to help his dwindling attraction. He offered horse racing, a merry-go-round, a beer garden, a chute-the-chute boat ride from tower to artificial lake, even an all-girl band, the Silver Cornets, dressed about as interestingly as the mores-and-morals of the day would permit.

Although a combination of a senior-citizen Bill Veeck and a junior-grade Gussie Busch of his time—uh-huh, and with a bit of P. T. Barnum's theatrics thrown in—Von der Ahe was not equipped for life's own chute-the-chutes. His W. C. Fields proboscis lit up like a Christmas tree as he dallied over drinks and dames.

Seven successive years after the Browns returned to the National

Der Poss Bresident: Chris Von der Ahe, who hit the heights and the shoots—the chute-the-chutes, too—as a colorful saloon keeper "too late schmart" with his four-time champions.

League in 1892, after the American Association folded as a major league, Von der Ahe finished twelfth in a twelve-team league twice and got as high as ninth just once. Der Poss Bresident changed managers so often that one year he had SIX.

Finally, a fire destroyed the Vandeventer-and-Natural Bridge ball park, later Robison Field, to which Von der Ahe desperately had moved in the return to the National League. (The park had been put up by Henry V. Lucas, old John R. C. Lucas's nephew, when the younger Lucas nobly sought in 1885-86 to establish the Union Association without player contract restrictions.)

For Von der Ahe, the end came when he couldn't even draw enough with the "Pretzel Battery," a popular Germanic combination of lefthanded pitcher Theodore Breitenstein and catcher Heinie Peitz. The National League and many creditors forced Chris to sell out after the 1898 season for only $33,000.

The Cardinals, as the Browns had been rechristened, played a benefit for the old showman in 1908, but he was broke when he died in 1918. All he had then except for memories of better days with Comiskey was the huge gravesite statue he had had erected for himself earlier in Bellefontaine Cemetery when the suds-and-cents were flowing.

If I only had room for more on Der Poss Bresident, but maybe one story will do. Once at an American Association meeting, Von der Ahe complained in high dudgeon to his fellow clubowners that they had scheduled too many of his home games on days when it rained.

Huffed old Chris in his heavily accented South Side Dutch, "I don't vant to be greedy, but next year let it rain in Zinzinnati or on that 'dumkopf' in Baltimore (Von der Horst)."

The Pretzel Battery: Theodore Breitenstein (left) and Henry Peitz weren't baseball's best, but Ted and Heinie went together in St. Louis and Cincinnati by the Germanic nickname that fit them as nicely as a good head of suds.

2

Lady Bee & the Birds

King of the Mountain: Denton True "Cy" Young, winningest pitcher ever (511), spent two of his 22 seasons (1899-1900) with the Cardinals. Old Tuscarawas, elected to baseball's Hall of Fame its second year (1937), had only one beef. He thought he won 512!

Years ago when the Philadelphia Phillies' "Slidin' Billy" Hamilton was the Lou Brock of his day, a good batter and an even better base-runner, Hamilton bragged to a big Cleveland pitcher that the previous day he had fouled off twenty-nine straight against Baltimore. The husky Cleveland pitcher nodded. First time up that afternoon against him, Hamilton fouled off three successive pitches. The Cleveland pitcher walked down toward the plate and said:

"Listen to me, Billy; I'm putting the next pitch right over the heart of the plate. If you foul it off, the next one goes right into your ear."

Years later before his death at age eighty-nine in 1955, Denton "Cy" Young, the winningest pitcher in baseball history, would remember with a smile:

"Hamilton got the message. He sent the next pitch on a weak dribble to second base."

Young, who should have been called the "Oldest," was durable as well as baseball's most consistent pitcher. From the gloveless era of the pitcher's box in 1890, when the distance to home plate was ten feet shorter, his career spanned twenty-two seasons.

And he had won, as a cub reporter found out when the old sod-buster from Tuscarawas County in Ohio's fertile hill country was a watery-eyed, pipe-puffing old man. The kid from the press wondered if Young had ever played ball.

The old man, amused and annoyed, said softly:

"Sonny, I won more games than you'll ever see."

True, which, by the way, was Cy's middle name. He won 511 games, far more than any other pitcher, including five seasons over thirty and eleven more over twenty, two of these in St. Louis.

Young's two seasons with the Cardinals, sandwiched neatly almost halfway between his two trips each with Cleveland and Boston ball clubs, resulted from one of baseball's oddities.

When Chris Von der Ahe sold out, a St. Louis attorney bought the ball club for the Robison brothers, who had operated streetcar companies in Fort Wayne, Indiana, and Cleveland. Frank DeHaas Robison and brother Stanley Mathew also owned the Spiders, Cleveland's ball club, then in the National League.

Such syndicate or twin-team ownership would not be tolerated now. What the Robisons did next

Of the Brothers Robison: Stanley Mathew Robison and elder brother, Frank, actually the more authoritative, bought the Cardinals through the blind cover of an attorney. The former Ft. Wayne, Ind., and Cleveland streetcar-company executives helped change uniform covers and, above all, ball clubs. The Robisons made the granddaddy of trades—entire teams.

was even more startling than Frank's opulent habit in a period when a silver dollar looked as big as a jelly doughnut. (He drew out $100 every morning and sought to spend it before calling it a night.)

The Robisons simply—or not so simply—traded their entire ball clubs. Annoyed that the Spiders hadn't drawn, they sent their big-name ball club to St. Louis for the poor-relation Browns.

Overnight, overjoyed St. Louis wound up—lock, stock and jock strap—with a ball club that had the likes of the mighty Young as a pitcher, Bobby Wallace as an outstanding shortstop, and Jesse Burkett and Emmett Heidrick among the out-fielders. Why, Young even had his favorite catcher, Lou Criger, and there was also Ossie Schreckengost, who later would catch the great George "Rube" Waddell for Connie Mack at Philadelphia.

This was truly a marriage made in baseball heaven for St. Louis. "The Crab," i.e., Burkett, twice previously a .400 hitter, would bat a glossy .402 here. Wallace, who would spend the next twenty seasons in St. Louis, most of them in the American League when the NEW Browns came to town, batted .302, fielding flawlessly. And big Cy, short for Cyclone and not because of his bucolic appearance, won 26-15 and then 20-18 here.

The OLD Browns, who shuffled off from the Mississippi River to Lake Erie, en masse, were unbelievably inept in 1899. They won only twenty games and lost 134, the first of which was a memorable home opener in St. Louis for the NEW Browns or rather, former Spiders.

To get away from the brown taste left in the mouth because of Von der Ahe's last sad seasons, the Robisons brought out their ball club in bright red-trimmed uniforms, including red socks. There was, of course, already a team known as the

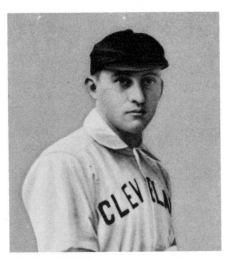

A Belting Best: Jesse "The Crab" Burkett, little lefthanded-hitting outfielder moved from Cleveland to St. Louis, became as a Cardinal the first of only three players (Ty Cobb and Rogers Hornsby) ever to hit .400 three times.

Mound City Landmark: A brilliant shortstop, Rhoderick "Bobby" Wallace spent 20 of his 25 major league playing seasons in the uniform of St. Louis's National League and American League ball clubs. He was 45 when he fielded his last ground ball in 1918.

Cincinnati Red Stockings, and when reporter Willie McHale of the old *St. Louis Republic* heard a woman fan remark, "Oh, what a lovely shade of cardinal," Mac put two and two together and came up with a new nickname.

Years later when Branch Rickey was a luncheon speaker and a woman host had perched a red bird on a bat as a souvenir place card, the new nickname was switched from mere color to a perky bird. It was an apt nickname, because the cardinal is seen so frequently in Missouri that it ought to be the state's official bird.

In 1899, to get back to Cy Young and associates, a record crowd estimated as high as 18,000 by Fred Lieb, author of G. P. Putnam's 1943 history of the Cardinals, crammed Robison Field, despite a streetcar strike, for a delightful opener. Young handcuffed the "Exiles," as the transplanted old team had been tabbed in Cleveland, and the Cardinals cuffed 'em, 10-1.

The Cards got off to seven straight season-opening victories, a home-town National League record still not topped, but then they tailed off and finished fifth. When they could do little better in 1900 and won fewer games, manager Oliver Patrick Tebeau of St. Louis's Goose Hill district was fired.

Actually, even before the season, Frank Robison had offered the job to John McGraw, player-manager of the slick Baltimore Orioles, but McGraw turned him down. Still, when Baltimore, Louisville, Washington and Cleveland were cut as the National League reduced to eight clubs, McGraw had no choice. The clever-hitting, aggressive third

Man with a Mission: John J. McGraw, one of baseball's most famous and feared names as a tough-nut New York Giants' manager, won 10 pennants in 30 years. Before that, he starred for 16 seasons at third base, including one (1900) in St. Louis when he hit .344—and threw his uniform into the river.

baseman, who had a date with destiny in New York as a thirty-year manager, accepted his sale to St. Louis.

"Muggsy"—oops, he hated that nickname—would go only if he got $100 a game and if the hated, restrictive reserve clause were removed from his contract. "I'm going to stay only one season," cautioned McGraw, who felt his legs beginning to slip.

Belatedly, accompanied by his long-time friend and later bitter Brooklyn managerial rival, catcher Wilbert Robinson, McGraw arrived in early April. He played only ninety-nine games and reportedly wasn't too enthusiastic, because he knew that Cincinnati newspaperman Ban Johnson was planning to upgrade the Western League into the American League and to bring back Baltimore to big league status.

At his best or only so-so, "Little Napoleon" still was some ball player. He hit .344 for the Cardinals, but he was true to his word. Scarcely had the season ended when McGraw and Robinson were on a train back to the Chesapeake. Ceremoniously, as the train chug-chugged across the Eads Bridge, McGraw dumped his St. Louis baseball uniform into the Mississippi. So did me-too Robinson.

McGraw became manager at Baltimore, but he lasted little more than a season. His romance with Johnson was brief. The martinet was too tough on the umpires for Johnson. Ban would have liked McGraw in New York with the Highlanders, but Muggsy had other ideas. He jumped to the Giants in 1902 and won nine pennants, including four in a row.

Even though St. Louis had a race track across Natural Bridge—a prestigious jockey club in Fairground Park before reform five years later turned Missouri and the nation's fourth largest city conservative—the wagering McGraw didn't like St. Louis.

"To win in this heat," Muggsy muttered, "a ball club has to be at least twenty-five per cent better than any other team."

Cy Young didn't like the heat in St. Louis's kitchen either, but he liked a $600 raise offered him by Johnson to jump the tight-fisted National League to the new Boston Red Sox.

The National League then had a supposed $2400-a-player salary limit. Although Robison regarded himself as generous, he was staggered by the loss to Jimmy McAleer's Browns as the new American League team came to town from Milwaukee in 1902 with the old nickname. Burkett, Wallace and Heidrick jumped to the Browns, along with pitchers Jack Powell, Charley Harper and Willie Sudhoff and infielder Dick Padden. First baseman Dan McGann followed McGraw to Baltimore.

So—if you can follow the bouncing ball, Max—the new Browns finished second in the new league and the old Browns (Cardinals) sagged back to where they had been when they really WERE the old Browns.

Small wonder Frank Robison lost heart and interest. He even sent a young righthander named

Mordecai Brown to Chicago for what amounted to a box of Cracker Jack shortly thereafter, and "Three-Finger" Brown became a pitching ace of the Cubs' championship clubs of 1906-07-08.

When Frank Robison gave up the front-office ghost to brother Stanley in 1906, a couple of years before Frank died, Stan showed that he and his manager, Honest John McCloskey, could be as funny as the names of the one-time board of directors—Von der Ahe, Muckenfuss, Diddledock and Deck.

Robison No. 2 and his field foreman dispatched Babe Adams back to the minor leagues so that he could resurface at Pittsburgh and win three games in the 1909 World Series. No wonder the Cardinals didn't see the first division until the Twentieth Century was fourteen years old.

Even with bad ball clubs, there still was room for screwballs—capable ones, too, such as Harry "Slim" Sallee, a lanky lefthander. Slim was almost as colorful, if not nearly so good, as the rival Browns' elbow-tilting eccentric, Rube Waddell. "The Rube," acquired from a weary Connie Mack at Philly, was box-office worthy in a close fourth-place finish in 1908. From profits, Browns' owner Robert Lee Hedges built the first steel-and-concrete center section of Sportsman's Park. Rusty and rundown, that was still there when the Cardinals moved downtown to Busch Memorial Stadium in 1966.

While Waddell liked to chase old horse-drawn fire engines, Sallee, an off-season sheriff's deputy, liked the sunrise so much that he stayed up nights to help milkmen make their wee-hour rounds.

Another character who didn't burn the midnight oil but drank it was Arthur "Bugs" Raymond, who was good enough to post a 15-25 record for a 1908 team that was 'way last with only 49-105. Bugs figured in a deal by which John McGraw euchred the thin-talented Cardinals out of a fine young outfielder, Jack "Red" Murray, and Bugs.

Actually, McGraw was concerned about the future of his star catch-er, once big and fast Roger Bresnahan. Credited generally as the man in the mask who invented shinguards, Bresnahan, the "Duke of Tralee,"born in Ireland, had a big name. McGraw, loyal to his friend, unloaded him on an awe-stricken Stanley Robison for five years at a sizable salary for the period, $10,000.

"The Duke," only a part-time player with St. Louis at age twenty-nine, did return a managerial divi-dend after two seventh-place seasons. His 1911 Redbirds were so perky that they threatened for a time to make a pennant race of it before falling back to fifth, a heady one game over .500.

They even earned $165,000 on attendance of 447,768, more than pretty good for the times and smaller Robison Field. Besides, you could get in the ball park at times for just twenty-five cents or usually a half-buck up to a dollar. Some old debts

Screwball: St. Louis has had plenty, in-cluding Harry "Slim" Sallee, a lanky left-hander who was an imaginative insomniac. He liked to stay up nights to help milkmen make their rounds.

Don't Argue With a Lady: Roger Bresnahan tried and failed. As manager of the Cardinals, 1909-1912, the Duke of Tralee, as they called the Irishman, even got profane in his dispute and—zip!—he was gone. Big Duke invented shinguards when catching for John McGraw in New York. He lost his money in the stock market crash and wound up a turn-key in Toledo.

were paid off, but not by Stanley Robison. He died in spring training, only fifty-four years old.

The ball club was inherited by his niece, Helene Hathaway Robison Britton, his late brother Frank's daughter. Helene was a pretty woman with style. A press that might be dumb wasn't blind. Writers called her "Lady Bee."

Interested in women's rights, Mrs. Britton moved from Cleveland and, temporarily, installed her husband, Schuyler or "Skip," as they called him, a print-business executive, as front-office boss. But Skip skipped around and didn't spend enough time in the Britton mansion in the 4200 block of Lindell. Ultimately, they divorced, and Helene was a Mrs. Bigsby before her death years later in Philadelphia.

A good fan, Mrs. Britton brought petticoat-rule to baseball, actively running the ball club. In 1912 Bresnahan was acquitted of apparent sour-grapes talk of a "crooked" race charge made by Philadelphia's Horace Fogel. Fogel had insisted that the Duke hadn't played his best ball club against friend McGraw's Giants. Yet the episode left scars.

Lady Bee didn't like Bresnahan's rough, colorful language, acquired in years with the salty-tongued McGraw. She liked it less when the Cardinals slumped to sixth place. When Bresnahan raged profanely in a stormy post-mortem

Pretty Petticoat? Where?: That's what they called it in newspapers, then, "petticoat rule," when Helene Hathaway Robison Britton, Frank's young daughter, succeeded Uncle Stanley as president of the Cardinals.

at her house, "what-the-what any blankety-blank woman" could tell him about baseball, the livid boss lady took action.

Despite Rog's lengthy contract, she told club attorney James C. Jones to buy him out. Ultimately, St. Louis paid $20,000 as a compromise, and the Cubs bought Bresnahan's services as a player. Later (1915) he managed Chicago for one season.

The Cardinals, meanwhile, found themselves with a manager who would make a name for himself. Miller Huggins was a pasty-faced little second baseman, only five feet, six and a half inches tall and weighing just 140 pounds, but he was a scrappy giant. A lawyer from Cincinnati and a walk-wheedling leadoff man, he was a favorite of Lady Bee. Soon, "Hug" was everybody's favorite.

In 1914, even though dealing popular first baseman Ed Konetchy, the big Bohemian chocolate dropper as a former candy-factory kid, Huggins gave St. Louis its first significant National League success since the second-place finish in 1876. (After all, their Browns' antecedent victories were in the American Association.) Why, once, before finishing third, they even drew 27,000 for a doubleheader with the Giants. How? By putting 7000 in the grandstand, 10,000 in the bleachers and another 10,000 squeezed behind outfield ropes.

The '14 Cardinals finished third. Three years later, they did it again, 82-70. By then, Huggins had given up at second base to a fella named Rogers Hornsby, who'll be mentioned further.

Although happy, Helene Hathaway Robison Britton was also sad. A two-year battle against the Federal League, a third major league, had been expensive. World War I had frightening aspects. So Lady Bee asked lawyer Jones to find a buyer. Huggins leaped at the chance and hurried home to Cincinnati to ask the Fleischmann yeast family for help in raising the necessary $375,000.

When, however, Jones decided to compete, too, and scratched up the necessary cash from St. Louis businessmen and sports fans, the folks here got the club. Angrily, Huggins listened when J. G. Taylor Spink, Ban Johnson's friend who had named son Johnson for the American League founder, sold Hug on taking the job to help make the Yankees a match in New York for McGraw's Giants.

So Huggins became a persistent pennant winner before his untimely death in 1929 at just fifty. But he almost didn't get the Yankees' job. Jacob Ruppert, the brewer who owned the ball club, didn't like men who still wore peaked caps rather than hats.

An odd ending to an era, as odd almost as the way Bugs Raymond bowed out at New York, where McGraw finally gave him a rail ticket to nowhere, after the manager ordered him to the bullpen one day, and Raymond took the ball out a side gate and pawned it off for three shots of cheap-grade whiskey.

That was the end for a might-have-been pitcher, who was a two-town legend best remembered, probably, for the time McGraw cornered him with a private detective's report of what Raymond had consumed the previous night. Little Napoleon read off Bugs' order of the day (or night).

"Seven ryes, seven beer-chasers, cheese, eight onions and..."

"That's a lie, Mac," Bugs corrected indignantly. "I didn't have but two onions all evening!"

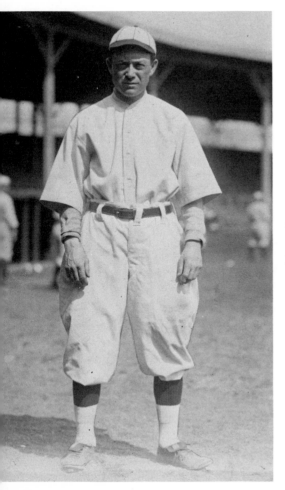

Little Hug: A smart, pee wee second baseman and born leader, Miller Huggins, a Cincinnati lawyer, might have been the Redbirds' best manager, finishing second twice in five years through 1917 at a time of little income. But, rebuffed when he sought to buy the club with Cincinnati capital, he quit and went to the Yankees for fame, fortune and an early death.

3

The Odd Couple

James C. Jones, the lawyer who saw to it that St. Louis money retained the Cardinals rather than Miller Huggins's Cincinnati capital, conceived a brilliant idea, when he passed a hat in 1917 and asked seven civic leaders and contributors to suggest candidates for club president. A blind man's buff, so to speak, and each of the seven wrote down the same name—Branch Rickey.

Wesley Branch Rickey, then business manager of the rival Browns, brought to baseball a former athlete's understanding, a lawyer's shrewdness, an English teacher's polysyllabics, a religious person's reverence and, "by Judas Priest," to use his normal expletive, a pioneer's footpath to baseball success.

For St. Louis, Rickey devised the farm system, the home-grown, mass-development method by which the Redbirds went from rags to riches. In Brooklyn, certainly with the knowledge that he wouldn't hurt his own pennant-winning chances but with a sense of justice that can't be challenged, he brought the black man back into organized professional baseball.

So Branch Rickey deserved Hall of Fame recognition that was given him shortly after he collapsed dramatically of a heart seizure while reciting a Biblical parable at Columbia, Missouri. That was in November, 1965, as the bushy-browed man, nearly eighty-four, accepted induction into the Missouri Sports Hall of Fame.

(Rickey would have had both awards long before, but he was not eligible for baseball's Hall of Fame because he was a valued member of the organization's Veterans' Committee. But when Stan Musial retired [1963], Missouri permitted persons not born in the Show-Me State to become members of its athletic Hall of Fame, thus making possible Rickey's elevation to that honor.)

"B. R.," which was probably

the best-known of Rickey's many nicknames, some gratuitous and others sarcastic, was a poor farm boy born in Ohio's "Duck Run" country of Sciota County. He taught school for thirty-five dollars a month, pedaling eighteen miles each way, as he began a pursuit of pedagogy and pennants.

A good athlete, he played football and baseball at Ohio Wesleyan University, reached the big leagues briefly as a catcher handicapped with a sore arm, and added a degree in law at the University of Michigan. He wouldn't drink, seldom cursed, refused to play Sunday baseball in respect to his mother's wishes and, his health impaired, prepared to spend his life as a lawyer in the more salubrious atmosphere of Idaho. Chances are, he'd have wound up heavily in politics.

But Robert Lee Hedges, who remembered Rickey for his intelligence even when a record number of bases were stolen off him with the 1905 Browns, persuaded Branch to put away his ten-gallon hat, to take down his shingle and to come back into baseball as business manager and assistant manager.

It was just in time for Rickey to obtain for the Browns the best player he ever handled, George Sisler, a poetry-in-motion pitcher and first baseman. The "Mahatma," as the New York press labeled Rickey when they didn't call him "El Cheapo," was "coach" to Sisler at the U. of Michigan. Ultimately, to Sisler as to most others, he was, whether respectfully or subserviently, "Mr. Rickey."

Apparently Philip de Catesby Ball, St. Louis ice-and-fuel magnate who took over the Browns when the Federal League folded, didn't share Hedges's affection for Rickey and relieved him as field manager. But he fought in court to retain B. R. in the front office when Jones approached Rickey to move from the Browns to the Cardinals.

The Cardinals were so poor then that they had to stay in St. Louis to train in 1918. Rickey, seeking to impress a visitor, even swiped the best rug out of Mrs. Rickey's living room for his bare office when lovely Jane was out of town.

The Redbirds needed a buck desperately then, and they got it from a man who knew how hard it was to come by a buck. Sam Breadon, a New York City kid who had skinny-dipped in the Hudson River, was a twenty-three-year-old bank clerk with a grade-school education, earning $125 a month. He heeded a Manhattan friend's advice to go West in 1902 for a crack at a new game with exciting potential, the automobile business.

Sam went as a $90-a-month grease monkey, but he was too ambitious and the "friend" canned

By Judas Priest: It's the Mahatma himself, Branch Rickey, the Ohio farm boy, athlete, scholar, lawyer, orator whose nimble brain and persuasive tongue did most to build the Cardinals into a team of double-decade destiny.

B. R.'s Counterpoint: Sam Breadon, the poor boy who struck it rich as an automobile grease monkey and then car salesman. In 27 years as Cardinals' president, he never lost his lower New York East Side accent or his fan's enthusiasm, including his predilection as a neatly attired man to change managers as often as shirts. He countered odd-couple partner Branch Rickey to form a dandy front-office, double-play combination.

him. He was down to a fifteen-cent-a-day budget when he sweet-talked himself into a deal with a confectionery for cases of Honey Boy popcorn. Near where Lady Bee had lived on Lindell, he cleared thirty-five dollars during a World's Fair parade.

Soon, proudly refusing to accept a tip for auto service, he became a partner with Marion Lambert, a member of a prominent St. Louis family, in the fast-growing field of auto sales. He did well in the World's Fair year. A baseball fan, he permitted friend Fuzzy Anderson, an auto associate, to talk him into contributing $200 for four shares of Cardinal stock.

At the suggestion of insurance man W. E. Bilheimer, a bleacher ticket was given to a needy boy for every share of stock. This was the forerunner of the Knothole Gang, a free-seat, week-day bonus for boys (and later for girls) that combined with the subsequent climb of the Cardinals to doom the rival Browns at the box office.

When Jones gave a dinner later for stockholders, seeking more money to pay off Mrs. Britton, Breadon enthusiastically subscribed $1800. He thought that was the limit —"Don't put good money after bad," he insisted—but at partner Fuzzy Anderson's plea, he came up with $5000 more. Showing considerable business skill, Sam soon headed the organization on Jones's insistence.

In 1920, therefore, Sam Breadon—"S. Breadon," he signed himself on checks — replaced Rickey as Cardinal president. B. R. stayed as vice-president and manager.

Breadon wanted to cut an unwieldy board of directors from twenty-five members to five, but he settled on seven.

He also wanted to get the Cardinals out of ramshackle League Park (Robison Field) with its rickety wooden stands. Although Phil Ball was a curmudgeon and didn't like Rickey, he was a sportsman. Finally, Ball heeded the persuasive Breadon's plea to share Sportsman's Park when the Browns were on the road. The Cardinals would pay half of the annual clean-up and pay $35,000 rent. Or maybe they'd build their own park.

Breadon sold the League Park site to the St. Louis Board of Education and to a transit company for a high school (Beaumont) and a street-car loop. The $275,000 realized from the sale paid off debts and helped associate Branch Rickey launch the plan that turned the baseball dwarf into a giant.

B. R. fumed that the wealthier clubs, particularly the Giants, got stronger by outbidding poor cousins for independently owned minor leaguers. And when Rickey planted a kid with a minor league club for seasoning, often an unscrupulous bush-league operator would ship the developed athlete to a team with more money. Worse, aware that Rickey himself and ace scout Charley Barrett were good judges of talent, other big league clubs lay back and simply let the Redbird super-sleuths find the best material for them.

The solution? Grow your own talent. With the money from the sale of the ballpark, Rickey bought eighteen shares of stock at Houston in the Texas League and then half-interest in Fort Smith, Arkansas, of the Western Association. By December, 1920, after a drinking bout at the baseball meetings in Kansas City,

Breadon owned half of Syracuse in the International League. Ultimately, after a franchise transfer (1928), Rochester would become the flagship of St. Louis's minor league fleet.

When the farm system reached its peak just before World War II, the Cardinals owned fifteen clubs outright and had working agreements with as many more. By then, the St. Louis ball club had its own sports concessions service, third only to Buffalo's national Sports Service of the Jacobs brothers and New York's far-flung ballpark-stadium-race track dispensers, the Stevens brothers.

So for nearly twenty years, Sam Breadon and Branch Rickey made a peach of a pair even though they were the "Odd Couple."

Breadon was neat and trim, a New Yorker who never lost his accent. Until his death, his Cardinals always were the "Cawd'nals." He was "Lucky Sam", "Singing Sam," a Democrat who lifted his elbow in the conviviality of barber-shop harmony. Rickey, as rumpled as an unmade bed, was two years younger, tousle-haired beneath a hat that looked as if he'd slept on it. He chewed cigars, but he didn't drink. He was a Bible-quoting, psalm-singing Republican.

They were totally unlike and yet they meshed marvelously, as Breadon okayed Rickey's better ideas and disapproved the most expensive or unpredictable. Together, they knew that as they went into the fast-track "Roaring Twenties" they had a good plan and a great player—Rogers Hornsby.

4

The Rajah & His Court

Rogers Hornsby WAS the Cardinals before their pennant-winning years just as Stan Musial was in the lean years between pennants. From the time scout Bob Connery saw him playing shortstop as a skinny kid with Denison, Texas, in 1915 and bought him for a magnificent $500, "The Rajah" was a prize. A dimpled darling, truly handsome, he was a tough-talking Texan and about as subtle as a punch in the kisser.

Greener than the family cemetery lot back home at Hornsby Bend, Texas, Rog thought Miller Huggins meant it literally when Hug took a look at the stringy 148-pound kid who played the tailend of the '15 season in St. Louis and said, "Looks as if we'll have to farm you out, kid."

Hornsby thought it meant to fill out, which indeed he did, and he took himself to his uncle's ranch, where he worked hard all winter, ate heavily of the steaks on which he ALWAYS based his base hits, and

drank more milk than he later would milkshakes. He came up at spring training, twenty years old, nearly six feet tall, weighing a surprising 180 pounds.

Huggins urged him to go down on the bat handle. Peculiarly, Rog stood deep in the righthanded batter's box and strode directly into the ball so that what appeared unreachable outside strikes were fat pitches. Years later he told me, "What I really didn't like was the ball up and in, but, going into the pitch, I'd pull back on the high-and-tight one and—at times—umpires called 'balls' pitches that really were 'strikes.'"

It really wasn't chicanery, because no player or manager ever treated umpires so objectively as Hornsby, who never believed in beefing about a call because, as he put it with great hitter's confidence, it took only one pitch to hit. And, oh, how he hit!

No shortstop, he hopscotched around for a proper defensive position, but his batting improved immediately to .313 in 1916. By the time Rickey and Breadon formed a front-office team in 1920, Rog was off and running—and few righthanded hitters ever got down to first base so rapidly—in a rousing rivalry with the neighboring Browns' graceful first baseman, George Sisler. For years, you made your choice and placed your bet: Rog or George, "The Rajah" or "The Sizzler."

In 1920, Hornsby hit .370 and Sisler .407 with a major league record 257 base hits, forty-two stolen bases and nineteen home runs, a distant second to Babe Ruth's eye-opening fifty-four total. Suddenly, the ball was juiced up, hypoed and whiter, the spit ball and other foreign substances barred from all except seventeen endorsed spit ball pitchers.

Sportsman's Park, home of the Browns and new residence of the Cardinals, was made to order for both men, especially Hornsby. Sisler, a lefthanded hitter, placed hits to all fields. Rog hit the ball harder as probably the greatest righthanded batter ever. He could pull the ball, but his best line drives to right-center took advantage of a relatively short (354 feet) distance to the right-center power alley.

During the next few years, the two players' averages soared like latter-day jets. In 1921, Hornsby hit .397, Sisler .371. In '22 The Rajah boomed to .401 with a home-run total that then was a National League record —forty-two—and Sisler matched the American League batting high of .420, stealing fifty-one bases. The stolen base then was on a decline that lasted until the Maury Wills-Lou Brock resurgence of the 1960s.

In 1923, Hornsby fell "back" to .384, but Sisler was troubled so badly by an eye infection that he was nearly blind. He would last until 1930, quitting at age thirty-seven, his career average still .340. But before his death at eighty in 1973, "Gorgeous George" would squint and almost snarl, "Three-forty! That wasn't hitting."

Hornsby kept going, spectacularly en route to .358, baseball's highest righthanded hitter's average for a career that ended with several fragmentary seasons. In 1924 and '25, he hit .424, the highest of any player in this century, and then .403. His AVERAGE for five seasons was .400!

Small wonder Breadon and Rickey, though still running a tight financial ship, couldn't afford to take tempting offers of first $250,000 and then $300,000 and four players from the Giants. The Chicago Wrigleys were willing to give many gum wrappers, too.

Small wonder, also, that Breadon, who had urged the Na-

A Peach of a Pair: Rogers Hornsby (right), the Cardinals' great line-drive hitting second baseman, and graceful George Sisler, the old St. Louis Browns' place-hitting first baseman. The batting stars created a civic rivalry in the early 1920s before Redbird pennants. Sure, early Hall of Famers.

tional League to adopt the official Most Valuable Player prize of $1000 that Sisler had won from the American League in 1922, was miffed when the bag of gold didn't go to Hornsby that first season, 1924, the year The Rajah achieved that twentieth century high (.424).

It turned out that a Cincinnati writer, Jack Ryder, had refused to name Hornsby among his top ten. The award went to Brooklyn's Arthur "Dazzy" Vance, a 28-6 winner for the second-place Dodgers. Ryder huffed, "How can you vote for a guy whose team finishes sixth?"

The excuse was as lame as Hornsby would be in later years from heel spurs after he suffered a broken ankle. Actually, he won the MVP prize a year later when the Redbirds finished fourth. However, the Cardinals were a disappointing yo-yo, up-and-down team just when Breadon thought Rickey's farm-system method had borne fruit.

B. R. had had some disastrous developments after successive third-place finishes in 1921 and '22. For one thing, he had tried to bring in a novelty, a bespectacled second baseman in '21. He would put Hornsby in left field and George "Specs" Toporcer would play second base. Specs, a lefthanded hitter and smart player who later helped develop farm systems for the Chicago White Sox and Boston Red Sox before early blindness forced him to become a skilled lecturer, never achieved anticipated stardom.

Death on the diamond is rare among active big league ball players, but the Cardinals and Rickey were twice stricken as a new ball club began to form. First, catcher Clarence "Pickles" Dillhoefer died of pneumonia, an extremely treacherous disease before modern-day drugs, at age twenty-eight in 1922.

Soon, the Cardinals were playing the Giants at the Polo Grounds. Other than Hornsby, Rickey's prize player and personal pet at the time was a smooth righthanded hitter, Austin McHenry, who in his third full major league season had blossomed forth with a .350 average, hitting seventeen home runs. Rickey watched in dismay as McHenry, a good outfielder, misjudged one fly ball. Then, another high fly fell behind McHenry. Puzzled, Rickey took the player to a doctor. Examination disclosed a brain tumor. Sidelined after batting .303 under handicap for half a season, McHenry was dead that fall at only twenty-seven.

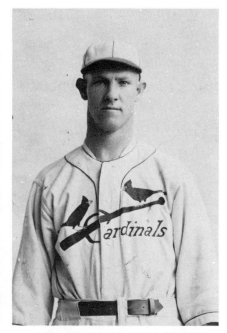

A Shooting Star: Death struck tragically a ball player about whom Branch Rickey always talked—Austin McHenry. A third-year man in left field, McHenry just had hit .350 with 17 homers when a fatal brain tumor was discovered in 1922.

Specs: That was the obvious nickname for George Toporcer, first infielder ever to play in the majors wearing glasses. A man of misfortune, Toporcer was a good ball player, but not good enough to beat out either Rogers Hornsby or Frank Frisch at second base and not able enough to play shortstop.

Years later—just after a salary huff by "Chick" Hafey and with Joe Medwick playing and, obviously, neither Stan Musial nor Lou Brock in sight, Rickey picked an All-Star team of Cardinals for me: McHenry was the left fielder!

B. R. was wheeling and dealing as well as hoeing on the farm with Charley Barrett as his Fuller Brush man of baseball. The Cardinals no longer could use a long-time pitching standby, Bill Doak, twice a twenty-game winner remembered by many because he had designed for Rawlings Sporting Goods in St. Louis an improved glove skillfully put together by Harry "Doc" Latina. The "Bill Doak" glove was a thirty-year staple, used even after bigger, better gloves had been architected by Latina.

Rickey had come up with a couple of pitching standbys for the Cardinals' early championship ball clubs. Bill Sherdel was a slender southpaw from McSherrystown, Pennsylvania, a pretty good hitter better known for his hard-luck, low-score losses in World Series play and a staff-leading 21-10 record in 1928.

A Famous Name: Yeah, actually a better name than pitcher even though spitballer Bill Doak pitched 17 seasons in the majors until 1929, including 11 with the Cardinals, and twice won 20 games. Doak's name prevailed because of a Rawlings glove improvement made at his request.

Wee Willie: Bill Sherdel came to the Cardinals when they were in last place (1918) and stayed through championship seasons. Sherry could do just about everything, especially throw a clever s-l-o-w ball.

Above all, "Wee Willie" was noted for a quick-pitch return delivery, later outlawed, and especially a masterful change-up. In Sherdel's day, they called it "a slowball."

As ball players learned when they tried to get an extra buck out of him, Rickey could talk an African into buying a fur coat or an Eskimo into a bikini. He sweet-talked Kansas City of the American Association out of a pitcher for $10,000 when he didn't have the ten grand.·

Jesse Haines became a Redbird landmark, an eighteen-season veteran until he was forty-four years old. By then, they called him "Pop" Haines. Like Rickey, he was an Ohioan, a native of suburban Dayton and later a long-time county auditor. He threw a knuckleball which he actually gripped with his knuckles, not his fingertips, and his quick-dipping, nonrotating delivery had more speed then many subsequent so-called "knucklers."

Pop was a sweet man, actually, neither alcoholic nor profane, but he hated to lose. Years later when Terry Moore was a wide-eyed rookie outfielder, an error behind Haines at Cincinnati turned him into a clubhouse tiger. Pop tore up the visitors' clubhouse at Crosley Field.

"It taught me," mentioned Moore, the take-charge leader of the Cardinals' early 1940s champions, "that if an 'old man' could become so intense, this was no kids' game."

Until Bob Gibson, Haines held the Cardinals' team record of 210 victories, topped by three twenty-game seasons, including twenty-four in 1927. He pitched a World Series shutout over the New York Yankees and hit a home run in 1926, gained a memorable second victory that will be mentioned, and came off a sore-armed list to turn back the hard-hitting Philadelphia Athletics in 1930.

In the early speakeasy-and-machine-gun era of the '20s when women began to smoke and make a move toward an ERA that wasn't earned-run average, Rickey began to win brownie points for the Cardinals.

Pop: Jesse Joseph Haines, good and reliable, pitched for the Cardinals from 1920 through 1937 when he was 44. Three times a 20-game winner, a moral man but hot-tempered, Haines made the Hall of Fame. Now, pitchers use larger gloves from which, often, the middle finger protrudes behind the flopping leather. Note that Pop pitched with what was called a three-fingered glove, one section covering the little and ring fingers.

With little help, he could do the unexpected. He could win a double-header with a barely remembered righthander named Johnny Stuart. He could startle baseball fans in 1922 by trading players between games of a Memorial Day doubleheader. Thus Max Flack played the morning game for the Cubs, walked to his nearby home for lunch and, returning to Wrigley Field, was told to try the visitors' outfield. He had been dealt for Cliff Heathcote.

Rickey could watch his big league ball club lose an exhibition ball game to a Mt. Vernon, Illinois, semi-pro club and spot little Ray Blades, who would become a good major-league outfielder. Blades might have been great if he hadn't twisted a knee trying to climb a chicken-wire fence that encircled the Sportsman's Park outfield before it was changed to rock-hard concrete.

Blades, a ten-year .301 hitter, was one of the many "Yes, Mr. Rickey" sycophants who learned much from the old master. Later a Redbird manager, Blades learned that the busiest and most exhausted man at any ball game, backing up throws toward first and second bases, should be the right fielder.

Rickey, walking the outfield at Fort Smith with Sid Keener, *St. Louis Times* sports editor, would hear a singing line drive and be told that it was off the bat of "a pitcher, Chick Hafey." Corrected Rickey, "A former pitcher, you mean. Turn that kid into an outfielder."

Charles "Chick" Hafey, who would oust Blades from his regular job, was a rangy righthanded hitter whose pull-hitting prowess was almost as awesome as his bazooka-powered throwing arm. By the time he won a batting championship as the only bespectacled hitting king in 1931, Hafey threw so powerfully that, as former teammates would concede, if he had played short right field, he would have held virtually all hits in his direction to singles.

Hafey was troubled by bothersome sinusitis each summer for a time. Said John McGraw of the swift outfielder, "With two good eyes, he'd be the best player in the game."

When Hafey barked a hot-shot double off "Fresco" Thompson's shins during one game and then bunted safely next time up as the Philadelphia third baseman backed up respectfully, Thompson sent over an ice-cream bar with a vendor who leaned over from the boxseats to the amused St. Louis dugout and said,

"For you, Mr. Hafey. If you bunt again, Mr. Thompson said he'll send another."

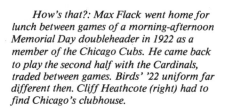

How's that?: Max Flack went home for lunch between games of a morning-afternoon Memorial Day doubleheader in 1922 as a member of the Chicago Cubs. He came back to play the second half with the Cardinals, traded between games. Birds' '22 uniform far different then. Cliff Heathcote (right) had to find Chicago's clubhouse.

Razor Sharp: Ray Blades, who once insisted he played on a semi-pro team at shortstop next to an Indian second baseman named Razor, was a farm-system pioneer signed out of Mt. Vernon, Ill. Blades, a graduate of a Post-Dispatch *grade-school baseball program, was hampered by a knee injury. Later, he managed the Cards.*

Some Chick: Charles "Chick" Hafey, first player to win a batting championship wearing glasses (1931), was a rangy, raw-boned, righthanded hitter whose pull-hitting power and strong arm took him to the Hall of Fame.

Who's on First?: Small wonder the Cardinals traded Jacques Fournier (left) to Brooklyn before the 1923 season. The kid standing on the bag, Jim Bottomley, just 23, hit .371 that year, en route to the Hall of Fame. But, gosh, he could have used another uniform. Here's Sunny Jim later, a Ladies' Day favorite.

Rickey was rolling. He was getting unexpected help. A naive kid from Nokomis, Illinois, wrote him an appealing letter for a tryout and B. R. had him scouted. So the wide-eyed farm boy tagged into town, so surprised when he saw a long, slender bat, that he asked Bill Sherdel with hayseed puzzlement:

"Pardon me, sir, but who's this man—this 'Mr. Fungo'?"

Before long, "Sunny Jim" Bottomley was the center of attention, the Ladies' Day favorite. He came in and ousted a good hard-nosed Frenchman, Jacques Fournier, the first baseman who'd hit .343 in 1921 and tested tough-guy Hornsby with his fists.

Within two seasons, the swaggering Bottomley, baseball cap tucked rakishly to the right, had belted the ball for .371. In '25 he

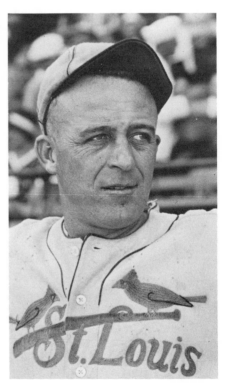

batted .367, and in '28 he won the league's MVP award with a .325 season more impressive by his total of 91 extra-basehits among 187 hits—forty-two doubles, twenty triples and thirty-one league-leading homers with a leadoff man's choked batting grip.

Bottomley broke many feminine hearts when he married, just as he broke up a lot of ball games. He remained a cracker-barrel philosopher. For instance, when trainer Harrison J. "Doc" Weaver opted for a long winning streak for the sake of "buckerinos" (a bastardization of American slang and catcher-coach Mike Gonzalez's Spanish for money—"dinero"), Jim disagreed.

"Naw, Doc," drawled Bottomley to Weaver, "you don't win pennants with long streaks. You win 'em by winnin' two games, then losin' one...winnin' two...losin' one...until you get up to a hundred victories. Heck, then you can throw away the rest!"

But, unfortunately, the Cardinals sagged before they surged. Restlessly, Sam Breadon, who had little patience with managers, wanted to make a change. He was aware that Hornsby and others thought Rickey was too scientific. Rog had had a knockdown-dragout fight with Rickey before Burt Shotton, B. R.'s "Sunday manager," halted it.

In spring training 1925 at Stockton, California, before setbacks to fifth and sixth places, Breadon urged Rickey to step down. B. R. insisted he stay on. The Cardinals got off to a poor start when Cincinnati's Pete Donohue shut them out opening day. By late May,

Rickey had made a good deal, sending Gonzalez and Ohio Wesleyan fellow alumnus Howard Freigau to Chicago for catcher Bob O'Farrell.

But it was too late. When Breadon found out there was no advance sale for a Memorial Day doubleheader, he took a train to Chicago and encountered his .400-hitting second baseman, Hornsby, then twenty-nine. Would Rog take over the club? Profanely, yes. Was the Alamo a Lone Star State shrine?

Rickey, angry, insisted that Breadon was ruining him. No, Sam insisted, the move to the front office exclusively would make Rickey. Miffed, B. R. would stay, but he wanted to sell his stock, which Breadon bought at a profit for the full-time general manager. The clubowner, by then with seventy-eight per cent of the stock, sold the par-value $30,000 stock to Hornsby for $50,000 and endorsed the new manager's note.

Hornsby, relieved to be out from under "the Ohio Weeze-leyan" so-and-so, as he derisively had described Rickey behind the back of a man whose lackeys always kept him posted, immediately ordered B. R's blackboard out of the clubhouse. "This ain't football," snapped Rog.

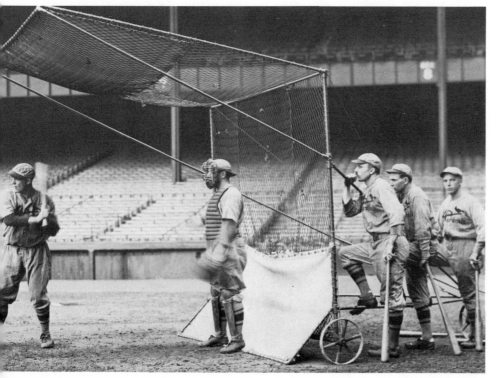

Choke-Up Slugger: Jim Bottomley, swinging a bat heavier than players use now, chokes up in batting practice on an open date at Yankee Stadium before the 1926 World Series. (Others are Bill Warwick, catcher, and behind the old-fashioned batting cage, Taylor Douthit, Les Bell and Billy Southworth.) Despite singles hitter grip, Bottomley in 1928 had 93 extra base hits among 187. Included were 31 home runs.

"T" Stands for Terrific: Tommy Thevenow, called up at Rog Hornsby's insistence, was the shortstop glove the Cardinals needed to win in 1926. A great fielder who was hot at the bat in the Series, too. Thevenow virtually ended his career when he suffered a broken leg in '27.

The Ballhawk: Taylor Douthit, a University of California graduate, came into his own in his first full season as a masterful center fielder in 1926, hitting .308.

He Rang the Bell: Inspired perhaps more by manager Hornsby than any other player, third baseman Les Bell led the 1926 world champions at bat, hitting .325 with 17 homers and 100 RBIs. National League teams wore golden-anniversary patches on left sleeves when photo was taken in '25.

The manager wanted young shortstop Tommy Thevenow, who had been optioned to Syracuse. But he'd been sent out for seasoning, said Breadon. "I'll season him my way," snarled Hornsby.

The farm system was producing. A University of California professor had recommended Taylor Douthit to the Cardinals and Rickey called him up, thanks to the honesty of a St. Joseph, Missouri, farm club operator, Warren Giles, who reminded Rickey that the Cardinals were about to let their option on the square-jawed ballhawk expire.

Hornsby took a shine to a righthanded-hitting young third baseman, Les Bell, and pumped confidence into him. He didn't have to take a shine to Flint Rhem, because the green-eyed righthander from Rhems, South Carolina, took care of his own moonshine. "Shad," the home-spun sobriquet for the green-eyed big guy, had a fastball that bothered opposing batters as much as his thick Dixie drawl did his teammates.

Rhem thought he could be another Grover Cleveland Alexander. In fact, when Alex came over to the Cardinals, Shad explained away his own inebriation with the syrupy suggestion that, sure, he'd drunk more than his share, but wasn't it more important to the club that he drink faster to keep more of the rotgut away from "Old Pete"?

In 1926—THE year—Rhem was the big winner, 20-7, but never again did he recapture the magic that began early at a spa at Terrell Wells, a cornfield outside San Antonio. The Cardinals trained there early before moving to SanTone, which Hornsby always did think was the best place to train a ball club.

Even before they threw out the first ball, Rog told 'em bluntly that they'd win the pennant. If they didn't think so, they could hustle their fannies into traveling secretary Clarence Lloyd's room and get their blankety-blank train fare out of there.

Opening day, Hornsby belted three hits and Rhem held on to beat Pittsburgh, 7-6, but by the trading deadline the Cardinals were fighting merely to stay out of the second division. Then Rickey made a brilliant stroke. He dealt a personal favorite, home-town outfielder Clarence "Heinie" Mueller to the Giants for veteran Billy Southworth.

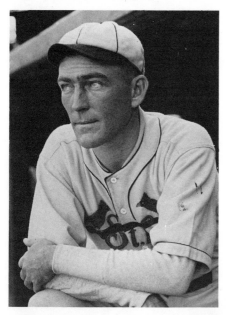

A Toast for Ol' Shad: That would be just great with Charles Flint Rhem of Rhems, S.C. The Cardinals' only 20-game winner in 1926, Flint loved to celebrate every victory by bending his elbow. Come to think of it, after every defeat then and thereafter, too.

Pals of a Different Stripe: Clarence "Heine" Mueller, colorful, often clowning home-town outfielder, went to the New York Giants in a 1926 deal that helped the Cardinals to their first pennant. A year later Heine's old boss, Rogers Hornsby, wore the Giants' uniform, too.

*Birds of an Ugly Feather: Billy
Southworth (left), veteran right fielder ac-
quired from the New York Giants for Heine
Mueller, had a destiny in the future as the
Cardinals' manager, but, first, he hit an in-
spiring .320 to help the outfield of Taylor
Douthit (center) and Chick Hafey in the pen-
nant drive. Here, working out for the 1926
Series, the great outfield looks pretty crumby
because the skimpily clad ball club won the
pennant in New York and stayed on the road.
New Series uniforms hadn't arrived.*

*Alex the Great: Grover Cleveland Alex-
ander was nearly 40 then, alcoholic, epileptic
and, indeed, his own worst enemy. But the
knock-kneed, long-wristed pitching legend
proved he still could master the baseball if not
himself. Old Pete won 373 National League
games, equalling a record, and won the 1926
World Series.*

Mueller, fleet and a good hitter,
made many a comic-opera mistake.
It's still not wise to steal third, for
example, with a teammate standing
there. But McGraw thought he saw
enough raw talent and, besides,
Southworth was a well-traveled
thirty-three, six years older, and he
couldn't play center field any longer.

But Billy the Kid, whose destiny
was with St. Louis, could play right
field. He hit a robust .317. Moreover, a week later the Chicago Cubs
asked waivers on a pitching great,
Grover Cleveland Alexander, who
was alcoholic, epileptic and his own
worst enemy. At thirty-nine, Alex or
"Old Pete," short for "Alkali
Pete," a nickname hung on him by
former catcher Bill Killefer when
Alexander fell off a buckboard on a
Texas hunting trip into a large pool
of alkali and mud, had angered new
manager Joe McCarthy.

Disrespectfully for one ordinarily shy and silent, Alex had
made it difficult for McCarthy, a
sensitive "busher" who hadn't
played major league ball. The climax
had come at a Cubs' squad meeting
to change their signs, since their
shortstop, Rabbit Maranville, had
been dealt to Brooklyn, whom they
played that day.

Said McCarthy, seriously, "The
first time Maranville gets to second
base today, he'll have all of our
signs."

Laughed Alexander, a late and
tipsy arrival, "I wouldn't worry
about 'Rab,' Joe," said Pete. "He
won't ever reach second base."

The waivers, then $4500,
followed. Four clubs had choice over
the fourth-place Cardinals. Rickey
was away and Hornsby not immediately available, but Breadon put
in a claim. "Hell, yes," said Hornsby, he wanted him. Rog hit Alex as
if he owned him, but he knew others
didn't. Besides, Alexander's old bat-

terymate and Rog's new coach, "Reindeer Bill" Killefer, could handle him. The lower clubs passed.

So baseball history was written. Grover Cleveland Alexander, three times a thirty-game winner earlier at Philadelphia and five times past twenty wins, came over to join the Cardinals. First time out, pitching before a sizable crowd at Sportsman's Park, which Phil Ball had expanded from 18,000 to 34,000 that year in the belief that HIS club, the Browns, would compete for the pennant, Alexander nipped his old Chicago teammates in ten innings before his own nip, 3-2.

Alex wasn't great in the regular season, but he was better than his 12-and-10 record, 9-7 in St. Louis, and the Cardinals kept coming. On August 31, they slipped into first place and then, with a full month to play, wound up their home season dramatically on September 1.

Hard-pressed, Hornsby used thirty-six-year-old pitcher-coach Allan Sothoron to beat title-contending Pittsburgh in the opener. The seldom-seen Sothoron pitched a three-hitter, 3-1, and then lanky left-hander Art Reinhart won the second game, 5-2.

On the road, the Redbirds with the red-pinstriped gray uniforms hung on over Cincinnati. First, Frank Frisch, New York's star second baseman who had entered McGraw's doghouse, hit a tenth-inning home run against the Reds that assured St. Louis a tie. Next, after several players had traveled by train to Philadelphia to see Gene Tunney lift Jack Dempsey's heavyweight title in the rain, Sherdel relieved Rhem. Southworth then hit a pennant-winning home run to beat the Giants, 6-4.

So the Cardinals waited a week in New York for the World Series as St. Louis raved over the city's first National League pennant since the infant season fifty years earlier, the first in any major league in thirty-eight years.

The World Series against the Yankees, managed by former St. Louis skipper Miller Huggins, saw Herb Pennock win a 2-1 opening duel from Sherdel. Next, Alexander beat former Browns' ace, Urban Shocker, 6-2. Finally, the club came home for a gigantic, open-car, ticker-tape parade downtown. And

They Also Served: Pitching replacements in '26 at a time the reliever lacked dignity, if not front-line ability, included (from the left), Herman Bell, Sylvester Johnson and Art Reinhart.

Memories Are Made of This: Down the stretch in 1926 when the Cardinals' pitching staff was shorthanded, manager Hornsby called on seldom-seen Allen Sothoron, virtually a pitching coach before such really existed. Sothoron dusted off the cobwebs for a key three-hit victory over Pittsburgh.

when Haines shut out "Dutch" Ruether and hit a home run in a 4-0 game, joy was spelled with a capital "J."

But "The Babe" had a capital "B," too, and Ruth prevailed. Not walked so respectfully that afternoon as Hornsby had ordered, the home-run slugger had a field day. He pulled Rhem's fast ball for a first-inning homer and teed off on a slow ball in the third, breaking Wells Chevrolet Company's plate-glass window across Grand Avenue. Finally, he hit one of Herman Bell's pitches in the sixth well up into the center field bleachers, 426 feet from home plate at ground level. So high, in fact, that romanticists had it carrying to the YMCA at the northeast corner across the street. Longest ever in St. Louis? Could be, but not THAT long!

From that 10-5 rout, the Yankees went on to win again in ten innings, 3-2, Pennock once more over Sherdel, and the show had to go back on the road again.

At Yankee Stadium, Alexander did it again in a 10-2 rout over Bob Shawkey. Hornsby asked Alexander to take it easy in celebration, just in case.

For Old Pete, "taking it easy," by his own evaluation, leaving aside late-evening snakebite, included a couple of shots of raw whiskey before brushing his teeth and, if the hotel elevator took too long, a mosey back for a third slug. So he dozed peacefully in the bullpen as the Cardinals used a key single by their lightest regular-season hitter and heaviest Series batter, Tommy (.417) Thevenow, for three unearned runs off Waite Hoyt.

By the seventh inning, Jesse Haines held only a one-run lead, and he followed one of the twelve Series walks to Ruth with a two-out pass to Lou Gehrig, loading the bases. Hornsby walked in from second base. Uncomplaining, Haines held up a finger, dripping blood from squeezing his knuckle ball too hard.

Alexander had stated that, if needed, he required only the minimum number of warmup pitches. He had a habit of pitching quickly, like a later Dizzy Dean or Bob Gibson. Hornsby wig-wagged that he wanted the old geezer sitting down in the red knit sweater, not the fellas warming up. Alexander got to his feet slowly and deliberately.

Old Pete was freckled and turkey-wattled from a long, hard athletic life, knock-kneed, wearing his cap perched on top of his head like a peanut. He ambled in a Great Circle Route from the distant left-center field bullpen. It was a raw, rainy day, and rookie New York second baseman Tony Lazzeri's nerves were raw, too.

In what still is regarded as one of Series history's most dramatic moments, Hornsby met Alexander on the outfield grass at shortstop, looked at watery old eyes that seemed reasonably clear and said, "There ain't no place to put 'im, Pete."

Alexander nodded. "Well, Rog," said "Alex the Great," "I guess I'll just have to get 'im out."

Alexander—aptly called "Old Low and Away" by Haines for ability to pinpoint pitches down across the lower, outer edge of the plate—short-armed Strike One at the far edge. Then, trying to lean Lazzeri back, he came up and in with a pitch, but almost got too much of the plate. Tony hit a long, deep foul into the left field seats. Strike Two.

Alex tried again for the low outside corner with his short, sharp curve, a close cousin to the modern-day slider. Ball One. Once more, though in baseball old age he had added the screwball to that once-darting fast ball, he threw that quick-dipping curve low and away. Lazzeri swung, missed. Strike Three.

Almost haughtily, as displayed on old game films in the St. Louis Sports Hall of Fame at Busch Memorial Stadium, Alexander flipped his glove into foul territory and trundled into the dugout.

In the ninth, with two out and none on, he went to a three-two count on the Babe. He threaded the outside corner, low and away. Umpire George Hildebrand hesitated and called it a ball. Alexander, walking in to take catcher Bob O'Farrell's throw, wondered about the pitch. Hildebrand held up two fingers, barely apart. "It was just that far outside," he said.

"If it was that close," grumped Alexander softly, "I'd think you could have given it to an old geezer like me."

Ruth, who rarely made a mistake physically or mentally, blew one. He tried to fool the Cardinals. A year later with lefthanded Lou Gehrig more impressive and batting fourth, he probably wouldn't have tried. Now, with Bob Meusel at bat, the Babe sought to surprise the Cardinals by stealing second. However, Alexander worked with a short delivery. O'Farrell had a great arm.

To Hornsby's delight, Rog, covering, saw the Babe coming. He grabbed the ball and thrust down his glove defiantly, tagging out Ruth. "The biggest thrill of my baseball career," The Rajah would say then and later of the tag-out title play.

Minutes later, he was headed to Pennsylvania Station to catch a railroad train back to Texas for his mother's funeral.

5

An Encore Named Frisch

When Frank Frisch was a fresh young feline from Fordham, a crooked-nosed cat like an early-day Garry Templeton in his speed and spectacular play, he helped lead the New York Giants to a record four straight National League pennants. One day when the team was traveling West, a stranger came into the Giants' Pullman and explained his unusual occupation and displayed a specimen. The man handled snakes. One he exhibited was a wriggler, tan and about three feet long.

Nodding to the interested ball players, the man said, "I know you are famous athletes. But if I were to release him in a field outside this train, not one of you could catch him."

Quietly, outfielder Ross Youngs, himself a fast man bound for an early death and late Hall of Fame induction, said:

"Frank Frisch could."

"The Flash" was spectacularly fast, a switch-hitter best in the clutch, a hell-for-leather former football player who dived into bases, including first base. He made sprawling stops, then leapt to his feet in one acrobatic motion.

He was the money player who had hit .300, .471, .400 and .333 in four straight Series, alternating between third base and second, wherever manager John McGraw needed him most. Through seven-plus seasons, he had hit as high as .341 and .348.

If you're fascinated with Frisch as a funny fella, hotly competitive, you can find almost a bookful in *The Pilot Light and the Gas House Gang*, written for Bethany Press of St. Louis in 1980.

But Frisch WASN'T Rogers Hornsby, certainly not to St. Louis. And happy Cardinal fans woke up one morning in December, 1926, to learn that the great-hitting manager of their brand-new world champions

The Fordham Flash: Frank Frisch hated to leave his native New York and to try to replace Rogers Hornsby, but he did both—and extremely well. He sparked the Cardinals to four pennants as a switch-hitting second baseman who has played more World Series games (50) than any National Leaguer. He was the pilot light of the 1934 Gas House Gang.

had been traded to New York. This surprise was likened by someone to a Christmas stocking filled with horse manure. Hornsby for Frisch and a "what's-his-name" pitching has-been, Jimmy Ring, who'd win only four of his final twenty-five decisions, none of them for the Cardinals!

For years, McGraw, always seeking to buy the best players possible to compete with the Yankees' box-office titan, Babe Ruth, had sought to acquire Hornsby. McGraw wanted to move Frisch back to third base in order to have both future Hall of Fame stars in an infield with another Cooperstown great, Bill Terry.

In 1926, however, as St. Louis made its move toward that first pennant, Mac had reverted once more to his cruel career-long habit of ridiculing his captain—then Frisch—for a mistake, whether it was the captain's or any one else's. In anger, Frisch had taken French leave, skipping the club in St. Louis. He'd been fined, and neither he nor McGraw had forgotten.

Sam Breadon hadn't forgotten, either, an episode with outspoken Hornsby. Down the stretch in '26 when the manager asked the club-owner to cancel an open-date exhibition for his weary ball club in New Haven, Connecticut, Breadon found New Haven owner George Weiss adamant. After a Redbird loss, "Singing Sam" made a tactical mistake. He walked into the Cardinals' clubhouse to tell Hornsby.

The Rajah blistered him bluntly as best described by the *St. Louis Post-Dispatch's* J. Roy Stockton. JRS wrote, "Hornsby recommended an utterly impossible disposition of the game..."

A reddened Breadon walked out, not to step into the Cardinals' clubhouse for twenty years. A proud man, he was hurt and angry. Perhaps tauntingly, aware that Hornsby wanted a three-year contract at $50,000, Breadon offered only one season—period. Two bullheads were on collision course.

Visiting St. Louis, Warren Giles, who was promoted by Rickey to run the Syracuse club on his way to prominence at Cincinnati and as National League president, never forgot the drama. He sat with B. R., who nodded to Breadon's closed door, where the boss sat once more with Hornsby.

"My fate could be settled right now," said Rickey, who didn't like the short shrift former physical opponent Hornsby gave to general managers he always demeaned as "business" managers. Rog always thought a clubowner and field manager could run a ball club's playing personnel.

Suddenly, Hornsby stalked out, the issue unresolved. Breadon picked up the telephone and called Charley Stoneham, then came out and told Rickey that the deed was done!

The Page One bombshell led to violent reaction. Angry fans festooned Breadon's Pierce-Arrow automobile agency and his fashionable West End home with black crepe. The city's Chamber of Commerce did a daring thing. It rebuked one of its leading citizens in a resolution. One sports editor, Jim Gould of the old *St. Louis Star,* wrote that he'd never cover another Cardinal ball game.

Hornsby was surprised; Frisch was stunned. Frank didn't want to leave his native New York to go anywhere, least of all to the St. Louis hot house. His father was a wealthy German in the linen business, but, hell, the Flash wanted to stay in baseball. He took his wife

Ada and went up to Lake Placid to ski, skate, bobsled, tramp through the snow and even sit out in the snow with his dogs and read.

When Rickey made a minor-league inspection tour and asked Frisch to meet him in Syracuse, B. R. needed only one look at the trim, determined twenty-nine-year-old angry ex-Giant, two years Hornsby's junior. "Tell Mr. Breadon I'll be ready," said Frisch, who, like Breadon, always gave the ball club that "New Yawk" pronunciation—"Cawd'nals."

Breadon sternly set out picking a manager to replace the popular Hornsby. In 1926, Rog had slumped to .317, only three points higher than Frisch, but he'd been injured. He'd hit only .250 in the World Series, but he'd won it all, hadn't he?

Breadon's first choice, coach Bill Killefer, turned down the job. "Reindeer Bill" didn't want friend Rog's job. He defected to the rival Browns. So Breadon turned to blond, bland Bob O'Farrell, the durable catcher who had been the National League's Most Valuable Player in 1926 when he hit .293, caught almost every game and blocked home plate as if he were the custodian of the Pearly Gates. O'Farrell, at thirty, was already a ten-year major leaguer.

For a time, there was a vexing financial and ethical question. Neither National League president John Heydler nor certainly that scowling commissioner, Judge K. M.

Landis, would let a St. Louis stockholder play second base for New York. Hornsby, who had paid $50,000 for Rickey's stock with Breadon as the endorsee, now wanted $120,000. The clubowner's limit was $80,000.

Finally, to solve the situation, each National League club was assessed $5000 to make up the difference, giving Hornsby a handsome sum for his one bad habit other than a tart tongue. He loved to play the horses, few as fast as the Rajah himself. With the Giants he showed that he hadn't lost his way with the wrong words, too.

On a train back to New York from spring training he was eating dinner with rookie shortstop Eddie "Doc" Farrell, playing in place of injured Travis Jackson. A New York writer wondered if the ex-manager of the defending world champions could see a pennant for McGraw's Giants?

"Not," said Hornsby, "with Farrell at shortstop."

Frisch, meanwhile, tempered

Not So Lucky Irishman: Bob O'Farrell, the National League's Most Valuable Player as Cardinals' catcher in 1926, became player-manager in 1927, but he did little playing, suffering a broken thumb. Worse, slick shortstop Tommy Thevenow was sidelined with a broken leg. O'Farrell won three games more than in '26 (92) but was canned as manager.

early spring-training coolness at Avon Park, Florida, with a gregarious guy's warmth. He had a great spring, but then in his first appearance in St. Louis, wearing the new black-circled "World Champion" shirt insignia over the single left-breasted Redbird on the Cardinals' proud 1927 uniform, the Flash pulled an immediate boo-boo.

Against the Browns in the traditional two-game pre-season city series, Frisch tried to work fast on a first-inning ground ball by George Sisler with two men on base. Although Frisch fielded characteristically with a squat to block balls he couldn't field completely, this one found daylight and slithered through—a two-run error! Head down, as he recalled, Frisch heard the crowd chant:

"We want Hornsby—WE WANT HORNSBY!"

Frisch didn't make 'em forget the Rajah, but he made 'em remember the Flash.

He won that first exhibition game at Sportsman's Park as a Cardinal with a late-inning base hit. Opening day, he tripled and homered off Pat Malone of Chicago in a 4-3 victory. He was devastating all season, setting a record still standing for most chances fielded by an infielder other than a first baseman, 1037.

He struck out only ten of 617 times at bat, stole forty-eight bases, got 208 hits, drove in seventy-eight runs and hit .337. If he hadn't jammed his right wrist in early September he would have hit more closely to Hornsby's .361 that was carried in a daily newspaper comparison of the two players.

Even though Rog hit twenty-six homers and drove in 125 runs, he lasted only that one season in the Polo Grounds, traded again because he couldn't get along with clubowner Stoneham or the big boss's subservient traveling secretary, Jim Tierney, and maybe not even with McGraw.

During that season, the Cardinals lost shortstop Tommy Thevenow with a broken leg, and O'Farrell became a bench manager with a broken thumb and sore arm. Nevertheless, the Cardinals almost won a pennant. Out of the stands, they plucked home-town catcher Johnny Schulte, a lefthanded hitter called "Eagle Eye" because he knew the strike zone at the plate and behind it.

Failure to come up with a shortstop other than twenty-one-year-old Heinie Schuble, trying to make the long leap from Danville, Illinois, in the old Three-Eye League, was a glaring omission. Frisch would walk off the field, arm around the nervous, error-prone kid, trying to buck

up the boy's spirits. Later, the Flash would complain:

"Crissake, if Rickey had brought up Maranville a couple of weeks earlier, I think we'd still have won it."

The 1927 Cardinals won three games more (ninety-two) than the '26 club. Haines had a career-high victory total, twenty-four, and Alexander, though past forty, won twenty-one. But with young Paul Waner hitting .380 and nosing out

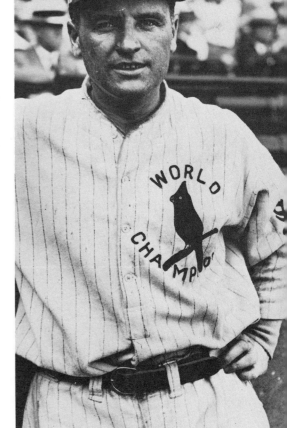

Johnny on the Spot: Johnny "Eagle Eye" Schulte, long-time St. Louisan, was plucked out of the stands to help the Cardinals' crippled catching in 1927. Later, he became Joe McCarthy's championship coach and confidante with the Yankees. Proudly, the Cardinals proclaimed their first world championship on the '27 uniform.

Frisch for the MVP award, Pittsburgh won the pennant.

The day the pennant was lost at Cincinnati, where little lefthander Jake May offset a home run by Frisch, 3-2, a tornado second only to that of 1896 devastated St. Louis, including Sportsman's Park. The pavilion roof in right field, only a year old, was ripped off and the twisted wood and steel dumped into Grand Avenue. A World Series could have been a problem.

To Sam Breadon, an increase in attendance from 681,575 to 763,615 WITHOUT Hornsby was eye-opening. Said Breadon, '' I knew then that it was the ball club that counted. I never again feared trading a player. But of all the players I ever had, the greatest was Frank Frisch of 1927.''

Despite O'Farrell's efforts, Breadon, a hard man to please out of the old third-base dugout, relieved Bob of his managerial job. Oddly, he gave O'Farrell a $5000 raise to $30,000 and kept him as catcher. For field foreman, Sam turned to a man who would become the first ever to win pennants in three cities (Pittsburgh, St. Louis and Cincinnati)—coach Bill McKechnie.

A banjo hitter with little major league playing time, McKechnie was forty-one and a patient, low-key operator, regarded as best handling pitchers and holding back his top pinch hitter until just the right moment.

Too Fast a Track: Heinie Schuble, called up at 21 from Danville, Ill., in the Class B Three-Eye League when Tommy Thevenow was hurt. The kid wasn't ready for the king-sized jump.

The Deacon and The Rab: Bill McKechnie (right), labeled the ''Deacon'' because he sang in his Pittsburgh suburban choir, found a shortstop and a pennant in a 37-year-old geezer, 5-foot-5 Rabbit Maranville, a colorful shortstop for 23 big league seasons.

Let George Do It: He did. George Washington Harper, winding up a long career, came over from the Giants in 1928, hit better than .300, including three homers in a key September series at New York—and thumbed his nose in John McGraw's face!

Ace High: Jimmy Wilson, nicknamed "Ace," came over from Philadelphia in 1928, hit timely and caught wisely for the Cardinals' next three championship ball clubs.

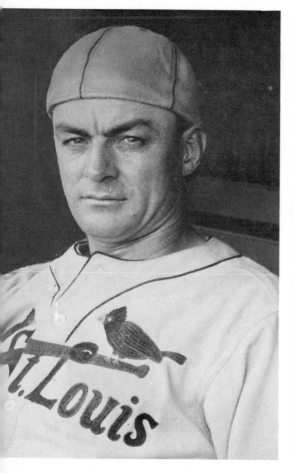

To help "Deacon Will" after peppery Billy Southworth was sent to be player-manager at Rochester, new home of the Syracuse franchise, Rickey acquired a veteran lefthanded-hitting outfielder from New York named George Harper.

When O'Farrell didn't bounce back to his former skill, B. R. made a key trade. He sent rookie catcher Virgil "Spud" Davis, outfielder Homer Peel and some of Breadon's cash to Philadelphia for a top catcher, Jimmy Wilson.

"Ace" Wilson, a Philadelphian whose green eyes flashed from behind a swarthy complexion and beneath thick, dark hair, had sturdy, soccer-developed legs, but he was a good hitter and fast. He handled a pitching staff on which "Wee Willie" Sherdel won twenty-one games, Haines twenty and old man Alexander sixteen.

A thirty-seven-year-old left-hander, Clarence Mitchell, came over from Philadelphia to help, too. Mitchell, who threw the last legal spitball by a lefthander in 1932, was the player who hit into five outs in two times at bat for Brooklyn in the 1920 World Series. (He grounded into a double play, then lined to Cleveland's Bill Wambsganss for the World Series rarity second only to Don Larsen's perfect game—an unassisted triple play.)

Because Les Bell had tailed off at third base without Hornsby's helpful hand, the Cardinals coveted Andy High at Boston, where Hornsby had turned up as player-manager. Breadon was afraid neither he nor Rickey could get Rog's attention without hitting him between the eyes like a balky mule, but a St. Louis writer, Ray Gillespie of the *Star*, served as go-between.

High helped in more ways than one because another native

A Man of Distinction: Clarence Mitchell, no less. Acquired by the Cardinals in 1928, a big leaguer since 1911, Mitchell threw last LEGAL spitball by a lefthander in 1932. He also hit into five putouts in two times up in a World Series (1920), including the only Series unassisted triple play.

St. Louisan, handsome, husky outfielder Wally Roettger, athletic pride
of the University of Illinois, suffered
a broken leg in mid-season and was
never the same athletically. He later
was baseball coach and assistant
basketball coach at Illinois before
his untimely death in 1951 at age
forty-nine.

With Roettger out, High could
play third base more often and versatile Roscoe "Watty" Holm could
move to right field to platoon with
Harper. George, who didn't like
McGraw, hit solidly (.305) that
single season in St. Louis. As a clincher, in a late September showdown
with the Giants, a club the Cardinals

beat out for the pennant by two
games, Harper hit three homers one
day at the Polo Grounds—and
thumbed his nose at "Little
Napoleon."

The less said about the World
Series, the better. The Yankees, crippled, almost blew the American
League pennant down the stretch to
the Athletics. Of course, they'd
whipped Pittsburgh four straight in
1927, but "Murderers' Row"
couldn't do it to the favored Cardinals.

Oh, couldn't they?

The Yankees clobbered the Cardinals in straight sets, 4-1, 9-3, 7-3
and 7-3. Babe Ruth and Lou Gehrig
were never better. Gehrig hit .545
with six hits that included four
homers and a double, driving in nine
runs. The Babe was awesome. He
went ten for sixteen—.625—and
drove in four runs, again hitting
three home runs in one game, even
teeing off on the hero of the 1926
Series, Old Pete Alexander.

Sherdel, the best of the shell-
shocked St. Louis pitchers, lost the
first and last games. He held a 2-1
lead into the seventh inning of the
Sunday final in St. Louis, but he
quick-pitched for Strike Three on
Ruth. "Sherry" stood on the pitching
rubber to return catcher Earl "Oil"
Smith's return peg without a
windup.

At the pre-Series adjudication
of Judge Landis, the quick pitch, il-
legal in the American League, had
been ruled out. So despite protests
of McKechnie, Frisch and Sherdel,
National League umpire Cy Pfirman
had no choice. As the decision went
against the Cardinals, the Babe
stood there laughing. He hit the next
pitch out of the park, and Gehrig hit
one even farther.

Mortified and perhaps mysti-
fied that the Cardinals had walked
Ruth just once compared with

*Twin Disasters: Wally Roettger (left), hit-
ting .341, suffered a broken leg in his first full
season, 1928, and never was the same. Roettger, later baseball and assistant varsity basketball coach at his alma mater, Illinois, was only
49 when he died. Wally's right-field replacement, Roscoe "Watty" Holm, who also could
play third base or even catch, was a handyman who died at the same young age.*

twelve times in '26, Breadon removed the pennant-winning manager by persuading McKechnie to swap jobs with Rochester's pennant-winning manager, Billy Southworth.

The Cardinals didn't think they needed old Rabbit Maranville any longer, and they shipped the geezer back to Boston, where he'd broken in back in 1912. The Rab, who had batted .308 in the Braves' famed 1914 World Series upset over Connie Mack's A's, had hit .308 also in the losing cause against the Yankees.

Maranville was a geriatric marvel who must have been bottled in bond in his drinking days. He would dive into a hotel-patio water fountain. In Japan, the little five-foot-five shortstop would march in a parade with Nipponese soldiers who couldn't say he didn't have the right height (or lack of it). And he made colorful belt-high basket catches later imitated by Willie Mays until at forty-four, still playing shortstop, he slid into Yankee catcher Bill Dickey at St. Petersburg, Florida, and suffered a broken leg.

The Cardinals thought they had the replacement for Maranville in Eddie Delker, who was, truly, a spring-training phenomenon or, as they put it in baseball, a "phenom," but Delker folded fast. Fortunately, because the farm system was beginning to flower, they had another one waiting in the wings—Charley Gelbert.

Gelbert, son of a great All-American end from Penn, had been a good athlete at Lafayette College, where he later coached baseball. If he hadn't been hurt later, Frisch thought he might have rated best ever. And the Flash had played beside some good ones: Art Fletcher, Dave Bancroft, Travis Jackson, Thevenow, Maranville and Leo Durocher.

Charley, My Boy: Like the old song of the same title, Charley Gelbert was a delight. When Eddie Delker fizzled as replacement for Rabbit Maranville, dealt back to the Boston Braves, the Cardinals tapped a great prospect who had played at Lafayette College.

Flowers That Bloom...: Tra, la, as the childhood song goes, but it was no fun to Eddie Delker—or, briefly, to the Cardinals—when the young shortstop, a spring-training phenom as successor to Rabbit Maranville, quickly faded in 1929.

In spring training the Cardinals thought that former teammate Southworth, no winning personality when drinking, was harsh and aloof. When, for instance, Wilson said he'd drive with his wife and young son, Bobby, to Miami for a series of exhibitions, Southworth tersely told him in front of the squad that it would cost $500, a robust sum at the time.

Still the Cardinals got off well. They led the league into June when they went on a killing ten-game losing streak interrupted by the highest-scoring game in history, 28-6, as reflected by this boxscore of the lively-ball carnage at Philadelphia's Baker Bowl bandbox:

CARDINALS

	AB	R	H
Douthit cf	6	4	5
Selph 2b	2	1	2
Delker 2b	3	2	1
High 3b	6	4	2
Bottomley 1b	5	4	4
Hafey lf	7	4	5
Holm rf	5	2	1
Wilson c	6	2	2
Gelbert ss	4	3	2
Frankhouse p	7	2	4
	51	28	28

PHILADELPHIA

	AB	R	H
Southern cf	5	2	2
O'Doul lf	3	2	2
Klein rf	5	0	2
Hurst 1b	5	0	2
Whitney 3b	5	0	1
Thompson 2b	5	1	4
Thevenow ss	5	0	1
Davis c	3	0	1
Susce c	2	1	1
Willoughby p	0	0	0
Miller p	0	0	0
Roy p	2	0	0
Green p	1	0	1
	41	6	17

Innings	1 2 3 4 5 6 7 8 9	
CARDINALS	10 1 0 2 10 0 0 5 0	–28
PHILADELPHIA	2 1 0 1 0 0 0 1 1	–6

E—Southern, Whitney RBI—High 2, Bottomley 7, Hafey 5, Wilson 3, Gelbert, Frankhouse 4, Douthit 2, Thompson 2, Southern, Selph, Hurst, Holm, O'Doul, Thevenow. 2B—Gelbert 2, Hafey 2, Green, Susce. 3b—Selph. HR—Bottomley, Hafey, Southern. SH—Selph, Holm.
DP—Thevenow, Hurst; High, Selph and Bottomley, Gelbert, Delker and Bottomley.
BB—Frankhouse 3, Willoughby 3, Miller 2, Roy, Green 2. SO—Frankhouse 2, Green. Hits—off Willoughby (3 in first inning, none out). Off Miller 0 in 0 (none out), off Roy 13 in 4⅓; off Green 11 in 4⅔. Left: Cardinals 10, Philadelphia. HBP: High (By Green). U—Reardon, Hart and Rigler. Time—2:26 LP—Willoughby.

Sam Muchnick, now the wrestling impresario, then covered baseball for the *St. Louis Times*. He remembered that at the finish, Jimmy Wilson wasn't even squatting to take pitches from Fred Frankhouse.

The bat-booming, history-making game failed to turn the team around sufficiently for Breadon, who showed he could own up to a "mistake." In July, he returned Southworth to Rochester and brought back McKechnie. Deacon Will, finishing fourth a few games over .500, faced unpleasantness first.

When he came back, Grover Cleveland Alexander just had come off a drinking cure. He looked pretty good and insisted on pitching immediately. Surprised, McKechnie okayed it, and Alex shut out Pittsburgh, tying the Giants' great Christy Mathewson for most National League career victories.

The Cardinals had a weekend series at Philadelphia, which then could not play ball on Sunday. The Saturday game was a skyhigh scorer typical of 1929 and '30. When the Cardinals tied, McKechnie asked Alexander to warm up for extra innings.

"Hold 'em, Pete, and we'll win it for you," said McKechnie.

He did for five innings and they did, 19-16, in fifteen innings. Alexander had 373 victories, one more than credited to Mathewson, and teammates hailed him. Old Pete said he'd like to run over to Atlantic City Sunday to see some old friends. McKechnie agreed.

"I won't take a drink," pledged Alexander.

McKechnie wasn't concerned. "I don't care if you take a drink, Pete," he said. "Just return Monday, fit and ready to work."

McKechnie had the forty-two-year-old gaffer down to pitch Wednesday in New York, but Alex showed up Monday unsightly and shaky. In addition, he shook off the coach hired to monitor him, Gabby Street. When he was bombed out quickly by the Giants Wednesday, McKechnie sent him back to Breadon, trying to cover up with a story of a sore arm.

Truth will out, of course, and Breadon, extremely fond of Alex-

ander, paid him off for the season and sent him home in August. Alex missed six weeks during which it was determined that Mathewson DID have 373 victories, too. Shipped to Philadelphia in the off-season, Alexander lost a tough season opener to the Giants' Carl Hubbell, 2-1.

But the magic was gone. Released to the minor leagues shortly thereafter, he never won again. He wound up pitching for the bearded traveling semi-pros, the House of David. I saw him wearing a neckerchief to protect a carbuncle as he pitched under the traveling team's portable lights at Sportsman's Park. It was the Depression of 1932, eight years before lights would be erected by the Browns with the Cardinals paying half ($75,000).

Breadon paid a hundred dollars a month to Alexander through National League headquarters until Breadon's death in 1949. Fred Saigh, then owner of the Cardinals, kept up the stipend and paid for Alexander's funeral a year later at St. Paul, Nebraska.

By 1930, the bottom had fallen out of the stock market. One-time paper-rich tycoons were taking the dry-dive out of downtown office buildings. Bread lines formed. Singers wailed a mournful tune, "Brother, Can You Spare a Dime." Sam Breadon, who feared ever being poor, quivered over the drop in attendance from the club record 778,147 to the fourth-place 410,921.

Singing Sam wanted McKechnie back, but Deacon Will had had enough of the shirt-changing managerial methods and stepped out to take a five-year contract with the Boston Braves. Breadon then turned to a pipe-puffing Alabaman, coach Charles E. "Gabby" Street, a World War I sergeant who had been Walter Johnson's batterymate and had caught a ball dropped from the Washington Monument. The "Old Sarge" hadn't been able to gumshoe Alexander all of the time, but everybody liked him. Besides, he'd take the job for $7500.

It was a hitting season, much to the embarrassment of clubowners trying to cut salaries. The National

Three of a Kind: Three men who managed the Cardinals get together in this photo. It's Rogers Hornsby, Bill McKechnie and Deacon Will's coach, Charles E. "Gabby" Street—the "Old Sarge"—who stepped into the job in 1930 when McKechnie preferred Boston's security.

League batted .303 as a whole, while the Cardinals set a National League record of 1004 runs or 6.5 a game.

Part-time player Ray Blades batted .396. An outfielder with an affinity for hitting the ball and failing to catch it, George "Showboat" Fisher, hit .374 in his one season with the Cardinals. The regular right fielder, as gaunt as Gary Cooper playing a lean, steely-eyed role, was George "Watty" Watkins, who hit .373.

The Cardinals had tried to farm out young catcher Gus Mancuso, but Judge Landis blew the whistle and Gus stayed to hit .366 as Jimmy Wilson's backup. Frisch batted .346, and Chick Hafey, though his playing schedule was limited by his eye trouble, drove in 107 runs in just 120 games, batting .336.

Hafey's replacement and also a first-base stand-in, Ernie Orsatti, the Hollywood stunt man, hit .321. Leadoff man "Sparky" Adams, acquired from Pittsburgh to help at third base, batted .314, while Wilson had .318. Jim Bottomley and Charley Gelbert finished at .304 each. Taylor Douthit played every game and hit .303.

Still, the Cardinals had to come from far back in a rally that ranked as one of the club's best, second only to the torrid stretch in 1942.

Until the Cardinals took four out of five from league-leading Brooklyn in mid-August, they were only one game over .500, still twelve games out, but Breadon felt good about the future and rehired Street for 1931, a departure for the rigid front office. To celebrate, the Old Sarge could have rushed out and bought a two-pants suit for only twenty-five dollars and two diamond rings for $16.85, fifty cents down and fifty cents a week.

By then, Breadon had completed the jigsaw puzzle. In a New York hotel suite at the trading deadline in June, with the press drinking Breadon's bootleg Scotch, Sam Muchnick had suggested that if Singing Sam could get Burleigh

Tattoo Tune: Beating a steady drum on the cozy wall at Sportsman's Park right field were two young outfielders. George "Watty" Watkins (right), who looked like a Texas ranger, batted .373. George "Showboat" Fisher was a classy guy who fielded as if first bounce were out. Imagine, Fisher hit .374 and was kaput.

Once in a Lifetime: A kid catcher named Gus Mancuso hit the lively ball in 1930 for .366, backstopping Jimmy Wilson, but then never came close again as a clever low-ball catcher for pennant-winning ball clubs at New York. Gus later succeeded Gabby Street briefly as Harry Caray's assistant on Cardinals' broadcasts.

Sparky: Earl "Sparky" Adams was a balding livewire at third base, traditionally the Cardinals' most uncertain position, but the little guy helped on two pennant winners.

Grimes from Boston to pitch, young Sam would bet old Sam ten bucks even that the Cardinals would win the pennant.

"Sammy," grinned Mr. Breadon, "if we win, I'll give you a hundred for ten."

Seconds later, the boss disappeared into his private bedroom. When he came out and said he'd done it, that he'd sent Bill Sherdel and Fred Frankhouse to the Braves for the veteran Grimes, he was left facing empty glasses. The press had rushed for phones.

Years later, hearty into his mid-eighties, Grimes would recall his first visit with Breadon. "Win me a dozen games, Burleigh," said the clubowner, "and maybe we'll have a chance."

But, the Cardinals had met with a setback at the end of August when Chicago had taken the lead. At Wrigley Field, the Cardinals and Cubs battled twenty innings, thanks to a great defensive play by Bottomley at first base, and Syl Johnson pitched twelve innings in relief. "Handy Andy" High's bloop single gave St. Louis an 8-7 victory.

Next day the Cards held a five-run lead into the ninth. Chicago tied it. In the eleventh, Bottomley hit a three-run homer. Chicago tied it. In the thirteenth, the Cubs won, 9-8.

When the Cubs flattened St. Louis in the series final, 16-4, with "Hack" Wilson hammering two home runs en route to his league record fifty-six, Chicago led the fourth-place Cards by seven and a half games. It looked as if the Redbirds had failed and fallen back.

But, as Gabby Street used to say, and others before him,—"Winners don't quit, and quitters don't win."

By late September, Chicago had faltered, and as the Cardinals moved into Brooklyn, the Dodgers led the Birds by only a game, the Cubs by two.

Although, as I wrote in *The Pilot Light and the Gas House Gang*, this was an era when the ball quivered like a jack rabbit and the pitchers quavered like quail, pitching always will out in any showdown, even one with a cruller twist.

Flint Rhem, scheduled to pitch the opener at Ebbets, showed up missing, which meant that when he reported, late and disheveled, he insisted that he had been "kidnapped" by gamblers and driven into New Jersey. So help his ancestors at Rhemsville, bad guys pointed a gun at his head and forced him to drink raw whiskey.

Even though the tongue-in-cheek story made good writing and reading at the time—Rhem blab-

Ol' Stubblebeard: Looking here more tired than tough, less menacing than when he faced batters unshaven, is Burleigh Grimes, the man who threw the last spitball that was offically permissible (1934). Grimes, a Hall of Fame pitcher, came aboard in mid-season, 1930, to help the Cardinals to a pennant that year and a world championship in '31. He mastered what Branch Rickey called the "purpose pitch," the knock-'em-down-and-make-'em behave intimidator.

bered at a reunion years later that the kidnapping story had been for the lower-case birds—a pitching change prompted a peerless hookup: Bill Hallahan versus "Dazzy" Vance.

Hallahan, a short, stubby left-hander, had been up and down since 1925, harrassed by his own wildness. A quiet, well-liked player, "Wild Bill" suddenly had become "Sweet William" in 1930. He threw a powerful fast ball and a jagged off-the-table curve. Vance, a big, ruddy-faced Florida cracker, had been among baseball's best pitchers.

Hallahan pitched with discomfort in his right hand, because a finger had been mashed when Ray Blades slammed a taxi door on it at the ball park. It was fortunate that the Binghamton, New York, pitcher threw lefthanded and that he was at his best, because Vance was too.

The game went scoreless into the tenth inning. With Gelbert limping because of an injury, Gabby Street sent up lefthanded-hitting High. Dazzy buzzed two fast balls past him. "I couldn't pull the trigger," said Andy. Vance's curve ball, like Hallahan's, dropped sharply, but "The Dazzler" switched to the hook and hung it a bit. High doubled off the fence in right-center.

Taylor Douthit's single scored

Andy. High then played third base as Sparky Adams shifted to short for the last of the tenth. The Dodgers filled the bases with one out. Brooklyn's catcher, Al Lopez, hit sharply to short, where the ball bad-hopped. Adams juggled it and, still not in control, shoveled the ball to Frisch, whose whirlwind pivot nipped Lopez at first.

So Hallahan's 1-0 masterpiece tied the race. Next day, with High again delivering a pinch double, the Redbirds rallied to win over a tough-nut Cuban curveballer, Adolfo Luque. They were in first place. Grimes recalled Breadon saying to him:

"I said a dozen, Burleigh; please make it thirteen."

Before Round One: Prior to the opening game of the pennant-deciding series in 1930 at Ebbets Field, the Cardinals' young lefthander, Bill Hallahan, posed with the Brooklyn Dodgers' great righthander, Arthur "Dazzy" Vance. In a high-scoring era, they pitched a 10-inning masterpiece won by Hallahan, 1-0, as a springboard to first place.

Handy Andy: Andy High, who served his country in two World Wars, served his home city well, too. The little lefthanded-hitting third baseman pinch-doubled to set up Bill Hallahan's opening-game victory over the Dodgers in September, 1930, at Brooklyn. He hit a key pinch double the next day, too.

He did, winning 5-3. The Cardinals, sweeping the showdown series, were in front to stay. They had won thirty-nine of their last forty-nine games for a torrid .796 pace, a two-length lead over Chicago. And when William Wrigley fired Joe McCarthy as manager, replacing him with 1929 pennant-winning star Rogers Hornsby, Wrigley kicked McCarthy upstairs into Yankee history.

Despite the twenty-one-out-of-twenty-five September for ninety-two victories, Hallahan led the pitching staff with only fifteen wins, but four others were in double figures: Grimes, Jesse Haines, Rhem and Syl Johnson. With the pennant won, a lean and lanky, high-cheekboned kid from Houston

"It's All Over Now": Never did a kid say so little that hurt so much as George Puccinelli's sing-song chant in the back of the Cardinals' getaway bus in defeat in 1930.

pitched a final-day victory. Dizzy Dean three-hit Pittsburgh, 3-1, and belted a double off the left field fence.

Although hitting was extremely heavy in 1930, the World Series was pitching-over-hitting if not over power. For instance, though Grimes allowed only five hits in the opener, Connie Mack's defending champion Philadelphia A's hit two homers (Mickey Cochrane and Al Simmons) and three doubles. Philly won 5-2 behind the great Lefty Grove, a 28-and-5 pitcher.

In the second game, Cochrane homered off Rhem to help George "Moose" Earnshaw, 6-1. When the Series moved to St. Louis, the Cardinals drew even. Hallahan shut out southpaw rival Rube Walberg, and Pop Haines outpitched Grove, 3-1.

Grimes was to throw the last legal spitball in the majors in 1934, and he covered his mouth with the glove on every pitch, but he threw a curve ball now and then rather than the sharp-dipping spitter. Early in the Series, he struck out Jimmy Foxx with the curve. In the ninth inning of a scoreless fifth game, Burleigh tried the hook again. Muscular "Double-X" looked for it. "Foxxie" hit one high into the bleachers off "Ol' Stubblebeard" to give the Athletics a 2-0 victory.

Back in Philadelphia, with Hallahan out early because of blisters on his pitching hand, Earnshaw and the A's breezed to the world championship, 7-1. The windfall losers' share of $3736.68 in the Series wouldn't look bad, but still—.

In the back of the bus after the sixth game, big George Puccinelli, who had batted .563 in sixteen times at bat in September, including three home runs and a double, set up a sing-song:

"It's all over now. . .it's all over now. . ."

Frisch growled. Another hard loser, Grimes, considerably shorter than the husky outfielder, got to his feet, walked back to Puccinelli and snapped:

"Listen, you big S.O.B., we know it's all over, but, dammit, we don't want to hear about it."

6

Pepper

Wild Horse of the Osage: Johnny Leonard Roosevelt "Pepper" Martin just didn't run the bases; he thundered. When he slid, which he did mostly belly-busting, the outfielder-third baseman of the Gas House Gang burrowed a furrow.

To Johnny Leonard Roosevelt "Pepper" Martin, life was a bowl of cherries with an occasional bourbon thrown in, but mainly it was the Bible and belly-busting slides. Rarely angry, the wide-shouldered, hawk-nosed man with the bronzed features of his Indian ancestry and the brashness of his familial Irish was hurt as he burst into Branch Rickey's office early in the 1931 season.

"John Brown," he exclaimed, using a proper name to substitute for an expletive in the same way Rickey employed "Judas Priest," "if you can't play me, Mr. Rickey, trade me."

Pepper had a point, because he'd been up and down for a few years, used mainly as a pinch runner when he didn't squirm restlessly on the bench. Martin had what Rickey liked and what the GM called the "spirit of adventure."

From the time the Cardinals bought him for $500 from France

Laux, a big league broadcaster later, but then coffee-and-caking in the baseball canebrake, Pepper was something as special as his nickname. It had been hung on him by Blake Harper, a hard-nosed former Fort Smith operator who became kingpin of the Cardinals' far-flung concessions operations.

Martin hitchhiked from Oklahoma to the Cardinals' spring-training camp in Avon Park, Florida, spending a night in jail en route. He reported, dirty and grimy, dressed as if he were about to stalk deer off the reservation back home. He hated neckties and any infielder who got in his joyous way on the bases.

A Rochester writer had dubbed him, aptly, the "Wild Horse of the Osage," but the awkward, aggressive athlete was really more like a Cape buffalo amuck. He'd thunder down to first base and stop with a lurch that would make an orthopedist groan. He hadn't had time yet to team with Dizzy Dean in hijinks and to drop bags of water onto Frank Frisch's bald pate outside hotel rooms on the road.

But, John Brown, he wanted to play. At the trading deadline in 1931, Rickey obliged him. Taylor Douthit, the center fielder, was only thirty, just three years older than Martin, but beneath those bushy brows, B. R. had dictated that "Tay" wasn't pulling the ball quite so well. Besides, he made $14,000

and Martin only $4500, and (ahem!) Mr. Rickey was credited with twenty percent of the annual profits.

Douthit didn't want to go, and over a weekend of rumors, he hit valiantly, boosting his average to .331 with eight hits in nine trips. All he did, though, was to make the separation more embarrassing, because he would be dealt on Friday to Cincinnati, then the Siberia of the National League, for Monday delivery.

So Martin and a towering rookie righthander named Paul Derringer were new regulars of '31. Rickey despised Derringer's living habits, but "Oom Paul," who would reach his pitching glory as the Reds went from the bottom to the top, had an 18-8 record his first season. Actually, no pitcher won twenty (Hallahan had nineteen), but the Cardinals won 101 games and Cadillacked to the pennant by thirteen and a half games.

As a novelty, Chick Hafey, the left fielder now wearing glasses, led the league with a .349 average, just a fraction ahead of teammate Jim Bottomley and defending champion Bill Terry. Terry had dipped from the National League's last .400 average partly because, to save salaries, the majors had dejuiced the ball and also eliminated the sacrifice fly, previously credited when a batsman advanced a runner from ANY base with a fly ball.

In St. Louis, after the landlord Browns erected a screen thirty feet high from the right field foul-line to right-center—from a point 310 to 354—the long ball also was affected. But Sportsman's Park rocked uncommonly on July 12, 1931. Just after a base-running scrape at Chicago, the Cardinals came back to play the Cubs, and a whopping crowd of 45,715 poured into the ball park, about 13,000 more than the

seating capacity. A doubleheader was a farce as the visitors won the first game, 7-5, the home team the second, 17-13. Of the thirty-three hits in the second game, twenty-three were doubles, ground-rule fly balls that fell in among spectators restrained by ropes in an arc from foul line to foul line. The record is as phony as a three-dollar bill.

But the Cardinals, well-seasoned and well-balanced, were indeed real, probably second only to the young 1942 whirlwinds. They proved their merit by topping Connie Mack's formidable foe that sought a third straight world championship with a Hall of Fame lineup of Mickey Cochrane, Al Simmons and Jimmy Foxx, led by Lefty Grove with a remarkable 31-and-4 season.

Before the Series, J. Roy Stockton, the *Post-Dispatch*'s pipe-puffing analyst, put the prognosis in the side pocket as easily as one of the best billiard players in Charley Peterson's downtown parlor. Stockton suggested that young, fired-up Pepper Martin, who had hit .300, well might be the World Series hero.

Pepper had prayed, "Please God, let me do well." In the opening game, he hit a two-run first-inning double off the great Grove and two other hits, but Derringer lost, 6-2.

Next day Martin was St. Louis's whole, limited show in a duel between Hallahan and George Earnshaw. Pep doubled, stole third and scored on a fly ball for one run. Later, he singled, stole second,

John Brown, Mr. Rickey: Visiting the office of the Cardinals' canny general manager with a package of venison to soften Branch Rickey at contract time, Pepper Martin wears a rare necktie—askew—and a handsome pair of new boots from down home in the Oklahoma territory.

Oom Paul: A towering rookie, Paul Derringer won 18 games for the Cardinals' pennant winners in 1931, but he contributed more to Cincinnati's champions of 1939-40.

moved to third on an infield out and eluded Cochrane's tag on Charley Gelbert's squeeze bunt.

The 2-0 victory was achieved with an incredible finish. In the A's ninth, with two on and two out, pinch hitter Jimmy Moore swung and missed an apparent game-ending third strike, a curve ball in the dirt. But instead of tagging out the runner as he stood there or flipping to Bottomley at first base, Jim Wilson arched the ball to Jake Flowers at third. The throw was off the bag with the runners in motion.

Alertly, Eddie Collins, coaching third, raced down to the plate as the Cardinals began to trot victoriously off the field and temporary-boxseat patrons and bleacher fans began to vault onto the playing surface. Collins shooed Moore to first base, and plate umpire Dick Nallin nodded. Yep, Wilson had trapped the ball.

Worse, as Flowers conceded later, the St. Louis third baseman, glancing quickly for a young nephew, would have flipped the ball to the kid if he'd spotted the boy's box seat. If Jake had thrown the ball into the stands, the tying runs would have scored.

When play was resumed, finally, Hallahan fortunately threw strikes to walk-wheedling Max Bishop, the leadoff man, who arched the ball to the belt-high box-seats installed for celebrities. Bottomley drifted over with Frisch hurrying behind him, yelling:

"Plenty of room, Jim, plenty of room. . ."

Bottomley banged into the wooden barrier and almost catapulted among spectators, reaching in for a brilliant game-ending catch. Shaken up, as he trotted off with Frisch gleefully pounding his back, "Sunny Jim" griped:

"What do you mean 'plenty of room?' "

Grinning, Frisch said, "Yeah, but you caught the ball, didn't you, Jim, old boy?"

Through the first five games, Martin was spectacular, collecting twelve hits, including four doubles and a home run. The Wild Horse ran wild, stealing five bases, scoring five runs and driving in five. If it hadn't been for Johnny—NEVER John, please—the Series wouldn't have gone to a seventh game.

In the windup at St. Louis, the Cardinals got only five hits, most of them bloopers. All were off the bats of the top two men in the batting order, Andy High and Watty Watkins. One of Watkins's was a two-run homer in the third inning when Earnshaw and Cochrane thought he'd be bunting. The Cardinals hung on to a 4-0 lead.

Grimes, the thirty-eight-year-old battler, had pitched a two-hit game earlier. Now, Mike Gonzalez, the third-string catcher-coach and a self-styled "smart dummy," strolled up from the left field bullpen after the eighth inning, ostensibly to get a drink of water. Mainly, Mike wanted to see Grimes's eyes before the decisive ninth.

Back in the bullpen, Gonzalez warbled to Hallahan in his cracked-

ice English, "Hey 'Moong' "—the closest Mike could get to Bill's in-house nickname for his round face—"Burleigh tire, you get rady."

So Hallahan, who had won two games, was loose and ready to save another. Suddenly, the Athletics scored two runs and had the tying two on base. Once again, Wild Bill was Sweet William as he faced Bishop. Max hit the ball sharply to left-center, but Pepper Martin thundered over, two-fisted the ball with gloved hand on top, juggled it and held on for a Series-ending catch.

Afterward, Judge Landis congratulated him in the clubhouse and said, "Young man, I'd rather trade

Say It With Flowers: They would have said it with flowers for Jake Flowers if the part-time third baseman had found a young nephew to whom to flip what should have been the game-ending third strike in a 1931 World Series boo-boo.

places with you than with any man in the country.''

The eagle-beaked guy grinned and said in his Southwest twang, ''Why, that'll be fine, Judge, if we can trade salaries, too.'' ($60,000 for $4500).

Money really meant only more spare tools or new gadgets for Pepper Martin's midget auto racer. Afterward, he went on a $1500-a-week vaudeville tour, a king's ransom for the Depression. But he tossed away the final five weeks ($7500) of a nine-week tour, explaining in his dressing room at Louisville:

''Heck, I ain't an actor, I'm a ball player. I'm cheatin' the public and the guy who's paying me the $1500. 'Sides, the huntin' season is on in Oklahoma—and that's more important.''

While Cardinal officials celebrated the world championship, Rickey sat thoughtfully behind a clouded cigar. They wondered why even a teetotaler showed so little enthusiasm. B. R., roused from his smoky reverie, said that he'd been thinking about Frisch.

Sure, though the Flash had been named Most Valuable Player in the National League with a .311 average, he had deserved the honor more at least in 1923 and 1927.

Frisch appeared to be aging gracefully. In September, running against young swifties, Martin and Ernie Orsatti, the old money player and base-swiper had jumped the gun and nipped them in a seventy-five-dollar race across the outfield.

''But what,'' mused Rickey, reviewing his farm system, ''what are we going to do when Frank gives out?''

In effect, they soon found out. Frisch went to Japan for an All-Star tour immediately after the World Series, then took his wife on a slow-boat trip around the globe. He got home overweight and heavy-legged and fell off in an injury-riddled 1932 season. Pepper Martin was even worse, a flop at only .238.

Typical of the Cardinals in that era, high-salaried gaffer Grimes was sold to Chicago and—worse!— Chick Hafey, the batting champion, was unloaded to Cincinnati.

Indeed, the Cardinals had a kid named Joe Medwick who would be coming up from Houston late in the 1932 season, but Hafey was a premier player, an angry one. Chick had been corseted with a three-year contract, pyramided modestly up from $8000 to $10,000, through the salad seasons before the Depression. He'd hit .337, .338 and .336, a paragon of consistency. He had twenty-seven, twenty-nine, and twenty-six homers and 111, 125 and 107 RBIs, even though he never played more than 138 games.

Smart Dummies: Mike Gonzalez's fractured-ice English of highest compliment was to use the appellation, which the capable Cuban coach of the Cardinals applied to himself and—reluctantly!—his long-time coaching sidekick, Clyde "Buzzy" Wares (left). To the Senor, Wares was "Cly" or "Bussy."

The Butler Did It: Choreographer of many madcap stunts of the Cardinals' Gas House Gang was the unexpected, switch-hitting first baseman, James "Ripper" Collins, who even carried around a typewriter to write columns for an Albany, N.Y., paper until manager Frank Frisch advised him one day to take a seat on the bench—or in the pressbox.

Stylish: Bill Walker, taking a throw at first base in spring training, was a neat, trim lefthander who looked a bit like the Prince of Wales before Edward became king of England and the Duke of Windsor. Walker, invited as the National League's earned-run leader in 1931 to pitch batting practice for the Cardinals in the '33 World Series, accepted graciously and soon pitched for the Redbirds from his East St. Louis home.

So he'd asked for $15,000 in 1930, just as the bottom dropped out, and the front office Mickey Moused until opening day. They signed him then and sent him to Danville to get himself in shape, docking him $2100 in pay. Consequently, he wound up with only $12,900. Now, he wanted that fifteen grand and the $2100 back, too.

In a huff, Hafey angrily drove his 1929 Auburn back from Florida to his chicken ranch in California, ninety miles an hour across the desert. Opening day, Breadon and Rickey dealt him to the Reds for a couple of warm bodies and cold cash.

The Cardinals were good and successful but also cunning in that period. For instance, obtaining Chicago's slump-shackled slugger, "Hack" Wilson, who had fallen off in home runs and fallen out with Hornsby, the Cubs' manager, Rickey offered Hack a salary cut from nearly $40,000 to $7500.

"Hell, Mr. Rickey, that ain't a salary cut; it's an amputation," said Wilson, promptly dealt to Brooklyn for $40,000 and someone to carry it. Hack never saw the inside of a St. Louis uniform.

To top off the trouble, Gabby Street suddenly began to believe his press clippings. At spring training, noting that Grimes was gone, he told other members of the so-called "brain trust," all of whom would be managers later, that from now on he'd call ALL the shots. Understand? Frisch, Wilson, Bottomley, et al. understood.

The Cardinals had more parties that spring than the country getting ready for the presidential election. The crowd booed baseball fan Herbert Hoover at the World Series in Philadelphia by chanting, "We want beer . . . we want beer."

The 1932 Cardinals dropped

farther than any world championship ball club in history, going from 101 victories to seventy-two, from first place to a tie with the Giants for sixth and seventh.

The situation worsened for 1933. The star young shortstop, Charley Gelbert, shot himself accidentally when hunting in the autumn, nearly ruining a leg. The shortstop position loomed as vulnerable as when Tommy Thevenow suffered a broken leg a few years earlier.

Because a banjo-eyed, switch-hitting power hitter from Rochester, Jimmy ''The Ripper'' Collins had come up in 1931 and outpowered Bottomley, the Cardinals traded good ol' Sunny Jim, a Hall of Famer. Actually, they'd brought up two more who would make the Hall of Fame, Joe Medwick and Dizzy Dean, but the ball club lacked balance as well as a major league shortstop.

Off-season, Rickey had outsmarted himself when he dealt Gus Mancuso to the New York Giants' new manager, Bill Terry. With a staff of low-ball pitchers (Carl Hubbell, Hal Schumacher, Fred Fitzsimmons, and others), Terry wanted an agile little guy who could hunker down like a kid in the sand for pitches that couldn't be hoisted out of the close-porch Polo Grounds' fences at the foul lines. New York won the pennant.

One of the ball players Rickey got—and of these only East St. Louis southpaw Bill Walker really helped the St. Louis cause—was a good-looking veteran outfielder, Ethan Allen, who would win a more permanent name as baseball coach at Yale, as the writer of instructional books on baseball and as the originator of clever baseball skill games that were more than children's toys.

But the erudite Allen pulled a dunce-cap play with the Cardinals. At New York, scheduled to bat behind Medwick, Ethan hit in front of him. He homered, too, but the Giants protested and the batting-out-of-turn appeal was upheld. The home run was canceled and—get this, because the hit-happy Medwick couldn't!—the proper batter (Medwick) was out. Out, mind you, without ever stepping up to the plate.

Allen, batting over, popped up and had to listen to the graphic protests of the muscular Magyar or ''Hungarian Rhapsody,'' as the more romantic called the outspoken Lord Medwick of Carteret, New Jersey.

To play shortstop, the Cardinals for a time even considered Frisch, who, by his own admission, as a shortstop was a helluva good second or third baseman. Who'd play second base? Why, bless his losing stack of race-track tickets, Rogers Hornsby was back, broke. Sentimentally signed as a free agent after he'd been released in August, 1932, as manager of the Cubs, who

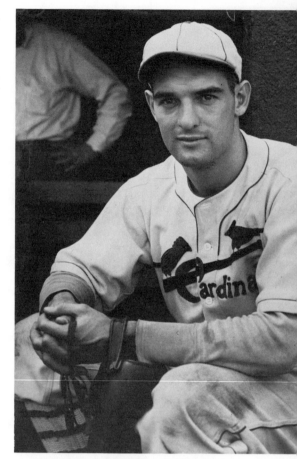

Oops! Ethan Nathan Allen, later baseball coach at Yale and inventor of scientific baseball games, was an intelligent man—yep, smart dummy!—but not the day he batted out of turn, lost a home run and a time at bat for angry, hit-hungry Joe Medwick.

Trivia Triumph: If anyone doubts that Rogers Hornsby (left) and Frank Frisch ever played TOGETHER, here's the proof. The Rajah joined The Flash temporarily in 1933, the year Frisch became manager of the Cardinals and Hornsby moved over to the rival Browns as field foreman.

didn't vote him a penny when they won the pennant for Charley Grimm, Rog had been rehired by the men who had let him go, Breadon and Rickey.

For a time, the Cardinals wanted to play Hornsby, but he was thirty-seven and had suffered a broken leg a couple of years earlier. He never had been able to go back on pop flies, prompting J. Roy Stockton to suggest, tongue in cheek, that the Rajah had a weakness handling pop-ups because he hit so few himself. But now, he couldn't move too well.

Frisch, in turn, was miscast at shortstop, explaining later, "I couldn't go to my left, and Rog couldn't go to his right. So we camped like conventioneers around second base."

Hornsby could still hit, though, as evidenced by a .325 average in July when he was released to become manager of the neighboring Dodier Street offices of the Browns. Rival Frisch had just become manager of the Cardinals.

Gabby Street resented Frisch's taking over even though his former captain had been, traditionally, his best player. The Old Sarge thought the Flash had "laid down" on him in 1932. Angrily, Frisch agreed, yeah, he hadn't been able to run out every play because he was swaddled on both legs with bandages. And, no, he didn't want the old buzzard's job, but, by God, if he ever did manage, he'd tell the press when he played a man under handicap. "Uncle Frank" did.

Breadon and Rickey brushed off Street's efforts to fine Frisch $5000—gadzooks, the former $28,000-a-year second baseman was down to $18,500 as player-manager in the Depression depths—and then they brushed off Street as manager in July, 1933.

Frisch improved the ball club with a bit of hypo, but it still finished fifth, 82-71, even though the outlook was fair and warmer. Noisier, too, because wheeling and dealing like a mustached old riverboat gambler—pardon the comparison, Mr. Rickey—Branch put together a trade that, essentially, sent Derringer to Cincinnati for light-hitting Leo Durocher.

Seated in his hotel bed, a heaping breakfast before him, Rickey expounded on the deal, then lit up a victory cigar. He knew that Durocher, a twenty-seven-year-old fashion plate with slicked-back hair and a booming voice, would be the answer at the most sensitive defensive position.

C'mon, Fellas, Smile: Shortly before Frank Frisch succeeded Gabby Street as manager in July, 1933, Street had suggested his top star had "laid down on him." Frisch, injured, resented it. Characteristically, The Flash always perched his cap high on his head.

Unannounced, uninvited, Durocher roared into Rickey's office later and did the unexpected. He called Mr. Rickey by his first name, which even Mrs. Rickey rarely did in public.

"Branch," rasped Durocher, "I'm glad to be aboard and I'll help you win pennants, but if you think I'm going to do it for a measly $6000 a year . . ."

Tall Tex: James Otto "Tex" Carleton was a better pitcher than fighter, hooking up in fisticuffs with Dizzy Dean, who couldn't fight, and Joe Medwick, who could.

Amused, Rickey, the past master at oratory, let Durocher have it about bad debts, alimony, child support, et cetera. "Lippy Leo" left the room abashed but unbroken. Thereafter, he would be the old man's favorite reclamation project.

Of Durocher, Rickey would say that "The Lion," whom he later regarded highly as a manager, "had an infinite capacity for making a bad situation immediately worse."

Their long-time association began shortly before the shift in field command, which followed a most unusual doubleheader at New York that proved two things:

"King Carl" Hubbell of the Giants could throw strikes all day, not walking a man as he beat Tex Carleton and Jesse Haines in eight-

een innings, 1-0. Rogers Hornsby could hit in the pitch dark at midnight, because, pinch-batting in the last inning of the second game, lost by Dizzy Dean also 1-0, the Rajah drilled a line-drive single.

It was so dark then, and Leroy "Tarzan" Parmelee of the Giants threw so hard that when Durocher batted, trying awfully hard to keep his derriere out of the third-base visitors' dugout, he stalked away from a blurring fast ball as the umpire signalled Strike Two.

"But that's only Strike Two," announced the man in blue.

"Hell," lipped Leo, finally forced to wave futilely at another one, "you take the third one."

You're Hooked, Diz: Although Dizzy Dean proved over the years a clever con man on the golf course and in other instances of good-natured chance, Ol' Diz never saw the day he could out-slick at the card table a fella who dressed and behaved as slickly as Leo Durocher (right). The guy in the middle is smart. Lon Warneke sits it out.

7

Ol' Diz
& the
Gas House
Gang

Dizzy Dean had three birthplaces, two first and middle names and one supreme ego that, "dawgonnit," as "Ol' Diz" would say when he was just a skinny kid, was almost as good as his high, hard fast ball.

A cotton chopper from Lucas, Arkansas, who tried to give New York nice-guy writers each "a scoop" by telling them he was born in Oklahoma and Mississippi in different years, was a poor public's fresh symbol of a gabby, flannel-clad Horatio Alger conquering all in the dry cesspool of drouth-and-Depression. Dizzy was one of the most colorful characters of the merry madcaps, baseball's "Gas House Gang."

Dizzy liked to say he'd gone no farther in school than fourth grade because, shucks, he didn't want to show up his pop, who had stopped at second (grade). It was Alfred Dean, wandering the cotton-country by-ways with his kids as poor-mouth itinerants, who bailed his son out of the Army at Fort Sam Houston, San Antonio. You could do that for a

hundred bucks in the peace-time Army before World War II.

Dizzy, nicknamed by an Army sergeant who should have been a sports writer, pitched for a San Antone streetcar company for thirty dollars a month and was seen by Frank Snyder, former Redbird catcher managing Houston.

So the skinny kid with the self-abiding faith broke in at St. Joseph, Missouri, in the Western League in 1930. There, spreading around his dough as if he had some, he rented three hotel rooms, which, after all, were at least one more than his Christian names.

"Ol' Diz," as he termed himself before he was old enough to vote, had been named Jay Hanna because, after all, Pop knew there was a big-money big shot who could stand a little more publicity, too. But then a neighbor's kid had died young, and Jay Hanna, feeling sorry for the sorrowing old man, said, why, Mr. Herman, he'd be glad to be the old guy's kid. So he would become the second Jerome Herman.

Poetry in Motion: Before he became an overstuffed broadcaster, Dizzy Dean was a rawboned righthander who threw hard with a fluid, three-quarter delivery. He was, in truth, as good as he thought he was, which was considerable. Dizzy was the last National League pitcher to win 30 games (1934).

Truthfully, more baseball men, such as Branch Rickey and Frank Frisch, called Dizzy "Jerome" than "Jay." However, to Pat Nash, a sales clerk in a Houston department store whom he later married, he was "Jay." Brother Paul called him that, too.

Dizzy was such a big winner in the Texas League that the Cardinals brought him up at the end of their tail-end pennant triumph in 1930 and, as mentioned earlier, he pitched a final-game three-hitter to beat Pittsburgh, 3-1. He undoubtedly would have been on the great 1931 champions, also, indicating that the club might have finished further out of the league's sight, but he talked himself back to the bushes.

He overslept, overspent and wound up a dollar-a-day man, rationed by traveling sec Clarence Lloyd on high-command orders. He did get thrust into action against the powerful Athletics and struck out Cochrane, Simmons and Foxx in succession, telling Gabby Street that, golly, if the Old Sarge had had "Ol' Diz" in the 1930 Series, they'd be flapping the world championship flag at Sportsman's Park.

So they sent the "Great One" back to Houston, at which time Jim Lindsey, a big blond St. Louis relief pitcher, sighed derisively. "Gosh," he said, "I guess that's the first time a ball club ever lost thirty games in one day."

At Houston, Dizzy "fogged" in

his fast ball, to use his own descriptive verb for his high velocity pitch, and married Pat Nash, even though she refused a ceremony at home plate. Pat, over the years, could use all the language, and she would mother and wet-nurse the pitcher, for while Dean was a shrewd gambler and a con man on the golf course, he was a bit naive and open-hearted. Pat saved $1200 of the $3000 he made in 1931 and built his earnings into a secure fortune. Quietly, the Deans helped needy former players.

After winning twenty-six games at Houston, Dizzy was 18-15 with that lousy, far-down-low championship St. Louis team in 1932. When he missed a train and Gabby Street was set to fine him $100, Dizzy sweet-talked the manager into waiting until he had pitched against Pittsburgh. Dean shut 'em out, and Street forgot the fine.

In 1933, as the Cardinals inched up nine victories to fifth place under Street and Frank Frisch, Dizzy was 20-and-18. En route, he struck out seventeen Chicago Cubs, then a major league record at a time when choked-grip batters didn't strike out nearly so often.

For 1934, Frisch's first full season as manager, the talent-rich Cardinals brought up a young battery from Columbus. Bill DeLancey, the catcher, was only twenty-three and Paul Dean, Dizzy's younger brother, was twenty-one. Jerome… er, Jay…was firm about it. "If they give Paul the ball," he said, "me 'n' Paul will win forty-five games."

Frisch tried, aware that he not only needed another pitcher, but that a brother battery wouldn't hurt the sagging gate. Sam Breadon, concerned about giving away anything, had barred play-by-play radio, which had begun the year of the first pennant (1926). Competitive stations served the St. Louis area, but in 1934 they were not permitted to broadcast the games.

One announcer, Thomas Patrick (Convey), tried to bootleg the games from a step-ladder using binoculars atop the YMCA across the street in deepest center field, but Breadon stopped that. The only way you could get the results in '34 was in fast-flying, play-by-play presses of the two afternoon newspapers or by a similar quick-action rundown on radio immediately after the 3 p.m. games ended.

In right field, Frisch had placed an American League retread named Jack Rothrock, because Rothrock, too, acted as if he'd played under John McGraw. Rothrock, batting second, just ahead of Frisch, gave the Flash three switch-hitters among the top five batters. (Rip Collins hit fifth.) At one time Leo Durocher had switched, also, but he'd been talked out of it at Cincinnati. Frisch hammered at his young righthanded-hitting shortstop to hit to right field.

Steady as a (Roth) Rock: An American League retread, beating his way back up from the bushes after a broken leg, gladdened Frank Frisch's McGravian-trained heart. Jack Rothrock was a smooth right fielder and good No. 2-spot batter, a switch-hitter who could hit behind the runner to right field.

Behind the plate, Frisch wanted to alternate young DeLancey with "Spud" Davis, a good righthanded hitter. (Jimmy Wilson, Frisch's old friend, asked to be traded.) Frisch was delighted that the young, knock-kneed DeLancey threw extremely well and had the moxie to tell the great Dean not to horse around when "Dee" was behind the plate or he (Bill) would knock him (Dizzy) on his duff. Diz loved it.

He loved it, too, when Frisch stuck with brother Paul, advised by Mike Gonzalez, who had been brought back from Columbus to coach. Mike insisted that "Pablo" would win, "Frohnk." Long-jawed, not quite so tall as Dizzy and with heavier legs that made him subject to shin splints, Paul was completely

unlike Dizzy. He was never "Daffy"; that nickname was totally inappropriate. As a kid, he said little, except one day when Frisch was disciplining his older brother and Paul piped up, "Hey, Jay, why don't you punch that Dutchman in his nose."

But Paul really liked the "Dutchman," as most players called Frisch. With good reason, too. Frank started him once, twice, three times. Paul was hit hard and early.

Finally, in mid-May on a Ladies' Day against the world champion Giants, Frisch started P. Dean against New York's great lefthander, Carl Hubbell. Frisch, playing second base, helped with his own bat, and after a slow start, the younger Dean won in ten innings, 3-2. He was off to a nineteen-game season, throwing a heavy, sinking fast ball unlike Diz-

zy's high, lively fast ball that took off. J. Dean also had a better curve and change-up.

DeLancey began to catch more, even though Frisch kept insisting that the strong lefthanded hitter was swinging off-stride at the change-up and, dammit, he ought to take the pitch. At Cincinnati on Memorial Day, Dee timed a letup, hit it over the right field fence and, accepting congratulations, sat down and said loud enough for Frisch to hear:

"I wonder how the Dutch bleep liked that one?"

The Gas House Gang drove Frisch delightfully nuts. They called him John McGraw, Jr., and, in fact, the Giants had tried to lure him back from Sam Breadon in 1932, presumably to have him succeed the old man as field foreman. But one

You Can Do, Pablo: When Paul Dean (left) faltered early in his rookie season, 1934, the most optimistic other than Paul's older brother, Dizzy, was coach Mike Gonzalez. Mike had managed P. Dean the previous year at Columbus, O. Said Gonzalez to Frank Frisch, "Pablo can do, Frohnk." He did—19 victories' worth and two in the World Series.

Spud: He was big and slow, a base-running handicap, but Virgil "Spud" Davis was a good righthanded hitter (.308 for 16 years) and capable coming off the bench to hit, too. A heckuva No. 2 catcher, if not the most agile as No. 1.

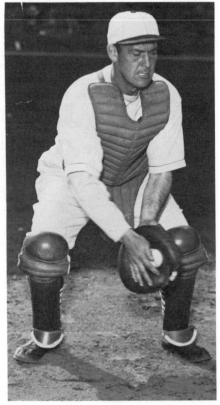

One Moment of Greatness: Bill DeLancey, a 22-year-old rookie, hit .315 as the Cardinals' catcher in 1934, taking over as regular. He caught every game in the World Series, sassed big-star Dizzy Dean whenever Dean horsed around and would have been, Branch Rickey predicted, one of the three greatest catchers ever. Tuberculosis hit him in 1935, however, and he was dead at 45.

New Yorker (Breadon) loved the other (Frisch). Frisch could be tough, as all McGraw-trained men were, but he had a sense of humor that made him enjoy hijinks and low comedy even if he couldn't show it.

He loved the aggressiveness of his swaggering left fielder, Joe Medwick, who had come up late in the 1932 season from Houston and hit .349. Later, "Jersey Joe" would bat .353, .351 and .374 in successive seasons, the last as the National League's most recent Triple Crown champion. In 1937, in his 237 hits, Medwick had fifty-six doubles and thirty-one home runs, driving in 154 runs.

But by 1934, hitching his left leg and swinging that big black bat at anything he could reach, the twenty-two-year-old Medwick hit to all fields and almost as savagely as he fought. Joe really wasn't quite so mean, but the hot-tempered Hungarian would be at a loss for words and—.

"Dawggonit," Dizzy Dean complained, "all a guy wants to do is sound off with a little chin music, and before you can open your mouth, that Joe whomps you. Ain't fair."

One day at Pittsburgh, Dizzy thought that Medwick, whose out-fielding at times could be indifferent, permitted a fly ball to drop inside the foul line as if it were land mined. Three runs scored. Afterward, Dizzy bitched in the dugout, and Paul joined him. One word led to another with the nasty Medwick. The Dean brothers got up and clump-clumped, spiked shoes on wooden floor, toward him. Medwick picked up his bat and said, "Step right up, boys, and I'll separate you brothers."

An inning later, Medwick muscled a grand-slam homer. He came to the bench, drank from the water cooler, then filled his mouth and walked over to where Dean sat. Joe spit the water on Dizzy's shoes and said, "All right, you big meathead, there's your three runs back and one extra. Let's see you hold the damned lead."

Another time "Joey," as Frisch called him, tangled with the first-baseman, Rip Collins. Frisch made the rest of the clubhouse stand by until they wearily punched themselves out. Frank stepped between them, threw his arms around them and said, smiling, "All right, you guys, now kiss and make up. I mean, shake hands. Dammit, fellas, you're on the same side. Let's fight the other side more and each other less."

Mostly, they'd clown, but Frisch blanched as Pepper Martin got a half-Nelson on Dizzy in a clubhouse "fun" wrestling match one day and nearly put Dean out of action. In a hotel lobby, Dizzy and Pepper would put pop corn in their mouths and fake a fight, spraying the corn as if it were flying teeth. They horrified little old ladies. And Frisch paid to have more than one suit of clothes dry-cleaned because he couldn't catch up with Pepper Martin as a water-target bombardier who'd drop a wet paper-bag block-buster and beat the Flash into the hotel lobby, sitting there reading the stock market or whatever made him look innocent.

They loved to play, day and night. Ernie Orsatti was a clotheshorse dandy. An habitue´of Hollywood, where his brother, Frank, was a prominent movie agent, Ernie doubled for silent screen comedian Buster Keaton. He drove a flashy, cream-colored

Auburn with red leather seats with as much showmanship as he played center field, making the easy catches look hard. But the little lefthanded hitter hit the great Hubbell as if they were kissing cousins.

Orsatti liked to outfox Frisch. At night in hotels, he'd tip hotel operators to switch late calls to him at a supper-club table so that when Frisch phoned his "room" as a bed-check, Ernie grumbled that, cripes, couldn't the Flash let a guy get his rest? But, hey Ern, what about that music in the background?

"Oh," Ernie would suggest sweetly, "I was just reading in bed again, Frank, and fell asleep without turning off the radio."

Pepper Martin would be off fight-managing an Oklahoma light-heavyweight named "Junior" Munsell or the Cardinals' batboy, "Kayo" Brown, who got so walloped one night that Paul Dean, scheduled to pitch a big ball game the next day, lost his ringside hot dog in sensitive upheaval and had to beat a hasty retreat.

The Gas Housers would "psych" the foe horribly in the sweat box of 1934 and 1936 when, for instance, with practically no air-conditioning for relief, the weather was hotter than the summer of 1980. Dizzy Dean and Pepper Martin would build a fire in front of the dugout, put Indian blankets around their shoulders and huddle as if freezing.

On a hot day or cold, Martin would wind up as center man of a tricky sideline pepper game, one filmed by trainer "Doc" Weaver and used as a billboard of televised

Muscles and His Mentor: Joe Medwick (left), dashing, hard-hitting young left fielder of the Gas House Gang, was molded into a well-dressed ball player by the smooth shortstop who couldn't carry Muscles' bat, Leo Durocher.

Hollywood: That was Ernie Orsatti, a razzle-dazzle showboat, fast and versatile, capable at first base and, trained by his off-season life-style, he made the easy catches look hard in the outfield. Pretty good hitter. He loved to needle Frank Frisch and to hit Carl Hubbell.

The Pepperpot: Lively Pepper Martin had a manly chest and liked to show it, whether facing a camera or knocking down a hot smash with his strong frame at third base. Yeah, and a strong, if wild arm.

games now. Pep would be sleight-of-hand center man with Orsatti and Rip Collins. Or they'd put on a phantom infield. Pretty good plays, too—without a ball!—or Pepper and Frisch would get into a burnout in which the manager would back Martin up past third base until Pepper surrendered by jumping into a box seat.

Pepper really could throw, too. He played third base without a jock strap much less a protective cup, but he'd knock down hot smashes with his hairy chest. At times he unfurled the hardest, wildest throws past a retreating Collins at first base. If the other side bunted, Martin didn't like that. If the game weren't in the balance, he might pick up the ball and throw it—at the runner, not the bag.

Actually, playing like a junior-grade, less-graceful Frisch, Pepper had a way with the manager. One evening after a tough loss at New York to the Giants, whom the Cardinals trailed most of the 1934

season, Frisch pulled a McGraw. Angrily, he refused to permit his players to change clothes. They sat there miserably, cooling clammily in sweaty uniforms, until Martin finally spoke up.

"Frank, can I ask a question?"

"Yeah, what?"

"I just wonder, Frank: Should I paint my 'midget' red with white wheels or white with red wheels?"

Frisch laughed. The whole team laughed. "Get your butts out of here," growled the Flash, ready to go home to New Rochelle and hit the cold beer and *kalteraufschnitt*, "and especially you, Martin."

In late August, the ball club came together as a team when Dizzy Dean led brother Paul in revolt. Dizzy, paid $7500 himself then, wanted Paul paid more than $3000, the rookie salary Bill DeLancey also got. The Deans skipped a charity exhibition game in Detroit. Frisch slapped a $100 fine on each brother. Dizzy tore up a uniform in disgust, and when a photographer asked him to tear up another, Dean obliged. Club

treasurer Bill DeWitt billed him thirty-six dollars for uniforms.

Fresh, Dizzy insisted, "I understand the Dutchman is good with a needle and thread." He refused to get into uniform. The brothers Dean were suspended.

Frisch had only twenty-one players that year, two under the tough-times' reduction to a twenty-three man limit, and two of his players were pitching geezers, Dazzy Vance, forty-three, and Jesse Haines, forty-one. Now, Martin was hurt, and Frisch moved to third base and played handsome young Burgess Whitehead, the University of North Carolina Phi Beta Kappa, at second.

"Dammit," Frisch said, spitting into his little glove and mechanically rubbing it in as he held a clubhouse meeting. "NOBODY, but nobody, is bigger than this game."

The Gang came through. Bill Walker was back from a broken wrist. Bill Hallahan came out of a

A Big Hand For Whitey: Burgess Whitehead, Phi Beta Kappa from the University of North Carolina, was so graceful that the Post-Dispatch's *J. Roy Stockton nicknamed him "The Gazelle." Although ham-handed Whitey wasn't regarded as durable enough by the Cardinals to replace Frank Frisch regularly at second base, he was dealt to New York and helped the Giants to pennants in 1936 and '37.*

slump. "Tex" Carleton helped. The Cardinals won eight out of nine games before Judge Landis, the commissioner, came to St. Louis for a hearing to make certain the ball club had been fair with the brothers Dean. They had.

Losing a Labor Day double-header at Pittsburgh, the Cardinals were seven games behind, but they were rolling. Dizzy Dean shut out the Giants. Then the Cardinals went East and continued to win as the Giants began to lose.

The deficit was five and a half games with fourteen to play including a doubleheader before a 50,000-plus crowd. Frisch singled home the winning runs in a 5-3 opener, and Pepper Martin's eleventh-inning homer gave Paul Dean his second extra-inning victory of the series, 3-1.

Then the Cardinals got permission to make up a doubleheader rained out previously at Brooklyn. This was the time Frisch argued with Dizzy how to pitch to certain hitters and Dean complained, "Frank, I don't see how a little old infielder like you could tell a great pitcher like me how to pitch."

Years later, laughing, Frisch would say, "The big jughead didn't know I was calling all his pitches. I'd signal past him to Bill DeLancey, who'd give him the sign. I'd give it quickly so that the other side wouldn't catch on, or Dizzy either.

At Brooklyn, Dean held the Dodgers hitless until the eighth, then coasted to a three-hit victory, 13-0. Brother Paul followed with a 3-0 no-hitter, causing Dizzy to apologize. "Gee whiz," he said, "if I'd known Paul was gonna do it, I'd-a done it, too."

In the final week of the season, with Branch Rickey's blessing and to Frank Frisch's annoyance, the Flash's partner in umpire-battling, Leo Durocher, was married to a chic dress designer, Grace Dozier. Ernie Orsatti was the best man. B. R. always did think marriage was a ball player's best friend—and mate. He was right. Light-hitting Durocher hit timely to help with two straight victories, and New York was tied in the race, even up with two games to play.

At New York the winter before, Bill Terry had said facetiously when asked about the rival Dodgers, "Is Brooklyn still in the National League?"

From Flatbush to Greenpernt, every joik in the jernt, as they pronounced it near the Gowanus Canal, seemed to come across the Brooklyn Bridge for the showdown, bearing signs taunting Terry. They did it, too. Van Lingle Mungo beat Hubbell, 5-1, as Paul Dean turned back the Reds, 6-1.

If Only These Were Talkies: If books talked, you'd hear Frank Frisch's high-pitched nasal squeal, probably profane, and Leo Durocher's booming, rasping voice, equally as descriptive, in a tirade against a p-o-o-r umpire. The Flash wasn't playing that day. See how smaller gloves used then fit into a player's hip pocket?

Even before Ol' Diz won his thirtieth game with a shutout flourish, whistles blew and automobile horns honked in an informal parade around town because the Giants' final-day 8-5 loss preceded St. Louis's wrapup victory, 9-0. Only 334,866, of which nearly one-third had shown up the final week, had watched a successful, historic pennant race in St. Louis.

Afterward, Rip Collins, whose .333 average, thirty-five homers and 135 RBIs led the '34 Cardinals, sang an appropriate Depression song hit, "We're in the Money." That night down at Jim Mertikas's old Grecian Gardens, an area that now houses St. Louis's Busch Stadium, Dazzy Vance couldn't get any strong-hearted teammate to share his belly-busting drink. The "Dazz-Marie" had rye, bourbon, scotch, gin, sloe gin, vermouth, brandy and benedictine in an over-sized, ice-laden glass, dolloped with powdered sugar and a cherry atop the witch's brew!

No wonder the Cardinals didn't fear the powerful Detroit Tigers in the World Series. From the time Dizzy Dean audaciously took a bat out of home-run hitter Hank Greenberg's hands at an open-date batting practice and hit one into the left-field bleachers at Navin Field, it was a Dean brothers' series.

On opening day, with movie actor-cowboy-newspaper humorist Will Rogers accompanying him, Dizzy was taken out to Henry Ford's home for breakfast with the automobile pioneer, the Series radio sponsor. Rogers urged Dizzy to be respectful to the grand old man, who held out a hand and said:

"Welcome, Mr. Dean."

"Put 'er there, Henry," Dizzy breezed. "I'm sure glad to be here, 'cause I heard so much about you; but I'm sorry, I'm a-gonna have to make pussycats out of your Tigers."

He did. Dizzy won the opener, 8-3. After misplays behind Bill Hallahan cost a game lost by Bill Walker in twelve innings, 3-2, Paul Dean came back home to St. Louis and gained a 4-1 victory. Tex Carleton and associates then were cuffed in a 10-4 game famous for Dizzy Dean's injury as a pinch runner.

Dizzy tried to break up a double play by going in straight up, and shortstop Bill Rogell low-bridged him, conking Dean on the forehead with a throw. Dizzy was carried off, but Paul was sure he was all right because he'd been talking.

Saying what?

"Nuthin! Just talkin'."

Dizzy came out from under the bedsheets to pitch well in the fifth game, but Detroit's king of the curve ball, Tommy Bridges, pitched masterfully, winning 3-1.

Me 'n Paul and "Edna": Dizzy and Paul Dean surround towering Lynwood "Schoolboy" Rowe, Detroit Tigers' ace, before the 1934 World Series. Rowe, 24-8, tied the league record of 16 straight.

So the Cardinals were down, three games to two, as they returned to Detroit to face Lynwood "Schoolboy" Rowe, who had tied the American League record of sixteen straight victories that year. The Cardinal bench had been sizzling Rowe's ears since they'd heard him say to his girl friend back home in Arkansas on a national radio broadcast:

"How'm I doin', Edna?"

With Leo Durocher contributing three hits and Paul Dean driving in his own winning run, 4-3, the Series came down to its moment of truth. It had been rough and ready.

Bill DeLancey had been fined fifty dollars for language unbecoming the ears of umpire "Brick" Owens of the American League. Judge Landis heard the language umpire Bill Klem of the National League and Detroit's "Goose" Goslin used on a hotel elevator, and he hit them for fifty dollars each, too.

Pepper Martin slid roughshod into people, putting even manager-catcher Mickey Cochrane into a hospital overnight. "Black Mike" was hailed in a sticky newspaper photograph as "Our Stricken Leader," and that brought a derisive hoot from St. Louis bench jockeys. When the Tigers' "JoJo" White bowled over old man Frisch, Durocher suggested that maybe he ought to cover second.

"No, next time," said the Flash brightly, "we'll BOTH cover." They

did. Frisch plopped heavily on White's vertebrae, and Lippy Leo sat on JoJo's head.

Before the final game, as Eldon Auker warmed up with his under-handed delivery, Dizzy Dean paused behind him and asked with calculated innocence, "You don't expect to get anybody out with THAT bleep, do you?"

Dizzy opened a decisive third inning with a single, and used speed, daring and a good slide to stretch the base hit into a double. When Pepper Martin grounded to Hank Greenberg's right at first base, Greenberg had no easy forceout at second. Pepper beat the throw to first and stole second. A walk to Jack Rothrock filled the bases.

By now, feeling his thirty-seven years, Frank Frisch had lost some of the old zip. In fact, Branch Rickey had suggested aloud that spring to publicist Gene Karst that he'd like to deal the Flash to Boston for catcher Al Spohrer, but he knew Sam Breadon wouldn't stand for that. Now, Frisch's old money-player skill came back.

Frisch fouled off seven pitches with a full count, then lined a three-run double into the right field corner. The Flash squatted happily at second base, as Cochrane made a pitching change in a seven-run inning in which Dean would hit safely again. The Dutchman thought about his clutch hit.

"Hey," he said to himself, "I ought to be over there on third base. If one of my men had 'sight-seen' this play, I would have fined him fifty bucks."

With the Cardinals ahead after six innings, 9-0, Medwick slid hard into third base with a triple. He and Marv Owen, the third baseman, kicked at each other. When Medwick trotted to left field after the inning, fans in the towering old bleachers vented their spleen on him.

In a Battle of Produce Row, Detroit fans fired empty boxes and box lunches, apple cores, bananas, hardboiled eggs and other items, hard and soft. Medwick stood there, a respectful distance from the barrier, hands on hips.

His mentor, Durocher, came out, put an arm around him and said, "They can't do that to you, Joe. Don't back off."

Snapped Medwick, "If you're so damned brave, why don't you play left field and let me play short-stop."

Ultimately, for Medwick's sake, Judge Landis removed the St. Louis left fielder, over the player's and Frisch's protest, when the commissioner could have declared the game forfeited.

The 11-0 final saw the Cardinals rewarded with a capital $5389.75 each, a whopping amount for the time, especially when it well-exceeded some players' salaries. Next highest to Frisch's $18,500 salary then was the $9000 paid two former World Series heroes, Martin and Hallahan.

No Kick Coming: When Joe Medwick tripled for his eleventh hit as the Cardinals romped in the seventh game of the 1934 World Series, his feet became entangled with those of Marv Owen, Detroit third baseman. Owen thought Medwick had spiked him and kicked at Joe. Muscles kicked back. So angry Tiger fans, sullen over an 11-0 defeat, threw everything except a fit at Medwick when he took his position in left field.

Afterward, even Dizzy Dean, the National League's Most Valuable Player, was astounded. "Just think," he said, "I really didn't know how good me 'n' Paul were. I said we'd win forty-five games and, dawggone, we won forty-nine in the season and four more in the World Series."

In 1935, Dizzy and Paul might have pitched the Cardinals to another pennant. Paul again won nineteen games and Dizzy another standout total twenty-eight. With Hallahan bouncing back to post a 15-8 record, the Cardinals actually won one game more (ninety-six) than in 1934.

They were stronger, partly because they had come up with a brilliant young center fielder, ruggedly handsome Terry Moore, who would rank ahead of even Curt Flood and Taylor Douthit as their best center fielder defensively. In addition, "Tee" Moore got off to a solid first-season start, batting .287.

Colorful and Capable: Two of baseball's finest, most glamorous stars, Dizzy Dean, just 24 years old, and Babe Ruth, finishing up bulging-bellied at 40 with the Boston Braves, after having been king of the home runs with the Yankees, meet in spring training (1935).

A Master of Defense: Terry Moore, Redbird rookie center fielder in 1935, became one of the great outfielders and over the years a steady hitter, too. Tee Moore inspired the St. Louis Swifties of the early 1940s.

With a fourteen game winning streak, longest in the Cardinals' history, the ball club caught the Giants again, but earlier this time. Manager Frisch, sidelined for too long early in the season with a nasty spike wound on his gloved hand, teamed with rookie Moore down the stretch.

The oldest player, thirty-eight, and the youngest, twenty-three, were the hottest. But, quietly, after losing a Labor Day opener, Charley

Grimm's Chicago Cubs began to win and win and win. In the final weeks, a broken leg suffered by Moore hurt the Cardinals, but they really never folded. Chicago just won twenty-one in a row, including a key 1-0 victory for Lon Warneke over Paul Dean on a home run by Phil Cavarretta in the final week.

It was Chicago, not St. Louis, in the World Series, won by Detroit. And Bill Lee, obtained by the Cubs from St. Louis's American Association farm club, matched Warneke as a twenty-game winner.

The Arkansas Hummingbird: Droll Lon Warneke, later a National League umpire and a municipal judge in Hot Springs, Ark., proved in spring training that his easy-does-it approach to life was a fact, not fiction.

A year later, disaster. Tuberculosis sidelined great young Bill DeLancey. Holding out for a $1000 raise to $8500, Paul Dean missed all of spring training until the team was barnstorming home from Florida and then tried to get into shape too quickly. His first time out, a fading Frisch hit a home run to give him a 3-2 win, and he rolled to five early victories, but then something snapped in the resilient right arm.

At only twenty-three, when it really should have been beginning for Paul Dean, it was all over and for DeLancey, too.

A dollar short in pitching, with Burgess Whitehead traded to New York (in time to help win two pennants) because Rickey didn't think he had enough stamina to replace Frisch at second, the Cardinals also were handicapped at second base. A stripling named Stu Martin, brought in to ease Frisch's way into retirement carpet slippers, became indisposed.

So even though a big young guy named Johnny Mize, who began to flex his muscles at first base, hitting .329 as an alternate to Rip Collins, shifted to the outfield, the Cardinals backed down into a second-place tie. When Lon Warneke and the Cubs beat twenty-four-game winner Dizzy Dean on the final day, 6-3, the clubs finished even with 87-67 records.

To boost the pitching staff for 1937, Rickey swapped Collins to Chicago for Warneke. The "Arkansas Hummingbird" with the outsized tobacco chaw giving him the look of Popeye the Sailor was a droll character, later an umpire and then a judge back home in Hot Springs, Arkansas. He won eighteen games, but his fast ball lacked some of its old snap, as witness a 4.52 earned-run average. The home-run ball began to plague him in a ballpark

Fore and Aft: Big Johnny Mize, slugging first baseman for the Cardinals, set the city's home-run record of 43 in 1940 and later belted the long ball for both the New York Giants and Yankees. He could hit for average, too.

with a short, beckoning right-field wall.

That wall was demolished, with most other barriers, by the "M" men in the middle of the lineup, Medwick and Mize. Joe hit .374 with thirty-one homers and 154 RBIs, and Mize, taking over regularly at first base, hit .364 with twenty-five home runs and 113 knocked in.

Mize was exactly what Casey Stengel, then managing misfit National League ball clubs, called him: "A slugger who hits like a leadoff man."

Mize had been dealt to Cincinnati with a spur in his groin, but the Reds had declined the damaged goods, thank you, and had returned him to St. Louis. Dr. Robert F. Hyland, the team doctor who had been described by Judge Landis as the "surgeon general of baseball," performed surgery that gave the Cardinals a new player.

But Frisch closed out his eleven-season career as a Cardinal player. He had benched himself and Durocher, too, using young players Jimmy Brown and Stu Martin in a dip to 81-73 and fourth place. To rally the Redbirds during one series at Philadelphia, he returned Durocher and himself to the lineup.

The Cardinals picked up one game and were leading the next day. Frisch was on second, fleet Terry Moore on first, when Medwick lined a drive into the close right field corner at doll-house Baker Bowl. By the time Frisch, breaking late for fear of a catch, reached third base, Moore had rounded second base and was approaching fast.

Coach Mike Gonzalez, viewing with a politician's alarm, waved on Frisch, warbling:

"He come, Frohnk, you go . . . he come, you go . . ."

As Frisch tagged home plate, Moore, sliding, took the manager's

feet from under him, and they tobogganed across to score.

Brushing himself as he headed to the St. Louis bench, Frisch groaned. "Any time," said the man who Ross Youngs thought could catch the fastest snake in North America, "any time they can outrun the Flash, it's time to quit. Brown, you go to second base!"

Frankie Frisch, the "Fordham Flash," never played afield again.

With the Cardinals' Gas House Gang running out of gas, Frisch blanched as the Redbirds went into Rochester for an exhibition and saw a sign that advertised:

"PEPPER MARTIN'S MUD-CATS HERE TODAY."

Sighed Frisch, "And it said in small type, P.S., that Medwick and Mize would be there, too."

Carolina Conquest: Ernie White (center), a talented lefthander whose career was cut short by injury, congratulates another Carolinian, busted-beak Jimmy Brown, popular infield hustler of the Cardinals' late 1930s and '40s. Manager Billy Southworth (left) also grins his happiness that Brownie hit a game-winning home run.

Frisch loved Pepper Martin, and when the Cardinals were winning he didn't mind the musical cacophony of Pepper on his guitar, pronounced "git-tar," and Lon Warneke, too, and he hadn't minded Bill McGee fiddling with his fiddle, Bob Weiland puff-puffing into a jug and "Frenchy" Bordagaray scrubbing up some kind of disharmony on a washboard. But now the Cardinals were losing, and two great hitters, Medwick and Mize, were listed as afterthoughts.

"Mr. Breadon," Frisch lamented, "Mr. Breadon, I'm the only manager required to carry his own or-chestra . . ."

So the Mudcats went into mourning, out of business, and then Branch Rickey, with a wild idea in mind for improving the team, lined up a pre-camp training session at Winter Haven, Florida, before the Cardinals trained for the first time in St. Petersburg (1938).

He proposed for Frisch and associates to try out the center field master Terry Moore at third base and to move third baseman Don Gutteridge to shortstop. Rickey wanted Frisch to make a catcher of big, hard-hitting outfielder Don Padgett. Frisch, released as a player, went to work. Demonstrating a hook slide, he immediately broke a bone in an ankle.

Two of the the three experiments failed, meaning Moore stayed out there where he belonged, and

Gutteridge never could play shortstop as well as third base or second. When the Cardinals came home and were given a Chamber of Commerce luncheon, Rickey got up and said:

"Except for pitching, this is the greatest ball club the Cardinals ever had."

Terry Moore leaned over to the player next to him and said, "Oh, oh, there goes the Flash."

In September, with the Cardinals sixth, Sam Breadon called in Frisch and tearfully said good-bye to his favorite player and former manager.

"Don't feel bad, Mr. Breadon," said Frisch, turning away. He was misty-eyed too.

"D" Stands for Dynamite: Don Padgett was a much better hitter than defensive player, as witness the three kinds of gloves the converted outfielder, shifted to first base and behind the plate, used in the big leagues. As a part-time player, the freckled redhead hit .399 in 1939.

Return of Billy the Kid

Frank Frisch's term as Cardinals' manager, the longest between Branch Rickey's six-plus seasons to the mid-1920s and "Red" Schoendienst's whopping twelve years through the mid-'70s, could have been considerably longer. More important, the success of the Gas House Gang would have been better and sustained IF—.

If the Flash himself, a Hall of Fame player and the National League's record holder for most years on title teams (eight), hadn't grown old.

If, more significantly, Bill DeLancey, Paul Dean and then, the unkindest cut of all, Dizzy Dean hadn't suffered career-ending injuries when they should have been barely entering the center-cut of their top seasons.

More than once, reflecting, Branch Rickey would say that he felt that DeLancey, who hit .316 with thirteen homers in just ninety-three

games as a rookie in 1934, would have ranked among the three best catchers B. R. ever saw.

Paul Dean, as observed, won thirty-eight games in just two seasons and appeared to be ready to hammer his way into the 20-Game Club. Dizzy Dean in just four solid seasons had achieved a spectacular 105-65 record before he was hurt.

Tagged for the All-Star game, an early Redbird tradition after Frisch had hit a home run in each of the first two, Dean was so reluctant to go in 1937 that he "innocently" followed his baggage to St. Louis rather than go to Washington. Sam Breadon offered to fly Dizzy to D. C. at a time when relatively few used planes to travel. Even Dean's wife Pat, though she once had called Branch Rickey "a stinker" in a contract hassle, advised Dizzy to go with Mr. Breadon.

So Diz flew with Breadon to Washington and almost had a

The One-Man Gang: Not only did they call Dominic Joseph "Mike" Ryba that because he could pitch AND catch when he was with the Cardinals—with the Boston Red Sox, as shown here with manager Joe Cronin—but in the Redbirds' farm system the Pennsylvania coal-mine refugee played EVERY position. He also managed Springfield, Mo., and drove the team bus. He later coached the Cards.

scoreless three-inning start at Griffith Stadium. But then Lou Gehrig, in one of the Yankee super-star's acknowledged top thrills, hit a two-run homer. Cleveland's Earl Averill, notorious for hitting hot shots through the pitcher's box, lined a blow back at Dean.

Like Bob Gibson later, Dizzy oomphed hard in his follow-through, relying on cat-like speed to recoil late into fielding position, but Averill's liner hit the planted left foot on the toe, breaking it.

Dizzy limped off. Dr. Hyland advised him to take plenty of time off for the toe to mend, but the Cardinals needed him. Dizzy, for all the noise and nonsense, was a team man first, "podnuh." He showed up ten days later at Boston, still limping a bit. The Braves' manager, Bill McKechnie, urged him not to pitch.

Suddenly, as he sailed through the seventh inning, he threw a pitch and something snapped. From the third-base coaching box, McKechnie wailed, "I told you, Jerome, I told you."

Dizzy never would throw hard again. Never would he charge down from the bench, glove in hand, to rescue a game, as, for instance, one day when Dominic "Mike" Ryba, an all-position virtuoso, was warming up to go in to pitch as the Cardinals rallied to take the lead.

"Here, Mike, you got the wrong glove," said Dizzy, throwing a catcher's mitt to Ryba, who warmed up with him and then accompanied Dean into the lineup—as his catcher!

Never again would Dean horse around happily as he had one day when he bet Johnny Perkins, fleshy East St. Louis nightclub comedian who traveled often with the Cardinals, that he would strike out Joe DiMaggio's older brother, Vince, four straight times.

The wager was amusingly small, but Dizzy was s-o-o competitive. He whiffed the older DiMag three times, but in the ninth, with the Cardinals leading by only a run at Boston, 2-1, with two out and two strikes on the batter, Vince lifted a high foul.

Astonishing rookie catcher Bruce Ogrodowski, Dean rushed toward the plate, yelling, "Drop it. Dammit, if you want to catch me again, drop it."

The startled kid let the ball fall. Frisch, sitting in the dugout, leaped up, hit his head on the concrete and plopped back, dazed, as Dean fired a game-ending third strike past DiMaggio.

But now it was 1939. Ray Blades, Branch Rickey's guy, was the manager. A year earlier, Dizzy had been dealt by Rickey to the Chicago Cubs for three players and a large sum for that time, $185,000. Ol' Diz could only sidearm with well-controlled slow curves then, but before an S.R.O. crowd he shut out the Cardinals the first week he was at Wrigley Field, lobbing the ball tantalizingly on the corners for only four hits.

Bothered by arm trouble, he was only 7-and-1 that season, but he helped Gabby Hartnett's Cubs to a pennant, beating Pittsburgh in a clutch game in the final week, 2-1. He might have slow-curved the New York Yankees into a World Series defeat, too, except for critical misplays that left him vulnerable to late-inning homers by Frank Crosetti and Joe DiMaggio.

When Crosetti hit his go-ahead home run, Diz cussed him all the way around the bases, concluding:

". . . And, furthermore, pod-nuh, if I'd-a had my high hard one,

Unappreciated Visionary: Francis Raymond Blades, the former hustling outfielder, was a smart, sign-stealing manager who believed Branch Rickey's view that the busiest man in the ball park, backing up plays, should be the right fielder.

What Do I DO? Bruce Ogrodowski, journeyman catcher briefly with the Cardinals after Bill DeLancey's death, decided the wise thing was to follow Dizzy Dean's insistence he drop a foul ball so that Ol' Diz could strike out Vince DiMaggio a fourth time—for a penny-ante bet!

you wouldn't-a seen it.''

Crosetti, stepping on the plate, turned and said, "Diz, damned if I don't think you're right."

Years later (1947), beginning to flesh out like a fat man in the circus, which he was when he died at sixty-three in 1974, Dizzy interrupted a colorful broadcasting career. He pitched for the old St. Louis Browns in the final game of the season. Cripes, he'd groaned over the mike, anybody could pitch better than those humpty-dumpties. Shrewdly, the Browns' boss, Bill DeWitt, had invited him to try.

Graciously, P. K. Wrigley, owner of the Cubs, gave him his un-conditional release. Wrigley never felt cheated in having Dean around, even though he'd continued to pay Dizzy the $25,500 league record (un-til Johnny Sain of the Braves in 1948) that Dean had shoe-horned out of the Cardinals.

"Having Dizzy," said Wrigley, virtually a Howard Hughes of baseball for later-life anonymity, "was like traveling with a brass band."

The guy who could lustily yodel "Wabash Cannonball" at the drop of a hint went out there overstuffed that final game of the 1947 season at Sportsman's Park against the Chicago White Sox. For four innings he gracefully eased his junk past the Sox, shutting them out. Then he hit a long one to left field and, to use his improper King's English, he "slud" into second base with a dou-ble and got up, gimpy.

Seated in the Browns' club box, Pat Dean leaned down to manager Herold "Muddy" Ruel and said, "For crissake, Muddy, get him out of there before he kills himself."

In Dean's place back there in 1939, Blades had come up with two pitchers who helped as the former outfielder introduced a unique win-today-and-forget-tomorrow medley of relief pitching that would become today's vogue. Curt "Dan'l Boone" Davis, a willowy righthander ac-quired from Chicago, gave a strong starting-and-relieving record of 22-16 and, in addition, batted .381.

Clyde "Hard Rock" Shoun, a tough lefthanded bullpen specialist, appeared in fifty-three games, a record at the time. A part-time player, Don Padgett, hit .399, and Johnny Mize, with Medwick tailing off, led the league in hitting with a .349 average and twenty-eight home runs.

Also, a kid who'd come up under Frisch the previous year figured strongly in the St. Louis surge to a healthy second-place finish with a 92-61 record. At Col-umbus, manager Burt Shotton had called him "Country." He was a round-faced twenty-two-year-old kid from Carolina named Enos Slaughter.

On New Year's Day, he'd been hunting with his father near Rox-boro, hurrying to get home so they could hear nearby Duke play Southern California in the Rose Bowl football game. After handling infected rabbits, Pop Slaughter became ill and died. Young Eno hovered between life and death.

Eager to overcome that first season .276, Slaughter came to

Weak Wonder: Curt "Dan'l Boone" Davis looked willowy, almost wan as a ball player, but, acquired by the Cardinals from Chicago in the Dizzy Dean deal, he had a fabulous year for a close runnerup in 1939. He won 22 games, lost 16 and batted .381.

Hard Rock: That's what they called Clyde Shoun, a hard-nosed Tennessee moun-taineer, a lefthander who was converted by Ray Blades into a full-time reliever.

spring training in '39 with painful boils still under his arm. He had hot and cold flashes. Now and then, the room would spin in a wave of dizziness. But he beat off the remnants of tularemia and wound up in right field with a robust .320 season.

Sam Breadon, a fair man if a hard one, upped Enos's ante a thousand more than Rickey's $9000. In '39, Breadon saw the Cardinals draw only 410,778 despite their strong second-place finish behind Cincinnati. More than 42,000 poured into the park for a late August doubleheader victory over the Reds. As one helping him hold back the crowd because he had no special guards

and the city police wouldn't do it, I stationed myself along the third-base line until the Reds' open-stanced slugger, big Ernie Lombardi, drilled a whistling foul over my head. I looked down. Gad, I was standing in fair territory!

Waving a mental white flag of surrender, I said to the boss, "I don't know about you, Mr. Breadon, but I'm getting the hell out of there."

"Me, too," crowed a veteran reserve, Pepper Martin, recognizing a good idea when he heard one. Breadon remained with only a more courageous (or stupid) kid, "Bing" Devine. Soon, the boss and "Der

Bingle" left, too.

In 1940, it was Blades who left, suddenly. The Cardinals got off slowly. Lights were turned on for the first National League night game in early June, 1940. (The Browns had played St. Louis's first official floodlighted game against Cleveland's Bob Feller.) The Cardinals were bombed, 10-1, by the Brooklyn Dodgers, managed by Leo Durocher, the old Gas House Gang shortstop who had been sent packing in a him-or-me dispute with Frisch.

The crowd of 23,000 booed, not necessarily because the Cardinals were unloading Joe Medwick's bat to Brooklyn. "Muscles," slumping, had been at odds with Ray Blades for using Lynn King as a late-inning outfield replacement for him. Some fans had been heckling the pouting slugger, too, because he had accompanied Durocher and his dress-designing wife Grace through a garment-factory picket line, hurling some caustic comments at striking workers. Besides, as Medwick would reflect later, Joe knew he'd worn out his contract welcome with the Cardinals.

"Yeah," he said, "Rickey would weaken me with all that double talk while shaving. Ever see a man shave without using lather? He bled so much he looked like one of Count Dracula's victims. And then I talked to Breadon over a couple of thousand dollars' difference, and he told me it was a matter of principle, not principal.

He said, "Why, Joe, I'd just as soon throw this $2000 out the window,' and I told him, 'Mr. Breadon, if you threw that $2000 out the window, your arm would still be holding it.' "

So Medwick was dealt with Curt Davis to Brooklyn for cash just after Breadon, stung by that booing night-game crowd, Joe's imper-

High Praise: Shortly after Ty Cobb (right) had written a controversial national magazine piece (1952) in which he said Enos Slaughter was one of the few players then who could have competed in the Georgia Peach's day (1905-28), Cobb was in St. Louis and presented to the Redbird right fielder a gift marking his 1000th RBI.

tinence and seventh place, flew to Rochester to re-summon Billy Southworth as manager without consulting Rickey.

Southworth actually was one of Rickey's pet reclamation projects. Bill had won four straight International League pennants after that first-try failure at St. Louis in 1929. Next, he'd gone back to the New York Giants as a coach, but, as one who fizzed over belligerently when he looked at the bubbling grape, he took a spring-training swing at manager Bill Terry and left camp unemployed.

"Billy the Kid" turned back to an old friend, Branch Rickey. B. R. got him back into the game as a special instructor at tryout camps, the mass method by which the Cardinals built a dynasty. (The second most successful club at farm-production development, the Yankees, went full-fledged in 1939.)

An early dividend came at a 1935 camp at Durham, North Carolina, where Southworth liked the sweet swing of a broad-beamed young outfielder but was unimpressed with the way he ran. Billy showed the boy how to get up on the balls of his feet, off the soles. Enos Slaughter learned how to run from the man who took over as Cardinals' manager in June, 1940.

Southworth picked up that '40 ball club and brought it home a strong third. The team, led by

Johnny Mize's St. Louis home-run record of forty-three, picked up as Terry Moore, too, became a .300 hitter. Moore could hit the long ball (seventeen homers) to the more distant left field stands at St. Louis, and he even hit two inside-the-park home runs in one game at Pittsburgh. There, too, he showed that he had learned to hit to right field as Frank Frisch had hammered at him.

Lining an inside pitch safely to right field, the righthanded-hitting defensive star hollered happily to the Pittsburgh bench, where Frisch sat, "Hey, Frank, I got it . . . I got it."

By 1941, Frisch's thinned-out remnants were almost all gone. Pepper Martin, brittle now, subject to more injuries, had been sent to

Sacramento to manage the Cardinals' Pacific Coast League farm club. Mickey Owen, who would become the perennial sheriff of Greene County at Springfield, Missouri, had been dealt to Brooklyn, where he'd have a date with a missed third strike, destiny and a Mexican hayride.

Trainer Doc Weaver missed the tobacco-chawing, curly-haired kid most of all. Doc recalled that Rickey liked to tell about the time Mickey as a rookie had said he'd like to go to college in the off-season. Fine, said B. R., and, pray tell, to study what?

"Public speaking," Owen said brightly, "and gymnastics."

Mickey might have added geography. When the Cardinals trained one spring in Daytona Beach

The Sheriff: Arnold "Mickey" Owen, a colorful kid catcher with the Cardinals, had a couple of dates with baseball destiny, jumping to Mexico at one time and missing a World Series third strike at another. But the conscientious Owen turned out not only to run a successful baseball school in Miller, Mo., but also to be the fifth member of his family since 1833 to be sheriff at Greene County (Springfield), Mo.

Mr. Shortstop: They called him "Slats," a tall, wafer-thin player, so skinny that he wore an extra pair of baseball stockings to make his long legs look thicker. But Marty Marion was one of the greatest-fielding shortstops ever.

Creepy: Dark-eyed, glowering Frank Crespi, who gives no indication of his hidden mirth, was regarded by master shortstop Marty Marion in 1941 as the greatest single-season second baseman he ever saw. A holdout handicapped the native St. Louisan in 1942, and severe service-connected injuries ended his career, preventing his becoming a valuable long-time infield reserve.

and Weaver took the kid on a tour, Mickey wondered what was the expanse of blue water they saw stretching beyond the white sands.

"Why, the Atlantic Ocean," the good trainer replied.

Owen exclaimed, "The Atlantic Ocean! Gosh, Doc, I didn't know it ran all the way down here."

In '41 the Cardinals ran all over the place. They were the "St. Louis Swifties," as New York cartoonist Willard Mullin portrayed them. And if ever a ball club lost a pennant it deserved to win, that was the team.

They had come up with a fast little outfielder-first baseman, Johnny Hopp, and an agile, quick second baseman, Frank "Creepy" Crespi, who that year was the best second baseman their slim-jim master at shortstop, Marty Marion, said he had ever seen.

A brilliant battery of blond lefthander Ernie White and a rugged, rawboned catcher, Walker Cooper, whose older brother, Mort, had been trying to get over the hump from good to great, came up from the minors, too. A mournful mountain-music man, Max Lanier, a chunky southpaw who had had a taste of playing with Pepper Martin's Mudcats, was back.

Although the Cardinals would need a scholarly young lefthander from Houston, Howard Pollet, when Mort Cooper was out for the elbow surgery by Dr. Hyland which turned him in August into the big man of the mound, the pitching outlook was very bright early in the season.

When's the last time you heard of a guy pitching an early-season trial, throwing a one-hit shutout and getting farmed out? That's what happened to Hank Gornicki.

But injuries were incredible. Jimmy Brown, the scrappy infield captain, went down with a mashed nose, then a broken finger. Crespi was hurt and sidelined. Walk Cooper broke a collar bone and shoulder blade. Slaughter, the hot-

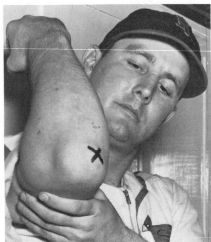

'X' Marks the Spot: That's where Dr. Robert F. Hyland, called "surgeon general of baseball" by first commissioner Judge Landis, operated to remove painful elbow chips from Mort Cooper. Big Coop had chewed aspirin when pitching to kill the pain.

Botoms Up, Crabby: A good sub outfielder and topflight pinch-hitter, lefthanded-hitting Estell Crabtree, is congratulated by Frank Crespi (left) and Ernie White after a key hit. Crabtree holds a soft drink popularized by clubowner Sam Breadon's fascination with thiamin chloride.

test hitter, dived over Terry Moore in right center and ripped his collar bone against the right-field wall. Finally, Terry Moore, the center field captain, was hit in the head by Boston's Art Johnson, a young left-hander, and sidelined with what was feared a skull fracture. Few players then wore batting helmets, then only thin fiber linings for the inside of their regular caps.

When Moore lay in the dust at Braves Field, big Johnny Mize, sitting out a thumb injury some of the more seriously injured resented, stood towering over him and mumbled:

"That's the final straw . . ."

They had some remarkable results, the 1941 Cardinals. For instance, only the lanky, skinny second-year man at shortstop, Marty Marion, played every game. A drawn-faced thirty-seven-year-old extra man, Estel Crabtree, came back up from the minors and hit a sizzling .341. And a jut-jawed young righthander, Howie Krist, another happy recipient of Dr. Hyland's surgical attention, posted a 10-0 record in relief.

In September, the Cardinals brought up an outfielder who, like Pollet, would help the Cardinals much then and more later. Pollet contributed five victories in seven decisions after a remarkable 20-3 record and an eye-popping 1.16 earned-run average at Houston.

The outfielder had begun the 1941 season near the baseball bottom in Class C at Springfield, Missouri, and for the Cardinals, a close second with a dazzling 97-56 record, he would bat a hot .426 in twelve games: Stan Musial!

A Young Smoothie: Howard Pollet was an old man young, a pitching craftsman as a kid. The polished lefthander came up at 20 to help the Cardinals in 1941 after a sensational season with Houston in the Texas League. He was fabulous until called into the service in 1943. As Eddie Dyer's meal ticket, he won 20 games each in 1946 and '49, but he was handicapped between times by a balky back.

Stan the Boy: Stan Musial was as young as he looked, just 21, at his first big-league spring-training camp with the Cardinals in 1942 at St. Petersburg, Fla. Manager Billy Southworth is with him, clipboard characteristically in hand.

9

The Redbirds Fly High

If Stan Musial hadn't come up and hit a half-ton the final couple of weeks of the 1941 season, chances are, he always thought, he wouldn't have started in 1942 with the Cardinals. By the self-analysis of a proud, confident, yet honest and humble man, the potential super-star was the lemon of the Grapefruit League in '42.

To get that far, "The Man," as he would become nicknamed by the fanatical yet fair-minded Brooklyn faithful who saw him treat Ebbets Field as his own dollhouse, had to make giant seven-league strides of progress. If you saw the Musial story in a movie, you wouldn't believe it.

He was the son of a poor little hard-working Polish immigrant and a sturdy, good-looking Czech migrant's daughter. Mom Musial, as a girl, used to row her father across the Monongahela River to the coal fields up from its confluence with the Allegheny at Pittsburgh. It was

from his mother that Stan obviously inherited the stamina that enabled him to hit .330 when he was nearly forty-two years old.

When "Stashu," as Pop called him with broken-English tenderness, was a boy in the hills of Donora, he was a kid playing with men, a strong-armed lefthanded pitcher and basketball star. He turned down a chance to play basketball at Pitt, and his angry father at first balked about pro baseball.

For sixty-five dollars a month during the summer only, he signed as a high school junior to play lowly Class D baseball. You couldn't do that legally now even if there were enough modest leagues, but in two summer seasons at Williamson, West Virginia, hitting better than he pitched, Musial was strong-armed and wild. Ultimately, he concluded later, process of elimination would have made him an outfielder rather than a pitcher.

In late 1940 at Daytona Beach, Florida, he was married to the former Lillian Labash, the home-town grocer's daughter who always teased that she fell in love with Stan's legs in a basketball uniform and that he fell in love with her father's milk and lunchmeat.

Times were tough all over then and Musial, with his first child en route, was making only $100 a month, but he never complained. He clerked for his in-laws in the off-season. Besides, who'd want to make even a partial living at a happier way than putting a round bat to a round ball?

Still, there was a crisis in spring training, 1941, because late in the '40 season, Musial had fallen on his shoulder playing the outfield between pitching turns. When he tried in '41 to throw in the Hollywood, Florida, camp of Double-A ball clubs, the arm was sore and weak and remained so when they dropped him down to the camp for Class B, C and D players at Albany, Georgia.

Just as Chick Hafey earlier and Ken Boyer later threw away their pitchers' toe-plates because they could swing a bat, Musial was being considered as an outfielder. But no one in Class B wanted a guy who couldn't throw, and nobody in Class C, but—wait!—Ollie Vanek stuck up his hand.

Vanek, managing Monessen, Pennsylvania, near Stan's home when the kid signed in 1937, was player-manager at Springfield, Missouri, in '41. Yep, he'd take a look.

So Musial started only about 230 miles physically from St. Louis, baseball eons away. For eighty-seven games he hit twenty-six homers and drove in ninety-four runs, wiping out Springfield's White Stadium. One night when Branch Rickey showed up, Musial arched those bushy old brows with a single, a triple and a homer.

Rickey, blessing his stork's-nest eye shields, said by "Judas Priest," we'll jump that slender, large-nosed lad to Rochester. Same results. A 7-come-11 natural.

At Rochester Manager Tony Kaufmann's merry eyes widened. In the eleventh inning of a game against Newark, Musial faked a bunt against charging third baseman Hank Majeski and doubled past him. In the thirteenth with a man on first, same setup. Again, Stan faked a bunt. Majeski didn't believe any guy would be sucker, or talented, enough to try it twice. He charged. Musial, a lefthanded hitter, whistled a game-winning hit past him.

Of course, Rickey had to see again to believe. He believed. The night B. R. was in the stands, Musial went four for four.

As soon as Rochester was eliminated from the pennant race, the Cardinals rushed an SOS that missed. Stan already was at home in Donora. The delayed news brought joy to his family and Lil's. Lil ironed shirts all night, then drove him into Pittsburgh, but—he missed the train.

Still, he was there in time, together with third baseman George Kurowski and outfielder Erv Dusak, Red Wing teammates, for Manager Billy Southworth of the crippled Cardinals. Timidly, the kid talked to captain Terry Moore. "Tee" broke into a grin and yelled over to Johnny Mize:

"Hey, John, remember when you and I hit home runs in succession this spring down in Albany, Georgia? Here's the kid we hit them off."

The Cardinals were only two games behind Brooklyn as Southworth started Musial in St. Louis against Boston, managed then by Casey Stengel. Stan came up to bat, standing deep in the box, crouched, eyes peeking over his right shoulder, looking, as someone put it, like a kid peering around the corner to see if the cops were coming.

First time up, facing the first knuckleball he'd ever seen, Musial popped up against righthander Jim Tobin. Second trip, he tattooed one to right-center for the first of his record 725 doubles and first of the 3630 hits that were still a National League high into the 1980s.

Before that brief encounter with the pennant—and he played on winners his first four full seasons in the majors—Musial gave them all something to remember: a double-header wrap-up at St. Louis against Chicago.

In the first game, playing left field, Musial made two catches and threw out a runner at the plate. At bat, he doubled off the right field screen, singled and stole a base, doubled again, and with the score tied in the ninth, singled and moved up on an infield out.

Four-Sack: Erv Dusak, a strong-armed righthanded-hitting outfielder who could play third base and even tried briefly to pitch, was regarded as an even better prospect than Stan Musial when they came up together from Rochester late in 1941. Obviously, despite a nickname almost facetiously given after a couple of key home runs in 1946, Dusak didn't measure up.

Gabe and That Other Guy: A popular player among his teammates was droll, lanky Ray Sanders—they called him "Gabe"—who was an easy-does-it, long-ball hitter with RBI skill in war seasons. A broken arm when traded to the Boston Braves in 1946 killed Sanders' career. The other guy? The current ballpark Stadium Club general manager and partner, Marty Marion.

After Creepy Crespi was passed intentionally, Coaker Triplett squibbed a little grounder toward third. Catcher Clyde McCullough pounced out, fielded the ball and fired to first base. "Safe!" on a close play, and as first-baseman "Babe" Dahlgren whirled to argue with the umpire and McCullough stood there defiantly, hands on hips, swish! Stan Musial, dashing from SECOND, had scored the winning run on a hit that traveled about fifteen feet.

In the second game, Musial moved to right field. He dived to his right for one line drive and charged in for a double-somersaulting catch of another. He bunted safely toward third base and singled to center for a six-hit, all-round day that caused Cubs' manager Jimmy Wilson to explode.

"Nobody, but NOBODY, can be that good," insisted the old Redbird of the club's brightest young star until Garry Templeton thirty-five years later.

As a result, Southworth, Rickey and all gave pause when the kid couldn't hit a lick in the spring of 1942. Wisely, they decided to withhold judgment. Good thing.

Once they got out of the wavy, high-sky background of Florida palm trees into the restful batting background of the big league park, Musial exploded again. He hit a triple and two singles Saturday against the Browns and a pinch double Sunday.

Branch Rickey called him in. About that $450-a-month contract for 1942 B. R. had had him sign when he came up the previous fall? Stanley, we're going to make that $700 a month. Joyfully, Musial rushed to a telephone and told Lil to pack her things and infant son Dick's and come on out. He'd go

apartment-hunting. They could afford it.

Still happy, Musial singled and tripled the next day off Chicago's Claude Passeau, but the Cardinals lost the opener, 5-4—what's new with the worst opening-day club in history?—and for months the Cardinals trailed Leo Durocher's defending champion Dodgers.

The Cardinals had dealt big Johnny Mize to New York, miffed in part because they'd felt the slugger might have played more when hurt a wee bit at a time other players were hurt more seriously in 1941. But, still, World War II had started, and sizable contracts had a way of

bothering the Cardinals' front office even in normal times.

Southworth opened with a rangy home-town kid, Ray Sanders, at first base, an easy-does-it former softball king who could hit a long ball in the clutch. Crespi was at second, the incomparable Marion at shortstop and doughty Jimmy Brown at third. Later, with Crespi handicapped from a holdout, Brown went to second. Versatile Johnny Hopp got in the game at first base, too, and a blond blockbuster, Kurowski, took over at third.

By George: A standout Redbird third baseman, though his career was limited by injury, was George "Whitey" Kurowski, whose ninth-inning, fifth-game home run won the 1942 World Series.

Classic Sentries: One of the greatest outfields ever, stars of the 1942 and '46 world championship ball clubs. From the left, Enos Slaughter, Terry Moore and Stan Musial.

Heroic Misfortune: Johnny Beazley was a 24-year-old Redbird rookie who had a sparkling 21-6 season in 1942 and won two World Series games. Here, he dresses to go back home to Nashville, Tenn., from his summer home at the old Fairground Hotel. In military service, Capt. Beazley hurt his great right arm. The handsome young righthander, good and tough, soon was through.

George—"Whitey!"—was a classic guy in a pinch, wearing "1," the uniform Pepper Martin had popularized. Kurowski's right arm was short, a result of boyhood osteomyelitis that required removal of bone from the forearm. He was thick-thighed, too, but, despite heavy legs and that arm deformity, which required him to hang over the plate, Kurowski could run and he could hit.

The outfield into which Musial fit as left fielder was one of baseball's greatest ever. With Terry Moore in center field, Enos Slaughter in right and Musial in left, it had batting strength, fielding ability and, above all, the hallmark of the 1942 club other than deep, A-1 pitching—s-p-e-e-d!

Even Walker Cooper, rangy then and catching brother Mort and the rest of that talented pitching staff, could run. The 1942 Cardinals didn't steal many bases, but they pressured the defense constantly by beating out hits in the infield and taking extra bases on plays in the outfield.

Some grumbled in mid-season when Breadon unloaded the team's highest salary, $15,000, selling Lon Warneke to the Cubs, but Breadon snapped back, "We've sold Lon to give Johnny Beazley a chance to work more often."

Lucky Sam! Next day Beazley shut out the Giants for his ninth victory. Tall, dark and handsome, Beazley was simply great. Max Lanier, Howard Pollet and, though ailing much of the time with a sore arm, Ernie White were standouts among the staff's lefthanders. Mort Cooper came up with a gimmick for a ball club that, though 47-30 for the first half of the season, was still eight games behind.

Big "Coop," never before able to get past thirteen victories, missed a couple of times and then shed his uniform "13." He borrowed "14" and won. So he went through the lineup, wearing larger-numbered flannel shirts, snug or not. Ultimately, Mort would wind up with twenty-two victories, one more than Beazley, and a dazzling 1.77 ERA that won him the National League Most Valuable Player award.

Against Brooklyn, in particular, the Cardinals found themselves in knockdown fights. Even Marty Marion got into a baseline battle, aided by hot-tempered Frank Crespi, with Medwick. Muscles probably had good reason to be angry, because the Cardinals' Bob Bowman had hit him in the head in a nasty 1940 mixup. Even Stan Musial charged Les Webber after the Dodger righthander, walking him, knocked the kid down with four pitches.

The Dodgers played an intimidating game, and the rest of the National League didn't like it. When other clubs began to retaliate, Warneke explained it from Chicago in his homespun way:

"When you got a sundae in front of you, and the other guy starts to reach for the chocolate syrup, you've got to stop him real quick or he'll start for the ice cream next."

The Dodgers began to lose— just a little!—and that's all the Cardinals needed. Ten games behind in early August, they played torridly and began to close the gap.

When Brooklyn came in for their final St. Louis series, Mort Cooper squeezed into catcher Ken O'Dea's "16" and went fourteen innings to beat Whit Wyatt, 2-1. Max Lanier, always great against the Dodgers, won by 7-1, and Beazley went ten for a 2-1 triumph. A Dodger victory in the windup merely delayed the inevitable.

The inevitable came at Brooklyn. Two down with two to play against the Dodgers, the Cardinals won the opener, 3-1, in another Cooper-versus-Wyatt duel. Then, with Kurowski hitting a two-run homer, Lanier outpitched lefty Max Macon, 2-1.

A day later the Cardinals could get only a Sunday split at Philadelphia, but the Dodgers dropped a doubleheader against Cincinnati. St. Louis led. Sourly, service-bound Larry MacPhail, president of the Dodgers, wired Reds' manager Bill McKechnie about his pitching rotation. Tartly, McKechnie wired back:

"Congratulations on your appointment as a lieutenant colonel. Please accept this as my application as your orderly. Believe I could be of great assistance in keeping you orderly. The Deacon."

Amazingly, the Dodgers won their last eight games and still lost ground. The Cardinals rallied time and again to snatch away ball games. A week before the windup, for instance, Hopp had to steal home to beat Warneke at Chicago, 1-0. On the final day, needing to win one game of a doubleheader, the Cardinals hit their former teammate hard, 9-2.

Hippety-Hopp: Johnny Hopp, a valuable blond handyman, was a swift, versatile player, most able to help the Cardinals at first base, in the outfield or on the bases.

As he passed between them in the third-base dugout, short cut to the clubhouses, Warneke walked head down, looking neither left nor right. "All right, you buzzards," he said, "there's your lead. Now, let's see you hold it."

Terry Moore had preached against over-confidence in the most remarkably sustained pennant drive ever, forty-three victories in the last fifty-two games, for a rousing 106-48 season that paid off with just a two-game edge. "I've never forgotten when Warneke and the Cubs caught us with twenty-one in a row in 1935," said Moore, inspiration for such young players as Musial, Slaughter, Marion and Harry Walker.

In the World Series the Cardinals faced a foe, the Yankees, who had lost just four games of thirty-six in winning eight straight World Series since Bob O'Farrell gunned out Babe Ruth in 1926.

The typical rout seemed on when Red Ruffing worked a no-hitter until the eighth inning of the opener at St. Louis, but then Terry Moore singled. In the ninth the Redbirds scored four times, knocking out Ruffing and bringing Spud Chandler to the mound. They left the game beaten, 7-4, but buoyed.

Next day the Yankee late-inning lightning struck when Charley Keller homered off Beazley in the eighth inning, to tie the score, but then Slaughter doubled and Musial singled in the home half. When Dickey singled in the ninth and "Tuck" Stainback ran for him, Slaughter made a great money play.

Enos raced to the right-field line, cut down Buddy Hassett's single and zipped a beautiful on-the-fly throw to Kurowski's shoe tops at third base, nipping Stainback. Ruffing's pinch-hit flyball was merely the second out. St. Louis won, 4-3.

In the third game, the first at Yankee Stadium, the circus came to town. Behind Ernie White's pitching, the Cardinals achieved the first Series shutout over the Yankees since Jesse Haines in the 1926 World Series, 2-0. And they did it because Slaughter leaped for a great catch, Musial made a good one and Terry Moore put the icing on the cake. Tee jumped over a fallen Musial in left-center for a backhanded, gloved grab of Joe DiMaggio's bid for an inside-the-park home run.

The fourth game was a toe-to-toe slugfest except that the Cardinals were niftier afoot. They blew a 6-1 lead but, recovering, ran wild on the bases and took it 9-6.

When Moore went up to home plate for the fifth game, Bill Summers, American League umpire, was apologetic. Yankee coach Art Fletcher, standing by with New York's batting order, reported that Joe McCarthy, the Yankee manager, had complained about the presence

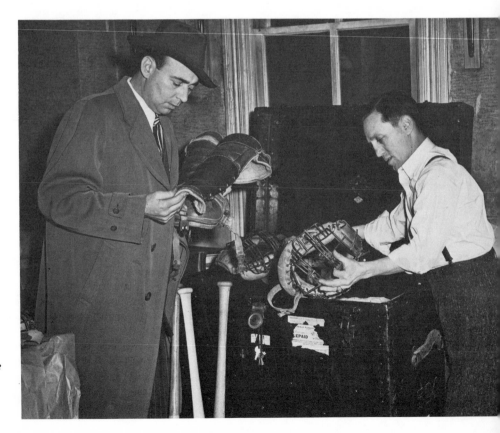

Indispensable Men: Little Morris "Butch" Yatkeman, a bat boy since 1924 and full-time equipment manager of the Cardinals since 1932, was honored as the "Indispensable Man" after a half-century and kept going. Here, he's shown before spring training one year with dapper Leo Ward, traveling secretary for 35 seasons.

in the Cardinals' dugout of Morris "Butch" Yatkeman, the club's bat-boy since 1924 and clubhouse manager since 1932.

"You mean Butch?" Moore asked, incredulously.

Yes, jut-jawed Fletcher said, Butch.

"Okay, 'Chisel Chin'," one Irishman said to another about a third, "you can go back and tell Mc-Carthy that there won't be any 'tomorrow' in this Series."

There wasn't, either. With the score tied in the ninth inning, Kurowski pulled one down the left field line for a home run to give Beazley and the Cardinals a 4-2 victory and a world championship.

Briefly in the New York ninth, the Yankees threatened. With Joe Gordon on second base, a runner on first and none out, the loosey-goosey kids on the Cardinals' ball club—only Moore in center field was thirty years old—implored trainer Doc Weaver to pull his "double-whammy." "Bucko" nodded. Yes, gravely, he could see the need for deep sorcery.

Solemnly, he extended his hands, back to back, and pointed double-decked first-and-fourth fingers at second base in a twin hook-'em gesture, the "double whammy." Suddenly catcher Walker Cooper pegged to Marion, who had shadowed in behind Gordon at second base. Out!

Double-Whammy Doc: Harrison J. "Buck" Weaver, shown here with his wife in 1939, was a master of psychology, of inventions and even of musical inspiration when trainer of the Cardinals from 1927 until his death in 1955.

Afterward, as the Cardinals planned to head back to St. Louis, Musial, whose .315 average had been second only to Slaughter's .318 that first full season, stood at train-side as his teammates prepared to go to St. Louis by special train. Stan and Lil had figured on a longer Series, and frugally they had saved so that she could see the anticipated wrap-up. Now, therefore, Musial was going back to Donora to meet her. For five Series days his pay was $6192.43 atop his full season's $4250 salary.

"And he cried like a baby," Marion would recall, merrily.

A year later Musial would win his first of seven batting championships, hitting .357 with twenty triples among eighty-one extra-base hits, and he waltzed to his first of three Most Valuable Player prizes, just as the Cardinals breezed to a pennant with a 105-49 record. Such stars as Slaughter and Moore were in service and Brown, Beazley, Crespi, Pollet and Murry Dickson would be called, too.

But how ya gonna keep 'em down on the farm? The Cardinals had more material than the rest. Harry Brecheen came up and George Munger and Al Brazle. Harry Walker moved into center field, and when Danny Litwhiler was acquired to play left field, Musial moved to the position he liked best and played least, right field.

Even though the Yankees had lost the great Joe DiMaggio and other service-bound standouts, the Yanks were favored in the 1943 World Series. The oddsmakers' viewpoint might have seemed strange, but it was correct.

Because Mort Cooper had had trouble in World Series and All-Star games, Southworth started Lanier in what would be a one-trip, save-the-mileage Series. Max's own error helped New York and Spud Chandler to a 4-2 victory at Yankee Stadium.

Dramatically, Robert Cooper, a rural mail-carrier and father of the brother battery, died at his home in Independence, Missouri. Sons Mort and Walk played. Mort hung on to beat the Yankees, 4-3, and hurried home. The catcher soon followed him.

For the third game, lefty Al Brazle had Hank Borowy beaten into the eighth inning, 2-1, but then Johnny Lindell singled and took second on Harry Walker's fumble in center field. When "Snuffy" Stirnweiss bunted to first, Ray Sanders's throw to third was in time, but Lindell barreled hard into Kurowski. Whitey dropped the ball. The second error led to a five-run Yankee rally, the strength of a 6-2 victory.

That one was pivotal. Back home, Marius Russo, New York southpaw, pitching back from a sore arm, won a 2-1 game from Lanier. Finally, M. Cooper and Chandler dueled scorelessly. The Cardinals got ten hits, but they couldn't bunch any. For the Yankees, limited to seven hits, Bill Dickey lifted a two-run homer in the sixth. The Bronx Bombers won the game, 2-0, and the Series.

Although Walker, second baseman Lou Klein and three pitchers, Brazle, White and Howard Krist, entered the service (and George "Red" Munger later), the 1944 Cardinals continued to have the most baseball ammunition. They were so far ahead that they won their ninetieth game earlier than even the 1906 Chicago Cubs and seemed likely to break the Cubs' record of

116 victories. But they stumbled repeatedly over Frank Frisch's second-place Pittsburgh Pirates in September and finished with the same record as in 1943, 105-49.

Like the American League's Connie Mack, Billy Southworth became a rare manager with three straight 100-game seasons. Mort Cooper went over twenty again, and Stan Musial, though tailing off after a collision with outfielder Debs Garms, hit .347 and finished ten points behind Brooklyn outfielder Fred "Dixie" Walker.

The Redbird hero, however, was shortstop Marty Marion. The towering drink of water was so brilliant at shortstop that he actually won the Most Valuable Player award with his glove. Over the years, Marion, descendant of the Carolina guerrilla warfare will o' the wisp of the American Revolution, General Francis "Swamp Fox" Marion, had a habit of sweeping his bat into big hits to right field in the pinch. But still, .267 was a light MVP average, indeed, for the long-armed octopus.

"Mr. Shortstop," they called him, and he simply ate up his harder-hitting St. Louis Browns' rival, Vern "Junior" Stephens, in the rare Streetcar Series. The Browns' Bill DeWitt had built shrewdly for the war seasons, and manager Luke Sewell knew how to handle the misfits and cutthroats who gave St. Louis its only American League pennant by knocking off—of all people!—the mighty Yankees the final four games of the season.

The underdog Brownies, sympathetic favorites, well might have upset the Cardinals in the World Series except for an incredible fielding play. After Mort Cooper had lost a tough two-hit opener to Denny Galehouse, 2-1, a result of a two-run homer by George McQuinn, the Browns knocked out Lanier in the eighth inning of the second game. The score tied, they had Mark Christman on second base with none out, but "Blix" Donnelly came out of the bullpen and pitched out of trouble.

Still, a two-game start for the orange-and-brown-trimmed American Leaguers seemed likely when McQuinn doubled to open the eleventh and Christman bunted beautifully toward third base. A hit seemed certain. Donnelly couldn't have thrown out the Brown's third baseman, but, springing off the mound to his right, Blix fielded the ball on the run near the foul-line, wheeled and threw blindly to third. He put a spike-high throw on the money to Kurowski so that McQuinn tagged himself out.

As a result, the rejuvenated Redbirds won in the home half, 3-2, against Bob Muncrief, a replacement for Nelson Potter. Sanders singled, moved up on Kurowski's sacrifice and, after Marion was passed intentionally, apple-cheeked Ken O'Dea delivered a pinch single for Emil Verban.

Professionally Speaking: Walker Cooper and brother Mort sit grimly in the 1943 World Series at New York after hearing of their father's unexpected death. Mort pitched and beat the Yankees that afternoon and entrained immediately for their home at Independence, Mo. The catcher followed as soon as the next day's Series game was played.

Actually, pinch-batting for the feisty, snappy-fielding second baseman, Verban, really wasn't necessary in the Series. Although a light hitter ordinarily, he'd batted .412 in the Series. His Yugoslav heart harbored resentment, because the Browns' owner, investment broker Don Barnes, had given the Cardinals poor seats for the American League home games.

The Cardinals, saved by Donnelly, then wrapped up the Series. Musial singled, doubled and homered off Sig Jakucki for a 5-1 win in the fourth game. In a first-game re-run, Mort Cooper struck out twelve and Denny Galehouse ten in a game won by the Cardinals, 2-0, on home runs by Sanders and Danny Litwhiler. In the sixth game Verban

singled in the go-ahead run by which Ted Wilks, relieving Lanier brilliantly, preserved a 3-1 championship triumph.

Verban, sneered at by Barnes when he appealed for help earlier to get his wife from behind a post, rushed to the first-base dugout rather than home bench on the third-base side and, looking at the crestfallen, moonfaced Browns' boss, the spunky little punk said, devilishly:

"Now, YOU are behind the post!"

For Musial, service bound, the championship was a going-away present, along with a couple of lumps on his head. As mentioned, the graceful batting star had had one outfield collision with fleet Debs Garms. Next, playing center field beside Pepper Martin, who had been

brought back at forty for outfield protection, he'd fought a bright sun one day and recoiled only at the last second as the ball glanced off his head.

Martin, racing over, retrieved the ball, fired it to second base and then solicitously asked the stunned Musial, "Okay, kid?"

Stan nodded, at which point Martin fell to the ground, trying without success to suppress his mirth.

"Then you don't mind," said the Wild Horse, "if I laugh. Hawhaw."

Feisty Fellow: Emil Verban (right), hitting hero of the 1944 World Series who gave Browns' owner Don Barnes a bit of lip, works out at Cairo, Ill., spring training in '45 with outfielder Augie Bergamo.

10

Old E·N·O & the Redhead

Surprise! The Cardinals LOST a pennant in 1945, but, then, they had lost two top stars, including the mighty Stan Musial. They also gained a guy who would be as colorful as his carrot-topped head, Red Schoendienst.

Toward the end of the war, the Cardinals couldn't even train any longer in Cairo, Illinois, their wartime spring-training site. Flood water backed them home. The idea, of course, was to minimize travel. Considering the colder climate and the loss of top talent, it worked pretty well. Baseball provided what President Franklin D. Roosevelt had suggested, a diversion.

For the Cardinals as for others, times had been topsy-turvy. Under a long-time agreement between Sam Breadon and Branch Rickey, the wedding between the sharp-eyed front-office boss and the free-spending general manager had ended in a contractual divorce.

Breadon, a forthright man who might frown over his traveling secretary's "waste" in installing an electric clock in his office, could pay Rickey as much as $88,000 in salary and bonuses, a staggering sum in 1941. But the war was coming then, and, besides, Singin' Sam was embarrassed that Judge Landis had ripped from the Cardinals 101 players in 1938, contending that Rickey had covered them up illegally in the minor leagues. Included was a St. Louis kid who became a Brooklyn star, Pete Reiser.

So Rickey had left at his zenith, that whopping 106-victory season in 1942, following a year in which the Cardinals won pennants or split seasons at Sacramento in the Pacific Coast League, Rochester in the International League, Columbus in the American Association, and Houston in the Texas League.

They were so great that, as broadcaster Bud Blattner, himself

Alley Oop, Red: Red Schoendienst, climaxing his first brilliant season at second base, leapfrogs in good dramatic action over Johnny Pesky's back to complete a double play throw to Stan Musial in the 1946 World Series. Red came up a shortstop who played left field in '45, then switched to second base.

one of the minor league graduates, put it:

"You probably could have taken the top players off our farm clubs and finished only behind the Cardinals and Dodgers in the National League, the Yankees in the American."

When Rickey went East—"A Brain Goes to Brooklyn," as J. Roy Stockton put it—Breadon ran the Cardinals with a competent minor-league staff. For 1945, Sam saw Musial, Walker Cooper, Max Lanier, Danny Litwhiler and others follow departed teammates into service.

A fortunate turn brought from the military a tall, slender, freckle-faced kid with big feet and an equally large instinct for playing the game. Back in 1942, Albert Schoendienst, a kid from nearby Germantown, Illinois, and boyhood friend Joe Linneman had decided to hitchhike to St. Louis for a tryout camp. Smart kids, they knew they'd get to watch the Cardinals play the Dodgers for free, too.

One night, they slept across the street in a park area near Union Station. When Joe Mathes and other scouts saw the natural form of Schoendienst, then a shortstop, Mathes hurried across the river to a bridge where Red's papa, Joe, was painting for the highway department. Pop wiped his hands on his Oshkosh-Bigosh, signed his name and the kid was on his way to Union City, Tennessee, without ever seeing a ball game in St. Louis.

Down there in Class D, Schoendienst got eight straight hits and then almost floored manager Everett Johnson with a crazy request: He wanted to turn around and bat lefthanded against righthanders. He said that he had a fuzzy spot in his left eye, and his nose got in the way when he tried to pick up a breaking ball.

At home in Germantown, Red had been such a good hitter that the kids made him bat lefthanded as a handicap and, sure enough, with a choked grip that would inch up the bat with the years, he could hit lefthanded, too. A year later when he was hitting hard at Lynchburg, Virginia, and Pepper Martin needed a shortstop, Red was dispatched to Rochester.

A timid knock broke up a clubhouse meeting, and Martin, answering the door, said, no, he didn't need a batboy. But, wait, the kid pleaded; he'd been told at Lynchburg to report.

"John Brown," moaned Martin, "you must be that Shone. . . er, something or other. Criminy, I'm in last place and they send me batboys."

But Schoendienst was as natural as the Huckleberry Finn he'd been when he played hookey from school to catfish along the Kaskaskia River. He had ricocheted a nail off that left eye in a boyhood fence-post accident when serving in a Depression project for young men, the Civilian Conservation Corps. But he was so good that when he got an early discharge from service before the 1945 season, the Cardinals welcomed the twenty-two-year-old lad to the big club.

Why the early discharge? A vague explanation, they gave then. I've always felt they detected then the first evidence of the tuberculosis that forced Schoendienst out of baseball in 1959. Even when he hit five doubles and a home run in a doubleheader in '48 or won the 1950 All-Star game with a homer, Red always tailed off in late season. Except, that is, for 1953 when he was forced out by a gashed brow when struck above his weak eye. Rested, he finished strong and almost won a batting championship (.342).

Though statistically only a .289 batter for eighteen-plus seasons, Red was actually a better hitter, a great adhesive-handed second baseman, a fourth outfielder on pop flies even though he disdained sun glasses. If he hadn't hurt his right arm, sliding headfirst with a shallow shoulder socket, he would have made a good shortstop.

But shortstop the Cardinals did NOT need when the high water of Cairo floods forced them back into the chill of Sportsman's Park to complete spring training in 1945. Schoendienst helped coach Mike Gonzalez by taking throw-ins as the "Senor" fungoed pitchers one direction after another for fly balls. Finally, Red invited Mike to hit him some.

Delighted, Gonzalez skillfully hit one fly ball after another, left or right, just out of the apparent reach of Schoendienst, but Red was a galloping gazelle. Finally, excitedly,

Homeric Feats: Red Schoendienst (right), of all people, considered a light-hitting, though good batter, wound up the dramatic 1950 All-Star game at Chicago's Comiskey Park by hitting a game-winning home run he had forecast. (Center) Burt "Barney" Shotton, Dodgers' manager who once played the outfield in St. Louis as Branch Rickey's "Sunday manager," points with pride both to Red and to a genuine home-run hitter, Ralph Kiner, whose homer in the ninth tied the game.

Gonzalez called out to manager Billy Southworth:

"Hey, Beel, you no worry about lef' field. That Rad, she can do."

Although he dropped the first fly ball opening day at Chicago, then had a hard time convincing the ticket taker that he was a ball player when the baby-faced kid came late from church on Sunday, infielder Schoendienst was spectacular in the outfield. The Cardinals' veteran coach, Clyde "Buzzy" Wares suggested he never had seen a left fielder since Fred Clarke of the early-century Pittsburgh Pirates so adept at cutting off base hits down the foul line.

By spring training, the stars were out of the service, many rusty from three years away. In Breadon's case, he had created one problem, and another had been foisted on him.

During the war, he had claimed a pre-war salary maximum of $13,500, Terry Moore's top dollar, as the club's individual ceiling. But then Marion, a master salesman as well as master shortstop, had become MVP and had talked himself around the ceiling to $15,000. Previously, Breadon had held back the Cooper brothers, but now when he offered to go to fifteen G's for them, it was too late. Angry, Walker was in service; Mort, petulantly, left the Cardinals one day when scheduled to pitch.

Breadon then dealt him to Boston for $60,000 and a talkative, fleshy righthander, Charley "Red" Barrett, a soft-serving, control pitcher who found to his delight that the slick combination of Marion and Emil Verban turned base hits into double plays. As the Cardinals finished second to Chicago in 1945 with a 95-59 record, even though beating the Cubbies sixteen out of twenty-two times, Barrett won twenty-three games.

By spring training, loaded with talent, the Cardinals had a new manager. Billy Southworth, hurting Breadon's feelings, had asked to leave the Cardinals to take a better contract offered by Lou Perini and fellow new owners of the Boston Braves. Rather than charge Boston with tampering, Breadon turned to a loyal long-time associate, Eddie Dyer.

Dyer, a great football player and baseball performer at Rice, had been limited to demitasse in the big leagues because of arm trouble in Rogers Hornsby's era as manager, but he had managed winning minor-league teams for years and had become director of top minor-league clubs after Rickey left.

The "Ol' Lefthander," the Cajun-Irishman from Houston by way of Louisiana called himself. He had only one weakness, a flaming temper that manifested itself mainly when photographers asked him to pose for undignified pictures. Dyer, a well-to-do, off-season insurance salesman, quickly appointed the club's captain, Terry Moore, as his mediator with the cameramen.

Moore, troubled because of excessive weight and the strain on his legs of St. Petersburg's Waterfront Park, sandy from frequent wartime use by service troops, had another problem. He had to use restraint to keep himself and other champion-ship stars from teeing off on Barrett when the wartime wonder expostulated to stars on how to pitch and to play the game!

Worse, although heavily favored, the Cardinals were handicapped. Simply because catching star Walker Cooper had suggested he'd prefer not to play for Dyer with whom he had had what Eddie lamented was a minor-league misunderstanding that could be overcome, Breadon sold big Coop to the New York Giants for $175,000.

Equally bad, the brightest pitching prospect, Johnny "Two-Game" Beazley, the pitching hero of 1942, came out of service with a bad arm as did Ernie White. The Cardinals' best minor league pitching prospect, John Grodzicki, had a dropped foot, a result of a gunshot wound suffered in the upper hamstring when he was a parachute trooper.

Breadon soon built Southworth's Braves into the Cape Cod Cardinals, a contender. Sam dealt Ray Sanders, Johnny Hopp, Danny Litwhiler and, ultimately, Ken O'Dea to Boston. O'Dea would have been the insurance man as the veteran protection behind the plate.

Although he had a carry-over catcher, Del Rice, a good glove man, Breadon was counting heavily on two home-town kids to play first base and to catch. At first, he'd use George Sisler's big son, Dick, a husky hitter who had done so well in the Cuban winter league that Mike Gonzalez, who ran the Havana club, lost perspective. Miguel said:

"If she play every day, she hit thirty home run—ceench!"

Oh, His Aching Back: If Ken O'Dea's back hadn't acted up, limiting his catching in 1946, the Cardinals' problems after winter sale of Walker Cooper to the New York Giants would have been fewer and simpler.

A Pitcher's Best Friend: That's the double play, so many of which were started by Marty Marion (left) that Charley "Red" Barrett, garrulous, carefree righthander obtained from Boston in a 1945 swap for Mort Cooper, credited Marion and second-base sidekick Verban for much of his 23-game success.

110

Yogi's Pal Joey: National television celebrity Joe Garagiola was a 20-year-old kid, fresh out of the Army, when he was thrust into the Cardinals' catching in 1946, aided by Del Rice (at right). Garagiola would become famous for his bald head and ability to think quickly and speak wittily. Actually, Joey, as Yogi Berra called his St. Louis boyhood neighbor, never was nearly so bad as Garagiola portrays himself, but, as Joe quips, "I wasn't even the bad player in my block." The reference is to Berra with whom he's shown at a bowling alley in 1949, the year Joe was married to Audrie Ross.

Behind the plate, Breadon counted heavily on a kid the Cardinals had hidden under contract since they'd sent him to Springfield, Missouri, as clubhouse boy at age fifteen, where the mirthful young man said he'd broken in by washing Stan Musial's uniform socks.

This was Joe Garagiola, who would become a household word behind a radio and television microphone as a national wit as well as a baseball broadcaster. "Yogi" Berra's pal Joey from across the street on "The Hill," St. Louis's Italian section, had hit a gargantuan home run marked by a bronzed tablet in the Philippines, but he was unprepared for the pressure put on him by the club when he'd had so little experience.

One day out there in Manila, Garagiola and another future catcher, Joe Ginsberg of Detroit, listened to a radio vignette from the States in which an announcer outrageously built up a young player.

"And then, my God," exclaimed Garagiola, "the Paul Bunyan he was talking about turned out to be me!"

So Garagiola would need time. Meanwhile, Breadon had dealt Jimmy Brown to Pittsburgh and Blix Donnelly to Philadelphia.

In spring training, Dyer said solemnly that Schoendienst, the star rookie and base-stealing champion of 1945 as left fielder, would be his number one utility player, but,

throatily, Red had said "bee's-wax" to that or a more expressive example of barnyard vulgar.

When holdout Whitey Kurowski was out of shape opening day, Red played third base and performed well. After Kurowski came back and Marion's tender aching back acted up—Marty had to stop bending over to pick up so many pebbles in his

personal housekeeping—Red played shortstop pretty well, too.

What comes after third base and shortstop? Second base. On a train trip, I told Red he'd make a helluva good second baseman, but, though he wanted very much to play, he told me "horsefeathers" or the equivalent. But, to boost catching, the Cardinals sent Verban to Philadelphia as part of a three-club deal for Clyde Kluttz.

Lou Klein got the message. In late May, Klein and pitchers Fred Martin and Max Lanier jumped to Mexico. Lanier was the big loss, as

witness his 6-and-0 record. Then rooming with Schoendienst, he'd left a farewell note that concluded:

". . . and keep hitting those line drives, Red."

He did, promoted to a career at second base.

Meanwhile, with other clubs' players having jumped to Jorge Pasquel's league in Mexico, Stan Musial, Terry Moore and Enos Slaughter turned down offers. Musial, then paid only $13,500, saw $75,000 piled on a hotel bed as down payment on a five-year bid for another $125,000.

Breadon, defying new commissioner A. B. "Happy" Chandler's

South of the Border: Down Me-hi-co way, that's where pitching ace Max Lanier (right) fled in 1946, seeking more money. He was accompanied by second baseman Lou Klein (left) and rookie retread righthander Fred Martin. They're shown here in 1949, reprieved from major league exile for having jumped their contracts.

hands-off edict, flew to Mexico to meet an impressed Pasquel. Chandler levied a $5000 fine on Breadon and, technically, suspended the Cardinals from any activities other than game-playing for thirty days. Clubowners respectful of Breadon urged Chandler to desist.

Said Breadon, manfully, "I wanted only to meet the man good enough to take ball players from me."

Said Pasquel, "Mr. Breadon, you impress me. I no take any more player from you."

But the damage seemed to be done. The Cardinals were seven games out in August. Then Dyer's decisive move paid off. He asked Musial to switch to first base from left field. "The Man," as Brooklyn now had tabbed him, was en route to a .365 season. The Cardinals closed in behind Pollet, a twenty-one game winner.

By the final day, however, for the first time in baseball history, both teams wound up in a tie. Old teammate Mort Cooper shut out the Dodgers at Boston, 4-0. But even though Musial homered early, George "Red" Munger faltered, and an 8-3 loss to Chicago at St. Louis meant the first-ever pennant playoff.

In a coin flip, Leo Durocher bested his old boss, Sam Breadon. The Lip chose to give St. Louis the first game so that the Dodgers could have the best-of-three with only one train trip. They never got the third game.

Pollet, pitching with a bad back bound tightly, worked courageously, and his twenty-year-old batterymate and good friend, Garagiola, hit hard in a 4-2 opening-game victory over Ralph Branca. Terry Moore, like Garagiola, had three hits.

At Brooklyn, the Dodgers got a first-inning run off Murry Dickson, but the wiry righthander tied them down until doubles by Musial and Moore and triples by Slaughter, Dusak and Dickson had built an 8-1 lead. Dickson horsed around in a sloppy ninth before Harry "The Cat" Brecheen, scheduled to pitch the third game, if necessary, came in and struck out Eddie Stanky and Howie Schultz.

The 8-4 victory, the sixteenth in twenty-four games, sent the Cardinals hurrying back by train for the World Series with Ted Williams and the Boston Red Sox, who were 7-to-20 favorites.

This was supposed to be a Williams-versus-Musial series, between undoubtedly the best all-round hitters of the postwar era. Williams got only five hits, all singles, against Dyer's refined version of the "Williams Shift." (Shortstop Marty Marion moved to the first base side of second base so that only third baseman Kurowski stood in the normal shortstop position.) Musial was limited to six hits, but four were doubles, one a triple, and he drove in four runs.

For the Cardinals, the standouts were Slaughter, the right fielder whose 130 RBIs had led the National League in a .300 season, and Brecheen, a 15-15 pitcher of whom a Philadelphia gambler had told me, "I'm betting on St. Louis because you got a skinny little guy (Brecheen) who is a big-game pitcher."

Touche!

The Cardinals lost cruelly at the start. Scratch hits enabled Boston to tie in the ninth, and big Rudy York's solo homer beat Pollet in the tenth, 3-2.

St. Louis tied in the second game, beating lefty Mickey Harris, 3-0, behind the battery of Brecheen and Rice. Next, Boston won at home behind Dave "Boo" Ferriss, 4-0, as York ripped Dickson for a three-run homer in the first.

Off Tex Hughson, the Cardinals teed off for twenty hits good for twenty-nine bases in the fourth game. Slaughter, Garagiola and Kurowski tied the Series record of four hits each as Munger evened it, 12-3.

But when Joe Dobson defeated Pollet in the fifth game, 6-3, Boston had not only a three-to-two lead, but St. Louis's back was against the green, ad-covered right field wall Slaughter played. Old Enos had been hit so painfully with a pitch on his right elbow that Doc Weaver had spent the entire train trip treating the arm with hot-and-cold packs. Even so, though a medical man keenly aware of keeping athletes in action when possible, Dr. Hyland doubted the wisdom of letting Slaughter play a sixth game. Movement could disturb a blood clot.

Growling, Slaughter insisted on playing, and he contributed a good catch and a base hit to Brecheen's second victory, 4-1, over Harris.

So it was the big one in which the Cardinals routed Ferriss and, in turn, Dickson, aided by old-timer Moore's great catches off Williams and Mike Higgins, pitched a dazzling game into the eighth. Suddenly, quickly, he weakened, and Dyer wig-wagged for Brecheen, the artist of the screwball and an intimidating high-and-tight, look-out pitch.

The Cat got two big hitters, but then Dom DiMaggio hit a game-

The Cat's Paw: Pitching hero for the Cardinals in the 1946 Series was a bandy-legged lefthander from Broken Bow, Okla., Harry Brecheen. The Cat won two games and then saved the last one. In this photo, Brecheen turns over his wrist in what Branch Rickey would call the "reverse-curve" twist to show off his prize delivery—the screwball.

114

tying double off the right-center field wall and pulled up lame at second base.

For the Cardinals, a packed house of 36,143 roared as Slaughter, boosting his Series average to .320, singled off righthanded greybeard Bob Klinger. With two out, "Bosco" was still on first base, eager to go. He was off and running even before Harry Walker looped a fly ball to medium left-center, where Leon Culberson had replaced DiMaggio.

Even as Slaughter reached second, he'd said to himself he would go all the way. Earlier, coach Mike Gonzalez had held him up once, and Slaughter had groused characteristically. Eddie Dyer, the manager whose cutting remarks ten years earlier at Columbus, Georgia, had convinced him never to walk again on a ball field, listened to the rasping complaint and said, finally:

"All right . . . all right, if it happens again and you think you can score, go ahead. I'll take the rap."

So as the Country kid reached third and Gonzalez prepared to run up the red traffic sign, Slaughter burst past the arm-flapping coach and kept going. Just then, getting Culberson's throw, shortstop Johnny Pesky turned and froze. Cripes, that fool was trying to score!

Throwing late and off-balance, Pesky didn't get as much on the ball as expected. When catcher Roy Partee came out to smother the sagging throw, Slaughter actually scored easily, really on a single. Official scorers miscalculated the hit and called it a double. They probably didn't even notice that Harry Walker had slowed near second, hopeful of drawing a throw.

Slaughter's dramatic first-to-home dash was to become a baseball legend. Almost as an anti-climax, in Boston's ninth, that kid who didn't want to play second base, Red Schoendienst, rapidly fielded a bad-hopping grounder and then flipped the ball backhanded to Marion at shortstop for the out as the potentially game-tying run crossed the plate.

Too late, which was the way the pennant races would be for too many years thereafter for the Cardinals—too little AND too late.

11

Paradise Lost

When the Cardinals and Dodgers ended the 1946 season even-Stephen before that historic first pennant playoff, my old boss, J. Roy Stockton, sports editor of the *Post-Dispatch*, annoyed many of Sam Breadon's friends, including the baseball broadcaster, Harry Caray, and the restaurant man, Julius "Biggie" Garagnani, later Stan Musial's partner. At a season-ending party at Ruggeri's restaurant to honor Breadon, with whom Biggie had become friendly when espousing "days" and "nights" at the ballpark for big leaguers from St. Louis's Italian area, Stockton was called upon to say a few words.

"Sam," said JRS, addressing himself with light amusement to the honored guest, "it looks as if you sliced the baloney too thin."

The oblique reference to one-way deals by which players had been sold stung, but it was true. The Cardinals had come too close to losing.

They had no more cream left to come to the top. It's too bad, though few clubs drew so robustly before the end of World War II, that the Redbirds hadn't drawn their first million gate (1,062,553) before 1946. In '47 they attracted an even more robust 1,248,013.

Breadon had his problems. First of all, he wasn't feeling too perky physically. The thiamin chloride he'd taken after a fall from a horse in 1939 no longer was a magic elixir. To Dr. Hyland's amusement, Breadon had had everybody on the ball club popping vitamin pills or sipping B-1 soda. But by now, maybe, the cancer that would take his life in May, 1949, had made its early inroads.

He was down, too, because the 1947 Cardinals didn't win. In spring training he'd hassled with Stan Musial, trying to get The Man for $21,000, insisting he had paid the outfielder-first baseman only

$13,500 when Stan observed, dryly, that Uncle Sam had asked for his share of the $5000 "bonus" he had been given in late season at manager Eddie Dyer's request.

Musial signed, finally, at a $31,000 compromise, but, troubled physically, he got off to a horribly slow start. In late May, the reason became apparent. He was felled at the old New Yorker Hotel with an attack of appendicitis. Wan and weak, he was rushed back to St. Louis by plane with catcher Del Wilber as escort.

In St. Louis, Dr. Hyland met the plane with an ambulance, confirmed the diagnosis and suggested that he could freeze the appendix and remove it in the off-season so that Musial could rejoin the ball club.

Gradually, Stan pulled away from .140 to battle his way back uphill to .312.

Handicapped by light hitting otherwise at the outset, Breadon dealt the 1946 batting star of the World Series, Harry Walker, to Philadelphia for squat, powerful Ron Northey. Northey hit hard for the Cardinals, but Walker, tugging nervously at his cap to win the nickname "The Hat," merely went on to lead the league in hitting with .363.

To make things worse, pitching leader Howard Pollet's back was still giving him trouble. The world champions lost eleven of their first thirteen games. Panicky, Breadon took a train to New York to ascertain

from veterans Terry Moore and Marty Marion whether Dyer had lost control. The manager was annoyed that the long-time clubowner heard a rumor about a player taking an extra drink in public, and, unhappily, Dyer had to ask his athletes to keep it private. No beer in the clubhouse, either.

Breadon was concerned, too, that the Cardinals might be upset or distracted because Branch Rickey had brought back the black ballplayer for the first time since Moses Fleetwood Walker in 1884. Yes, there had been some gum-beating about Jackie Robinson, but nothing more than on any other club, including the Dodgers. Dyer, in fact, had urged his players to cool it.

As a football star, Eddie recognized the competitive fire in another. "He's like Frank Frisch," said Dyer of Robinson. "Don't get him mad."

Inspired by old Joe Medwick as a free agent, the Cardinals reeled off a nine-game winning streak in June, offsetting the losing stretch they'd suffered early in the season. (This one coincided with a streetcar and bus strike and the United States Open golf tournament, won at St. Louis Country Club by Pittsburgh's Lew Worsham in a come-from-behind conquest of Sam Snead.) The Redbirds' four-game sweep over the Dodgers closed the gap and brought out the house the rest of the season.

Painful Exit: Stan Musial (left), weaker even from an attack of appendicitis than the wide-brimmed hat of the era would indicate, is accompanied by reserve catcher Del Wilber on a New York-to-St. Louis flight in May, 1947. Dr. Robert F. Hyland decided to freeze the appendix. Musial came back from a horrible start. After surgery that fall, he went on to his greatest season in '48.

But Brooklyn had a different temperament. They were managed then by Branch Rickey's old Sunday manager at St. Louis, Burt Shotton. "Barney" had replaced Leo Durocher when commissioner Happy Chandler suspended the Lip for his off-the-field conduct. The Dodgers struggled through to win.

All Sam Breadon had was second place and a lot of money. Now, he had nearly $2,600,000 in profits, including more than $1,000,000 in a ballpark-building fund. But in the post-war escalation the price of a new stadium had zoomed from forty dollars a seat to $100. Fiscally safe-and-sane Sam wasn't going to spend more than $4,000,000 for a park with a capacity of 40,000 plus.

Besides, he wasn't feeling well, and he didn't want the Cardinals to be run by a woman as they had in the days of Lady Bee (Helene Robison), nor did he want to see the Cardinals sacrificed for income-tax purposes as the New York Yankees had been when brewer Jacob Ruppert died. Now, too, Uncle Sam in Washington was suggesting that Breadon spend the $2,600,000 in the cash drawer or declare a dividend. Bless his pocketbook, he OWNED seventy-eight per cent of the stock.

On a second visit from a St. Louis lawyer named Fred Saigh, who originally had paid a call for a Houston group inquiring about a

The Hat, Etc.: Harry Walker, shown here in military service (left), was a good hitter, manager and a batting authority with the Cardinals and other clubs before stepping down to coach baseball at the University of Alabama-Birmingham, where he is in business. The other man, Howard Krist, a Cardinal pitcher who was 10-and-0 in 1941, had a remarkable 37-11 record for six fractional seasons before arm trouble forced the relief ace out.

Round Ron: Barrel-chested, waddling Ron Northey, a strong-throwing, power-hitting right fielder, replaced Harry Walker on a 1947 day with Philadelphia. Northey helped, all right, but The Hat won the batting title that year.

The New Order: Robert E. Hannegan, Postmaster General of the United States at the time and a former St. Louis University athlete, returned to his home town as club president in November, 1947. Hannegan and Fred Saigh (left), St. Louis lawyer and real-estate wizard, bought the club from Sam Breadon. A year later, Saigh bought out Hannegan.

possible sale, he said he had reconsidered. Yes, now he was interested. Saigh, a real-estate wizard who had risen through downtown building wheeling-and-dealing into financial prominence if not into public recognition, had come to the conclusion that he wanted the ball club himself.

Saigh was a small man, swarthy and neat. The son of a Syrian storekeeper, he had been born in Springfield, Illinois. He'd run track and played basketball at Kewanee, Illinois, High School. At college, he'd been too slight for any game except golf, but he'd been eager, and when he graduated from Bradley Tech at Peoria, he threw away the golf sticks and took law at Northwestern.

Now, at forty, his finances improved considerably through adroit handling of downtown real estate, he recognized a good thing in the Cardinals. He recognized, also, Sam Breadon's affection for a fellow Irishman, a jut-jawed fellow, hail and well met, Bob Hannegan.

Robert Emmet Hannegan, son of a former St. Louis police chief, was a convivial politician with an athletic background. He'd been a good football lineman on a St. Louis University team that gave Notre Dame's famed "Four Horsemen" a pretty good argument in a 13-0 loss. He'd made five bucks a game as an outfielder for a pretty good semi-pro ball club, Pants Store. But then he'd become interested in a game where they threw a bigger curve—politics.

At a time when Bob's political future seemed as dead as a ball club two games behind with only one to play, President Franklin D. Roosevelt rewarded party loyalty in 1941. He named Hannegan Internal Revenue Collector for eastern Missouri. Next, Bob became National Chairman of the Democratic Party and national IRS Commissioner. In 1944, at Chicago, the chairman wheeled and dealed to unseat the vice-president, not because he and his associates wanted Harry Truman in, he told me later, but because they wanted Henry Wallace out. They considered Wallace too progressive, and they knew that FDR was ailing. Truman was Roosevelt's ultimate unenthusiastic choice over Justice William O. Douglas.

Looking back now with an historic generation's vision, a guy can remember Hannegan's having said in 1948: "Harry (Truman) is having his problems now, but, you know, based on the big decisions he has had to make, I think he's going to be remembered as a great president."

Hannegan, who had said within Saigh's earshot that he'd like to be president of the Cardinals, was approached by the man who pronounced his surname to sound like "sigh." They conceived a wonderful, headshaking way to pay Breadon his capital gains $3,500,000 price.

They would form a new corporation and, using Saigh's downtown buildings as good faith, they'd borrow the money short-term to make the deal, using ball parks owned in Rochester, Columbus and Houston as collateral. They would

then inherit the cash drawer with its $2,600,000 assets and quickly pay off the bankers. Cost: Little more than $60,000.

At the last minute, aware that so many of his front-office associates were weepy-eyed in distress, especially the beloved secretary he called "Miss Moiphy" (Mary Murphy), Breadon wanted to change his mind. But old friend Hannegan pleaded:

"Sam, I've already resigned my cabinet post (Postmaster General)."

Breadon stepped down in November, 1947. Within two years, he would be dead of cancer at seventy-two and Hannegan would be dead of the effects of high blood pressure. He was barely forty-nine years old. Ill, he had sold out to Saigh after the 1948 season for $1,000,000, a handsome return for what was, in effect, a $15,000 investment.

Considering the ravages to the infield, a second-place finish in Hannegan's one year as president was commendable. That old arm injury flared up on George Kurowski. Red Schoendienst was hurt often, too. Marty Marion's back went pop like the weasel more and more. And even the old center field inspiration, Terry Moore, reached the end of the line.

120

Catching continued to be a problem, too. Del Rice couldn't hit, but he caught Harry Brecheen regularly. Wilber was Murry Dickson's favorite batterymate. Joe Garagiola, facing the brunt of the criticism as the catcher from whom the most was expected, even had to be shipped out temporarily to Columbus, where he rebounded well.

Garagiola was an innocent victim of broadcaster Gabby Street's catching omniscience, droned in dreadfully repetitious color commentary to Harry Caray's play-by-play. Breadon had yielded, as the owners had previously done at Chicago and New York, where they began broadcasting all ball games. Breadon had aired games only when the rival Browns weren't playing. At one time Johnny O'Hara and Jim Bottomley, then Dizzy Dean had aired major league home games competitively in St. Louis over KWK, France Laux and Cy Casper over KMOX. Then Harry Caray had come back to St. Louis with Street as his mentor. Breadon had liked Caray's melodramatic style.

Thus an exclusive agreement, set up temporarily with KXOK as the flagship, gave one St. Louis station the right to set up a far-flung network. Ultimately, of course, returning to St. Louis at CBS-owned KMOX, Bob Hyland, the former college-outfielding son of Dr. Robert F. Hyland, saw greater interest and wisdom in baseball broadcasts than soap-opera radio. KMOX became the kingpin of Cardinal baseball.

Merry Magician: A wiry little righthander Murry Dickson was an off-season carpenter whose hobby probably kept his pitching arm in shape longer than most players.

In '48, the first year broadcasters began to travel late in the season, the Cardinals prevailed as contenders partly because Brecheen led the National Legue with twenty victories and a 2.24 earned-run average, the reliable "Old Warhorse" Enos Slaughter hit .321, and Northey belted the long ball against righthanded pitching. Essentially, however, it was because Stan Musial had the greatest season of his career. Operated on by Dr. Hyland immediately after the 1947 season, Stan reported fresh and so strong in '48 that he gave up that slightly choked grip to reach the knob of the bat, increasing his power. Yet, as Ted Williams noted, he continued to be the only free-swinging star who really didn't strike out very much.

Musial hit .376, handsome enough, but, in addition, he had a devastating .702 slugging percentage and 103 extra-base hits. He led the National League in hitting (.376), base hits (230), total bases (429), doubles (46) and triples (18).

Emerging as a home-run hitter with thirty-nine, he missed by a rained-out homer becoming the first player EVER to lead in ALL major batting departments. In 1948, more than any other years, it was true, as Marty Marion put it, that "as Musial goes, so go the Cardinals."

Fred Saigh almost got home a winner in his first solo season, 1949, an incredibly successful one, that missed by a twinkling in a once-upon-a-time ending.

Sensitively, Saigh resents any suggestion that the sale of any ball player helped buy out Hannegan's interest. However, the fact is that shortly before Saigh bought out Hannegan, righthander Murry Dickson was sold to Pittsburgh for $125,000. The Pirates then were operated by Hannegan's successor as Democratic National Chairman, Frank McKinney, a Pittsburgh banker.

The Pirates' manager at the time, Bill Meyer, would explain privately that McKinney told him he could get either big Red Munger or little Dickson from the Cardinals. Surely, Meyer would prefer husky Munger, who had been 26-16 over the previous two seasons to dwarfish Dickson, 25-32.

"No, no," said Meyer, firmly, "I'll take the little one."

Dickson was a bone in the Cardinals' throat all season. A 12-14 game winner at Pittsburgh, where later he would post a twenty-game season with a seventh-place club, the "Merry Magician," who would deadpan that he sprinkled "woofle dust" on the ball, beat the Redbirds five precious times.

Nice Guys Finish...: Not last, but not first often enough, either. Despite a menacing chaw of tobacco, a great pickoff move and a good mixture of pitches, George "Red" Munger just didn't have the fire to be great rather than pretty good.

The Cork and The Spirit: Maybe that's what they should have called it when Ted Wilks, the Cardinals' ace relief pitcher of the late 1940s, met the New York Yankees' celebrated bullpen man, Joe Page, in spring training. Joe Garagiola nicknamed Wilks as "The Cork" because he stopped rallies. Page was indeed a free spirit with the Yanks.

Spelled Backwards: Eddie Kazak's name came out the same, fore and aft. The blond third baseman got off to a great start in 1949, but then he suffered a broken leg that reduced his potential. Still, he hit .304 in 96 games.

Manager Dyer was angry when he came in to see the new boss, but it did look as if he'd win. His pitching pet, Pollet, rebounded magnificently to pitch as he had in 1946, winning twenty games and losing only nine. Yes, and Munger did well, too, with 15-8. Also, Ted Wilks, the wide-shouldered reliever, was at his best with a 10-3 record and nine saves.

The pitching got a late pickup, too, as Saigh, working to solve the outlaw label of players who had jumped three years earlier to Mexico, helped baseball avoid a lawsuit by briefly signing outfielder Danny Gardella. Then Lanier, Martin and Klein came back.

Despite a recurrent bad back, "Nippy" Jones, the handsome first baseman, hit .300. Schoendienst, though tailing off late, hit nearly the same. Until he suffered a leg fracture, a blond third baseman who spelled his name the same fore and aft, Eddie Kazak, hit hard. He finished at .304.

Musial, though starting poorly, came on strong to bat .338 with thirty-six homers and 123 RBIs. Slaughter was robust with .336, but the two lefthanded hitters whose presence invited every soft-throwing, cunnythumbed southpaw in the league—even though Stan and Bosco hit them better than righthanded Redbirds—lost the batting title.

Jackie Robinson won the championship with a .342 average, and the Dodgers won the pennant, too, in a race cruel for the Cardinals except at the box office. In Sportsman's Park, then reduced to barely more than 30,000 capacity because of improvements made by Dick Muckerman of the Browns, the Cardinals averaged better than 20,000 a game. They drew the best ever by far in the old ballpark—1,430,676.

En route, a couple of games that were S-O-O vital got away from them. At home against New York, they were stopped, in part, by an astonishing throw from right center to the plate by rookie Monte Irvin, throwing out Red Schoendienst on a double by Musial. Essentially, though, the 3-1 loss to Adrian Zabala and the Giants resulted when Nippy Jones hit a two-run homer off the New York lefthander just as umpire Jocko Conlan at third base called a balk. Now, the hit would take precedence over the balk.

Afterward, Dizzy Dean, then doing Browns' broadcasts, came into the Cardinals' clubhouse, shaking his head. "Podnuh," he said, "Ol' Diz pitched too soon. Now, you can call back a home-run ball."

During the same season at Pittsburgh when a red-hot Pirate rookie outfielder, Dino Restelli, was hitting hard and arguing the same, he twice stepped out to dispute strikes by top umpire Larry Goetz. Angry, with Restelli out of the box, Goetz tried to get the Cardinals' Gerry Staley to pitch, ready to call a third strike. But, wool-gathering, Staley missed the significance of the gesture and, off the mound, lobbed the ball to Garagiola.

Men of Destiny: Gerry Staley (left) and Vernal "Nippy" Jones couldn't quite give the Cardinals a pennant. Gerry was a good pitcher in the 1949 near-miss; Jones hit .300 at first base despite a back that eventually required surgery. Seven years later, playing at Milwaukee, Nippy insisted by a dirtied ball that a Yankee pitch had nipped the shoe polish off a shoe and that he was entitled to base, helping win a Series game.

Signed and Sealed: Eddie Dyer (seated left) had plenty of witnesses when he signed his last contract with Sam Breadon a couple of months before Breadon sold out. Standing from the left, Harry Brecheen, George Kurowski, Enos Slaughter, Terry Moore, Ron Northey and Howard Pollet.

Joe fired the ball back, frantically urging Staley to pitch, but, automatically, Gerry checked two base-runners before pitching. Aware, just in time, that Goetz wasn't fooling, Restelli stepped right up into the box to hit a so-so serve on the nose for a game-winning double.

Said Goetz afterward, "Crissake, I couldn't throw the ball for St. Louis."

Yeah, that one game that got away TWICE proved so important. The Cardinals lost four of their first five games in a 96-58 season, but they never lost four in a row again until the final week. Then, two up on the defeat side with five games to play, compared with the Dodgers' four remaining, they lost their knockout punch.

At Pittsburgh, lefthanded-hitting Tom Saffell came up in a late-inning jam. Righthander Red Munger served a pitch that Saffell lofted against the right-field foulpole, barely fair, for a grandslam homer. Final: Pittsburgh 6, St. Louis 4.

Before the next game, Dickson said to hunting pal Brecheen, "I hope you win, Cat, but you're not going to beat ME." Final: Pittsburgh 7, St. Louis 2.

At Chicago, now out of first place but with a chance to regain a tie as the Dodgers were idle, the Cardinals lost again. Lanier, who had won five in a row, was hit hard and Munger failed in relief as a Chicago spear-carrier, "Monk" Dubiel, stopped the Redbirds, 6-5.

On the next-to-last day, Chicago scored three quick runs off an old nemesis, Brecheen, but the Cardinals failed time and again with men on against a herky-jerky nuthin'-ball lefthander, Bob Chipman. They now needed their own victory and a Brooklyn defeat in the final game to save a playoff for the season in which Saigh already had sold World Series tickets.

Ironically, that last day, the Cardinals' bats boomed. Musial belted two home runs and a single. Pollet breezed, 13-5. But, even though Don Newcombe blew a five-run lead in the first inning, the Dodgers won over Philadelphia on a base hit by Carl Furillo in the tenth, 9-7.

So a ball club picked to finish fourth, one which had struggled along in seventh place in May, had lost four in a row for the last time and six out of nine since Lanier out-duelled Newcombe in a late September classic, 1-0.

On the deadly silent train ride back to St. Louis that final Sunday evening, I dropped in to the compartment where Eddie Dyer sat talking quietly with his wife, Gerry.

Philosophically, I said, "Well, Colonel, after so many years breaking so many other teams' hearts down the stretch, I guess the Cardinals had this one coming."

Dyer nodded.

"But," I wondered, "when will we get this close again?"

Dyer shot a knowing glance at his wife. "That," he said, "is just what I finished saying to Gerry."

12

Skid Row

From the fabulous '40s, when they'd finished second or better nine consecutive seasons, the Cardinals drooped into the fumbling '50s, obviously handicapped by what Branch Rickey used to call a lack of "quantitative quality." Rickey had a way with words. Ask anyone who roared chestily into his office to seek a raise and slunk away glad the old man hadn't touched him for a loan. B. R. had a couple of more apt expressions, too.

Of a deal in which a player of questionable ability was removed, Rickey called it "an addition by subtraction." He talked, also, of "anesthetic ball players," those who lulled you into thinking they could do more for you than they really could.

Take, for instance, Sam Breadon's last personal favorite, Tommy Glaviano, an engaging brown-eyed California kid, a billiard ball-sized-tobacco chewer with hair that stood as upright as if he'd met Dracula or Jack the Ripper or the Frankenstein monster in a dark alley. "Harpo," they called him with an appropriate bow to the horn-tooting, bewigged Marx brother, and he was a lovable comic. When most guys dressed conservatively in business-suits, Glaviano looked as if he were suited up for a vaudeville song-and-dance act.

Small wonder that Joe Garagiola, who liked characters, was taken with the carefree butcher boy from Sacramento, California. Trouble is, as a third baseman with just a bit of power, Glaviano didn't hit or throw for average.

Throughout the '40s whenever the Cardinals needed to get well, all they required was a trip to Brooklyn, where Stan Musial had batted over .500 the last two seasons and where they won regularly. But first trip in for the '50s, they lost two games and then appeared to have found the old

Flatbush touch with an 8-0 lead into the eighth inning behind Howard Pollet. The game could have been called because of rain, darkness, cold weather or wet grounds.

But the umpires hadn't stopped it. Glaviano made a critical error in a shaky eighth inning and then three more in the ninth when the Dodgers scored five decisive times. Their windfall 9-8 victory did something else. Thereafter, it turned around St. Louis's luck in Brooklyn. The Cardinals became the home-field cousins for the Dodgers.

Compassionately, manager Eddie Dyer told Garagiola and Pollet to take charge of Glaviano so that he wouldn't do a Brodie off the Brooklyn Bridge. But next morning, after a late-evening departure on an overnight train ride to Boston, Glaviano got off at Back Bay, chipper and puffing a cigar.

He grinned. "How about those guys," he said. "They took me to a movie before we left New York. Know what it was called? 'D.O.A.'—Dead on Arrival!"

Dyer didn't have many laughs that season. Nippy Jones hadn't recovered from back surgery. Ted Wilks needed hemstitching on his right elbow. Marty Marion continued to have back miseries, and even his replacement, surehanded Eddie Miller, was hurt. And Musial, though he would lead the league with a .346 average, hitting twenty-eight homers and driving in 109 runs, missed his best chance ever to hit better than .400.

Early, hitting .448 in April and actually lucky more often than good, Stan, then twenty-nine, slipped in loose dirt rounding first base and heard something pop in his knee. "Thank God for the restaurant," he said, unable momentarily to get up.

Harpo: If you wanted to know why they called Tommy Glaviano "Harpo," it's a shame this isn't a movie for which the bright-eyed pixy would be glad to remove his cap and show his stand-up curls.

His knee bound in a protective cast, Musial still hit so well that he had dropped only to .442 in June. Then, pitcher Al Brazle fielded a ball near first base and threw too hard too close to Musial, who had made his "annual return to first base," as the *Globe-Democrat's* Martin J. "Mike" Haley wrote dryly. The ball was wild. Stan reached up and grabbed it with his bare hand, the throw ripping a deep gash between Musial's second and third fingers. He played hurt. His batting suffered, too.

Suddenly, Garagiola's bid for stardom ended at only twenty-four. Married to Audrie Ross, attractive organist at the Arena's roller rink, he'd settled down. He was hitting .347 in June when, attempting to hurdle Jackie Robinson at first base so that he wouldn't step on the Brooklyn second baseman's foot as Jackie fished for first base on a bunt play, Joe tripped and landed heavily on his left shoulder. Surgery never brought back the smooth swing of the kid who soon would give up the comfort of a $16,000-a-year contract with the world champion New York Giants for a $12,000 flyer on KMOX radio.

Catching would continue to be a black cat for the Cardinals. Ever since Pickles Dillhoefer's death in the early 1920s and Bob O'Farrell's broken-thumb and sore-arm troubles

Resilient: Bill Sarni, a pro at the tender age of 15 back home in Los Angeles, then a minor league baseball town, was washed up at 29, a result of a heart attack suffered after the Cardinals had dealt him to the New York Giants. He switched to become a prosperous stock broker in St. Louis.

in the championship '20s, they had felt the sting, notably in Bill DeLancey's ultimately fatal illness and now in Garagiola's disability. It continued, too.

Bill Sarni, an attractive Los Angeles kid who had caught briefly in the Coast League at only fifteen, had climbed to .300. Then, dealt to the Giants in one of frantic Frank Lane's manpower upheavals, he'd suffered a heart attack at only twenty-nine. He was forced into a new career as a stockbroker and made it a good one.

Hal Smith, too, went out the same unusual way for a young athlete. Bright-eyed, smiling "Chitlins," nickname for one of his songs, was barely thirty when he was stricken with a heart ailment a few years later (1961). Smitty was a good catcher and a funny one. He wrote—or said he did—western ballads, such as "Sittin', Spittin' and Whittlin'," "I Got a Belly Full of Chitlins and a Churn Full of You" and the one I liked best: "I'm Madly in Love With What's- Her- Name."

But back in 1950, there was nothing funny to Eddie Dyer as pitching folded, too. George Munger had failed often to be the big-game stopper on whom the manager had relied much. One day I walked into the Cardinals' clubhouse to find Munger, lying on the trainer's table,

Hands of a Receiver: Hal Smith (lower photo) and Hobie Landrith were the Cardinals' catchers in a close call chase of Milwaukee in 1957. Smitty, a quipster with funny song lyrics, was forced by a heart disturbance to hang up his talented glove early. He became a good scout, a description intended both ways.

second-guessing Dyer with a most agreeable single witness, Gabby Street.

Hell, Dyer owed me nothing and vice-versa, but I couldn't resist a comment. "Dammit, George," I said, "if he (Dyer) DOES lose his job, he'll lose it in part because too many people think you're his 'pet.' And, Sarge, (Street) I'm surprised at you. You wonder why Dyer gives (Harry) Brecheen a fifth day between starts. Heck, when you had Jesse Haines, you did it for the same reason—age!"

I'm lucky, I guess, that Munger, almost too pleasant, didn't drop me on my over-stuffed seat cushion. Gabby was too nice an old-timer. Or too old, anyway.

The sun set in the West for Dyer as the Cardinals dipped into the second division for the first time since 1938. Eddie agreed to resign gracefully, which was what Fred Saigh wanted, but on the appointed day when the manager saw Harry Caray waiting in an impromptu ballpark press room, he balked. If Caray, whose comments he felt had been excessively negative, were in the room, then, by gosh, pal, as Dyer would phrase it, the manager would have a no-holds-barred exit with Saigh in front of the media. Caray waited in a side room.

Although Johnny Keane thought he might get the job and some mentioned coach Terry Moore, Saigh turned to the playing ranks. Marty Marion, the thirty-three-year-old ailing whiz at shortstop would become a bench boss, and he brought back as coaches the minor league manager he respected highly, Ray Blades, and the popular old one-man gang, Mike Ryba.

Marion got the usual big year from Musial, who settled salary differences with Saigh, largely as a result of a decision that a Wage Stabilization Board ruling which limited club salary increases to ten per cent during the Korean War period did not apply. Musial, ten years after he'd fed his wife and first child on a hundred dollars a month, was up to $80,000.

Stan sought to become the first National League batting champion to succeed himself since Rogers Hornsby in 1925. He did, hitting .355 with thirty-two homers and 108 RBIs, but an opening-day 5-4 loss rookie Tom Poholsky suffered to Murry Dickson in the midst of snow flurries might have been most expensive to the ball club.

The Cardinals quickly were invaded by a flu bug. They toured the East with regulars bed-ridden. The sickbay incursion took its toll in the standings. Musial, literally getting out of bed to hit a game-winning home run at Cincinnati, applied the right label to the solid blue stockings Marion had decided the club should wear on the road.

"Know what they are, Marty?" Stan said. "Mourning Socks."

Marion continued to have Eddie Dyer's hard luck with young pitchers. Dyer had come up with a big blond who looked deceptively innocent. Cloyd Boyer, tabbed "Junior" by W. Vernon Tietjen of the old *St. Louis Star-Times*, threw extremely hard with an odd, flopping sidearmed delivery. Quite so, innocent looking or not, he'd made old hearts glow by spinning caps with a fast ball high and tight. But Boyer, whose younger brother, Ken, was working his way up in the ranks as a pitcher-converted-to-infielder in the minors, soon encountered arm trouble. He wound up as a long-time big league pitching coach.

For Marion, another pitcher came in fantastically. Joe Presko, a slight, olive-skinned kid also from western Missouri (Kansas City), had an easy-does-it delivery and a singing fast ball. Until hurt, "Baby Joe," as Tiej christened him, looked as if he might be the staff stopper, lacking since Pollet had lost his zip and Brecheen aged.

For Presko—and the Cardinals—futility reached a new high (or low) in a trading-deadline defeat at home against Brooklyn. The Redbirds were unbelievably bad. In one five-inning stretch, they put five men on base and failed to score. Presko and even Red Schoendienst, a clever runner, were picked off second base.

In another instance, with men on first and third, Joe Garagiola grounded hotly to Gil Hodges at first. Hodges's throw home nailed one man. Garagiola—to this day he doesn't know why!—froze in the batter's box. Double play! Nippy Jones's single then scored only one run.

That's all the Cardinals got out of fifteen hits, two walks and an error—one run! In the Dodgers' ninth, with one on and two out, Hodges hit a long home run to snap Presko's bid for a sixth straight victory, 2-1.

Baby Joe: Joe Presko was 22, looking as if he were still in his teens, when he threw a blazing fast ball for the Cardinals in 1951 before arm trouble did him in.

Junior: Don't let the nickname fool you or the youthful look. Cloyd Boyer, older brother of Ken, came up to the Cardinals with an odd arm delivery, but with plenty of speed and willingness to keep the hitters loose. Arm trouble shortened Junior...er, Cloyd's career, but he became a big league pitching coach.

Next day, at Marion's behest, Saigh dealt old friends Garagiola, Pollet and Wilks to pussycat Pittsburgh. The Cardinals got Wally Westlake, who, like third baseman Billy Johnson from the Yankees and shortstop Stan Rojek of the Buccos, wasn't the answer.

Lefthander Cliff Chambers, also obtained from Pittsburgh in the three-for-two deal, helped until he suffered a broken wrist a year later. By then, Marion was gone, surprisingly fired after a three-game and two-position improvement to 81-73, third place.

Saigh, noting that the club still had finished farther behind stretch-driving New York than Philadelphia the previous season, cited alleged lack of fire by Marion and Marty's failure to give the greenpea clubowner enough help in the office. The boss sympathized, he said, with the flu bug early and the sore arms late, but, oh, yes, here came the clincher:

"I still can't understand how we lost eighteen out of twenty-two to Brooklyn." Ah, Harpo Glaviano!

Boots and Saddles and The Brat: Eddie Stanky (right), taking over as manager in 1952, recognized early that leathery, angular Al Brazle, i.e., "Boots and Saddles" or the "Durango Cowboy," had the sidearmed control lefthanded to be a good relief pitcher. Old Alfie pitched until he was 40—at least!

Saigh had been impressed by the Giants' "Little Miracle of the Coogan's Bluff," the surge from thirteen games out on August 13 to win a storybook pennant on Bobby Thomson's playoff home run against the Dodgers. One little man liked another, the championship cheek of Eddie Stanky—"The Brat!" Eddie had been a key man for Leo Durocher's team in the stretch as, seeking to overhaul the Brooks, the Giants played a unique makeup game in St. Louis.

As the only ball club ever to play two separate opponents the same day, the Cardinals beat Sal Maglie and the Giants in the afternoon, then lost to Warren Spahn and the Boston Braves at night.

Saigh had to pay through the nose to make the thirty-six-year-old Stanky manager. The Giants obtained old lefthander Max Lanier and a clever fly-chaser who never hit adequately, Chuck Diering.

Stanky came in an elbow-flying iconoclast. He seemed determined to bury Cardinals' customs, but he stayed to become a smart, imaginative manager who was better handling kid players than older ones he thought would know better. Like Frisch, he was a team-ball master at going to right field with none out and a runner on second or third, moving up the runners. Branch Rickey hadn't raved about the pint-sized player's "intangibles" for nothing.

I began nearly fighting Stanky. With his cold, blue-eyed glare he would take out his temper on the press at times, but after one particularly stormy argument, I appreciated him better and I believe he did me, too. We became friends. I learned more inside baseball from the little man in his three-plus seasons as Cardinals' manager than from all the others.

If Stanky wasn't at his best handling pitchers—and I don't know, Mr. Rickey, whether he had the quality to achieve sufficient quantity—he applied the best combination lefthanded-righthanded, one-two relief-pitching punch. I refer to Al Brazle and Eddie Yuhas.

Brazle, a seamy, square-shouldered Colorado cowboy facetiously called "Clark Gable" by Chicago's Charley Grimm because he obviously wasn't, was an angular lefthander who just seemed to flip the ball to the plate sidearmed with nonchalance, but that fat serve was a tricky sinker. And the sidewheeling motion made good lefthanded hitters, such as "Dixie" Walker, Tommy Holmes and Earl Torgeson weep in frustration at a five-cent curve.

One night after a day on which "Old Boots and Saddles" had struck out Torgy four times, the Braves' first baseman stuck his head in the Cardinals' clubhouse and flipped in

Rawhide: Aptly nicknamed, Eddie Yuhas had one touch of greatness with the Cardinals in 1952, teaming with Al Brazle for a brilliant righthanded-lefthanded relief pair as the club won 88 games and lost only 66.

two plaid jock straps for Brazle, bringing a chorused squad guffaw when he yelled:

"Here's one for each of your heads, you skinny so-and-so."

But if Brazle baffled so many lefthanders, he was clobbered unmercifully by Brooklyn's slugging righthanded-hitting catcher, Roy Campanella. If "Campy" didn't hit at least the fence when he swung at Alfie's junk, he wasn't even trying. One night he even drilled one into Sullivan Avenue, over the hot-dog stand next to the bleacher scoreboard.

Yet it was Eddie Yuhas's pitching so skillfully against Campanella in a spring game at Miami, getting Campy to hit into a game-ending double play with the bases loaded, by which the rangy, rawboned rookie righthander quickly won a spot in Stanky's method-in-madness maneuvering. If only he had not hurt his arm. . .

With a combined total of a hundred appearances in 1952, the Year of the Relief Pitcher in the National League because New York rookie Hoyt Wilhelm and Dodger newcomer Joe Black also were great bullpen men, Brazle was 12-5 with sixteen saves, Yuhas 12-2 with six saves.

Except for staff leader Gerry Staley, who would win his biggest reputation as a game-saver himself for the Chicago White Sox in 1959, the starters were lean and green. Wilmer "Vinegar Bend" Mizell came in, overpublicized as another Dizzy Dean. Mizell was droll, all right, and a country kid who

ultimately would win his way into Congress, but he was wild. He walked in a rolling gait acquired from long practice making certain the turpentine sap taken from tall southern pines didn't spill out of buckets balanced on each of his shoulders.

Mizell walked the first two batters and, as a result, lost 2-1 in his first game at Cincinnati on an April night to remember. In the midst of a squabble with Eddie Stanky's alter ego, shortstop Solly Hemus, plate umpire "Scotty" Robb got into it with the manager and pushed him. Gosh, a man biting a dog, an umpire attacking a player! Equally stunning, clubowner Fred Saigh, stopping en route from Washington to see Mizell's debut, learned he had been indicted for income-tax evasion.

To finish with an 88-66 record, pretty stout for a third-place team in the old eight-team, 154-game route, Stanky had sweet-talked a solid .300 season out of a former baseline foe, Enos Slaughter. He got a .303 out of Red Schoendienst, too, and had benched both players the last day of the season to preserve their records. He'd conned Del Rice of the upper-cut hitch in his swing to go to right field more often.

Stan Musial, achieving a third straight batting title with .336, was disturbed mostly because he'd failed to get 100 RBIs (91) behind a good batting order. He really hadn't liked it, either, when as a last-day-of-the-season gimmick, he'd been asked to pitch against the Chicago outfielder, Frankie Baumholtz, he had just beaten out of the batting title.

Baumholtz must not have been pleased, either, because he switched to righthanded to face the former pitcher whose arm had healed sufficiently for him to throw reasonably well from the outfield. Stan merely lobbed the ball, and Baumholtz, hit-

ting it sharply, was safe on an error by Hemus at third base.

Hemus, actually a second baseman temporarily at third, was a shortstop by necessity. Stanky, taking over as manager, thought he could play second base and Schoendienst could be the shortstop, but he was wrong on both counts. Eddie couldn't cut the mustard to play regularly, and Red was superb at second base. Besides, the "Mighty Mouse," as Marion had nicknamed Hemus, showed Stanky something.

Although he lacked the great shortstop cruise or arm, Solly was a battler. Into the pug-nosed kid, Stanky poured his own enthusiasm and challenge. As a walk-wheedling little leadoff man, taught by Musial to use a thinner-handled bat, Hemus also could hit the long ball.

Solly hit fifteen home runs, a Redbird record for a shortstop, and, needled by Stanky to reach base 250 times, Hemus got there 268 times on hits, walks and as a human backstop hit by pitches.

One day at New York in the greatest Redbird rally I ever saw, the 1952 Cardinals trailed the great Sal Maglie 11-0 in the opener of a doubleheader, and Stanky actually began to think of resting his regulars. But on a sudden hunch, he said, no, let's wait.

Slaughter drove in five runs, Hemus three and Musial two. By the eighth, the Cardinals trailed by only a run. Hemus led off, facing a new pitcher, George Spencer. Solly trotted toward third to ask Stanky if Eddie wanted him to take a strike?

Three Squirts: Three little men, physically, Dick Schofield (left), Eddie Stanky and Solly Hemus (right) lasted a long time in the majors. Both Stanky and Hemus managed and Schofield, if you will, managed to last 19 years in the majors even though he got into more than 100 games only three of 19 seasons. Here, in 1953, Ducky, a shortstop, just has signed a big bonus at Springfield, Ill., and joined Stanky, who hammed it up with a grin in Brooklyn.

"No," snarled Stanky, the bit between his teeth, to use one of his own pet expressions. "Attack!"

Solly hit a game-tying homer on the first pitch. Later, Slaughter hit a single to drive in the go-ahead run. In the ninth Hemus hit a two-run homer off Monte Kennedy, climaxing a staggering comeback for a 14-12 triumph.

That was Hemus—and Stanky—at their best. Eddie was at his worst in handling a pasty-faced kid who came up from Columbus and, using a peculiar headfake that discombooberated the best hitters, he flummoxed them with pitches that were slow, slower and s-l-o-w-e-s-t.

Stu Miller was magic, like the professor throwing the chemically wood-repellent ball in the movie *It Happened Every Spring*. Miller broke in with a 1-0 shutout at Chicago, pitched another shutout and was within one inning of a record third straight no-run game for a rookie when there was an error behind him. One night he struck out Roy Campanella, and Campy leaned on his bat at the plate, shaking his head in disbelief.

Stu Miller was hard to believe. Once, pitching an All-Star game at San Francisco, he was blown off the mound by a stiff wind for a balk. Stanky didn't like Miller's independent attitude or his bridge-playing in bed. Eddie nicknamed him sarcastically "The Stenographer" and "Gertrude."

H'mm, all Gertrude did was to last sixteen-plus manful seasons in the majors as a pretty baffling relief pitcher.

Stu-pendous: Stu Miller, later heckled by Eddie Stanky, whom he fooled by becoming a durable relief pitcher elsewhere, broke in astonishingly with the 1952 Cardinals as a starter, throwing slow pitches with a disconcerting head-jerking manner. As he beats the New York Giants, 3-1, missing a chance to become the third pitcher to break into the majors with three straight shutouts, he is congratulated by third baseman Billy Johnson (left), first baseman Dick Sisler and catcher Del Rice.

13
Gussie

When Gussie Busch got his first field-inspection tour of Sportsman's Park, walking so fast he forced Redbird vice-president Bill Walsingham to dog-trot out of breath to keep up with him, the fifty-four-year-old beer baron had come to one of his quick, shoot-from-the-hip conclusions.

"I'd rather see my ball club play in Forest Park than here," he rasped.

It wasn't Busch's ball club, of course, as former owner Fred Saigh was fast to note, because the brewery, Anheuser-Busch, had bought it. But the reaction was the same because August Anheuser Busch, Jr., then WAS the "Big Eagle."

Hurrying the heck out of second place behind Schlitz in the brewery business, Busch would have preferred late brother Adolphus's keeping his nose to the hops and barley while Gussie enjoyed his personal *gemütlichkeit*. But fate in-

tervened. Gussie was in competitive haste to make the brewery No. 1 and, hopefully, the ball club, too.

Busch, who had attended former Smith Academy and the world's playgrounds in a fast-living spin into middle age, preferred his family and animals and riding show horses or to the hounds. Certainly, he would rather hold the reins of a handsome coach-and-four than those of the operation at 721 Pestalozzi Street. He also liked to slam the living bejesus out of whomever he could get across the table in a gin-rummy game. But as his son August later would prove, Gussie was a Busch first, a brewery traditionalist.

Business WAS business, the beechwood-brewed foam of the family-spawned beer game in which his grandfather had moved in the last century. Grandpa Busch, marrying into the Anheusers, had shown his father-in-law showmanship and business acumen. Gussie had much

The Big Eagle and the Old War Horse: August A. Busch, Jr., was Anheuser-Busch's Big Eagle and the little Redbirds', too, when the 54-year-old brewer sportsman signed 37-year-old outfielder Enos Slaughter to what would be the Old War Horse's last Cardinal contract, 1954.

of old Adolphus in his makeup. Less flamboyantly, Gussie's son, August, would show some of the same business schmaltz-and-smarts, sponsoring Budweiser growth, speedboats and a faster-than-sound automotive marvel.

Just as his great-grandfather Adolphus I had given a financial hand when San Francisco burned after its historic earthquake, August also reacted to national crisis. The brewery came through with canned fresh water in 1980 after a hurricane. Gussie had also been generous when the city or something else needed a lift. He had given a compassionate hand and a boost in tribute to the brewery's rapid growth as a beer-and-entertainment leader.

Indications are that August doesn't give high priority to baseball in the company's climb from five million barrels a year to nearly 50,000,000 as the 1980s begin. But, then, Gussie didn't know much more than a foul from the fowl he shot in season out there at his duck preserve at St. Peters, Missouri.

Oh, sure, the senior Busch had known Leo Durocher—he once had married a Dozier, too—and he knew Frank Frisch, another Dutchman who knew where to put Bud-wise-ah, as the Flash labeled the brewery successor to prohibition *heimgemach*. But baseball couldn't hold a pig's knuckle to a *schlagfest* in Gussie's life.

Then, suddenly, Anheuser-Busch owned the Cardinals.

Fred Saigh, who had loved the thrill and the limelight of the game, reluctantly had been willing to sell after a fifteen-month sentence and $15,000 fine on income-tax charges to which his lawyer obviously expected only a financial penalty. He had pleaded *nolo contendere* (no contest). To avoid embarrassment to baseball and unwilling to turn over his holdings to a trust, Saigh agreed unhappily to sell the Cardinals.

Later, miffed at the implication that Anheuser-Busch had come forth to save the ball club when he had indicated all along he would take less money to keep it in St. Louis, Saigh gave Busch a rough time of it—as a stockholder in the brewery. (When he was paid a reported $3,750,000 by the brewery for the National League ball club, nine farm clubs, five minor-league ball clubs and a two-story Dodier Street office building next to Sportsman's Park, Saigh wisely took some 28,000 shares of brewery stock. The stock later split about 4-for-1.)

To keep the Cardinals, I'm sure Fred would have given it all back. Ultimately, he expressed warmer feelings for the man who wore the comfortable moccasins of ownership he had enjoyed and, besides, who could deny that Anheuser-Busch had come forth when others in St. Louis held back?

Among others, Stan Musial, who knew Busch as a sportsman, had mentioned the ball club to Gussie, but, evidently, John L. Wilson, former streetcar-company head then in an executive position at Anheuser-Busch, brought forward the proposal officially.

Even before the stockholders could ratify the February, 1953 decision, Busch had taken that first tour, angered by the age, the wear-and-tear and lack of maintenance given Sportsman's Park by Bill Veeck,

then a shoestring operator of the Browns. Veeck, the promoter deluxe who had drawn handsomely leading up to Cleveland's long-awaited 1948 championship, had bought out the brothers DeWitt, Bill and Charley.

Privately, Veeck thought he could heckle and annoy Saigh and the Cardinals out of town. (St. Louis, Boston and Philadelphia would cease to be two-team towns within three years.) Saigh had been annoyed, though victorious, in a hard-boiled business sense when the DeWitts sought to improve that modest old Breadon-Ball lease at the ballpark. He'd seethed, too, when Veeck quickly grabbed up Marty Marion as a player who soon replaced a returning but quickly fired Rogers Hornsby. And he recognized the goat-getting when the Browns offered aging Harry Brecheen more to try to pitch than the Cardinals had offered The Cat to coach.

But the Browns as a ball club were almost as funny as Veeck's use of a three-foot-seven midget, Eddie Gaedel. To Veeck, there was nothing funny, however, when Anheuser-Busch bought the Cardinals. He immediately wooed Milwaukee which, having built a new ballpark and sought the Cardinals, now needed anybody's team.

Baseball hadn't had a franchise switch since Milwaukee was moved by the American League to St. Louis in 1902. Now, with the Braves having floundered at the gate in Boston, only four years after Billy Southworth's former Cardinals and others had won a pennant, the National League moved to protect Lou

The Kitten: Later more famous for a 12-inning perfect game he LOST for Pittsburgh against Milwaukee, Harvey Haddix was a talented, wiry little lefthander, nicknamed after "The Cat" he resembled, Harry Brecheen.

Perini. They gave him permission to move into Milwaukee, the Braves' minor-league territory. The American League, meanwhile, gave the back of its starched-cuffed hand to Veeck, the organization's hairshirt. The Browns were refused permission to move to Baltimore.

By then Wilson and others had pulled a gaffe by offering Veeck $800,000 for the old ballpark, $1,100,000 if the Browns moved. How could anyone risk offending American League beer drinkers even if that WAS a sad-sack AL ball club?

Ultimately, the brewery got Sportman's Park and immediately made safety repairs. A year later, after an 83-71 tie for third (with Philadelphia) behind Brooklyn in a 1953 season highlighted by young Harvey Haddix's twenty-game season and Red Schoendienst's .342 average, Busch spruced up Sportsman's Park considerably.

Even if efforts to rename it Budweiser Park seemed too commercial, the place richly deserved the Busch Stadium name, because about $2,500,000 was needed for new box seats, a new balcony chairs section, longer and better dugouts and, above all, better rest-room facilities.

Busch, a scrubby Dutchman, liked the eye-soothing effect of removing all circus-like advertisements off the outfield wall, favoring only the big Redbird-and-Eagle on the scoreboard, but he was pleased most with cleaning up those crumby ballpark toilets.

Gussie, then, was in a hurry except in traveling. He didn't fly at the time, but, rather, either used a private bus-sized van or, more often, first a private railroad car lent to him and then one built for the brewery. His ports o' call paid off for Anheuser-Busch AND the Cardinals. The guy had a caviar pocket-book, but cheese-sandwich taste.

Hastily, the brewery sought to bolster the Cardinals, but haste made waste. It was—too bad—not the financial free lance of the 1980s. The club's overdue first black player, Tom Alston, a tall first baseman bought from San Diego, was fast and a brilliant glove man, but he swung a startlingly weak bat. Later, he proved to be ill with a malady that might have caused his inferior play.

Before the Cardinals finally gave up on him, Fred Hutchinson, by then balking inwardly because he recognized no playing future in Alston, agreed to take "Tall Tom" to Vero Beach, Florida, for a spring game, but the long guy forgot to bring his uniform pants, so Hutch couldn't use him.

The manager growled, "If you want a clown, Mr. Busch, why don't you get Emmet Kelly?"

Historic: Tall Tom Alston (center) was the Cardinals' first black ball player, 1954, shown here with two other rookies who prospered more, right fielder Wally Moon and shortstop Alex Grammas.

No Bull Here: Ulysses Brooks Lawrence —"The Bull"—joined the Cardinals in 1954 and was a solid success, 15-6, but he wound up traded to Cincinnati, where he did even better.

The Cardinals had far better luck with an early black pitching acquisition, Brooks "The Bull" Lawrence, strapping son of a hulking Pittsburgh policeman. Lawrence was a 15-6 pitcher and only rapidly-reacting Frank Lane's temptation to trade anything, even a bag of gold for a bucket of ashes, let Lawrence away too soon to Cincinnati.

Early efforts to buy rather than build were sad, a reflection as much on scouts hard-pressed to show Busch something as on immediate lack of a responsible general manager. For one, "Memo" Luna, son of a Mexican border-city mayor, came along at a fancy price. The kid couldn't blacken your eye with a fast ball that wasn't.

By the time refurbished Busch Stadium was ready for the fans in 1954, the year Jack Buck came aboard to join the Cardinals' radio team, everything was set except the ball club. Still, the 1954 Cardinals showed me something. Even though a distant twenty-five games out with a 72-82 record, they drew better than the previous three third-place teams, 1,039,698 for sixth place. Obviously, an improved, clean ballpark, even if no larger, would attract customers, too, especially in a one-team town.

For the season, the Cardinals had paid a pretty penny to Cincinnati to acquire a shortstop, Alex Grammas, frozen on the minor-league level, and they arranged a cash deal with the New York Yankees to acquire Vic Raschi, who

had been a twenty-game winner for three straight pennant seasons, 1949-51.

Stanky could comment, privately, on the intensity of Raschi and what a competitor Vic must have been, but his high hard one didn't have championship velocity any longer. As a National League pitcher, Raschi might be remembered best as the man who served up the first of Henry Aaron's 755 home runs.

The hairy-chested Cardinals could hit, all right, and Stanky, in an exhibition game at Rochester, even fingered a first baseman, Joe Cunningham, now the sales director of the ball club. Cunningham was a good first baseman who sacrificed the position to try to make it in the

Fans' Favorite: Jolly Joe Cunningham, a talented first baseman who gave the outfield a game (if exciting) try to help the cause, was a good hitter for the Cardinals. Later, he managed in the minors for them and became director of group sales.

No Sale: Vic Raschi had been three times a 20-game winner and a big-game victor, too, in years with the New York Yankees, but he had really only his resolve when he came over to the Cardinals for a reported $75,000 in 1954.

outfield, where he was interesting more than he was good. He had a myriad of batting stances, but the good-natured guy really could hit.

Breaking in spectacularly, Joe hit three home runs in his first two games, including two off the Cardinals' No. 1 nemesis, the career-leading lefthanded winner, Warren Spahn, winner of 363 games. Ultimately Cunningham would hit .300 for the Cardinals in three successive seasons, including .345 one year.

The twelve-year man, who finished just under .300, could chuckle, too, at how Stanky had snapped:

"Cun'ngham"—running the surname together in a British affectation—"swing the damned bat. We've got one 'base on balls' hitter (Hemus) and that's enough."

The Cardinals gave up on their Polish Falcons about that time. The Falcons were three unrelated players of Polish extraction—first baseman Steve Bilko, outfielder Eldon "Rip" Repulski and third baseman Ray Jablonski—who had added some color but not enough talent to the team.

Bilko, brought up first under Fred Saigh, was a blond blockbuster who almost ate himself out of Eddie Dyer's training camp before he could make the majors.

"The next Jimmy Foxx," Saigh had called him in exuberance. Bilko had Foxxie's size, all right, but not "Double-X's" ability to pull the ball. Steve's top shots were to center field, the deepest of any ball park. Stan Musial had listed the re-

quirements for hitting:

"Physical relaxation, mental concentration—and don't hit a fly ball to center field."

Repulski, a snub-nosed, well-scrubbed kid Stanky said he would have liked for a son-in-law, could run and showed power at times, but he did a double throwing hitch that slowed his outfield returns. Jablonski was an early-day Ken Reitz, but not quite so slow and not at all gifted afield. Stanky taught "Jabbo" to delay-steal masterfully, which he'd do now and then, exquisitely timing the catcher's throw back to the pitcher to take off. But even though Stanky puffed Jablonski up into successive hundred RBI seasons, Jabbo wasn't good enough. Not, anyway, as good as his mom's kielbasa when the Cards played in Chicago.

Jablonski figured in what was for Busch and his executive vice-president, Dick Meyer, an eye-popping experience on the eve of the Cardinals' first season (1954) as St. Louis's only big league ball club. (The Browns had been sold to Baltimore—without Veeck.)

The Polish Falcons: In the frustrating 1950s, Steve Bilko (left) could eat better than he hit; Ray Jablonski (center) could hit better than he could field and Eldon "Rip" Repulski, shown here with the Cardinals' long-time vice-president, Bill Walsingham, could hit and field better than he could throw. The Polish Falcons were fun, but not quite good enough.

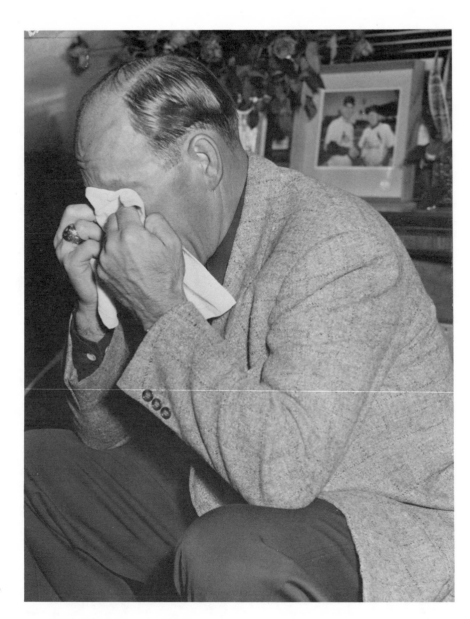

Crying for Joy?: No, Enos Slaughter really wasn't when told just before the season opener that he had been dealt to the perennial champion New York Yankees. He was shown in the Cardinals' front office on Dodier street when executive vice-president Dick Meyer gave him the good...er, bad...or, heck, the news.

Because Enos Slaughter was thirty-eight years old and Wally Moon had scintillated in spring training when the Triple-A outfielder had shown up there by mistake, the front-office triumvirate of Meyer, Stanky and vice-president Bill Walingham, Sam Breadon's nephew, thought a trade was in order.

Actually, they made a good move, acquiring Bill Virdon, permitted to ripen a year in Rochester, but the sale of Slaughter, one of the Cardinals' most durable players, an extremely good and highly emotional one, brought down the wrath of the fans. The brewery-and-ballpark switchboards would not be as lighted up like Chris Von der Ahe's red nose again until Lane dealt Red Schoendienst a couple of years later.

Slaughter was going to the New York Yankees, who had won championships four of the five previous years. The Yanks' manager, Casey Stengel, remembered Slaughter not only as a frisky kid in the National League, but as a gaffer who a year before had helped swipe the All-Star game at Cincinnati with his bat, glove and well-preserved legs.

For all of the Yankees' reputation and Stengel's regard, Slaughter broke down when told the news after a pre-season game at Busch Memorial Stadium.

Afterward, Slaughter and Stan Musial met on the Spring Avenue parking lot across from the old third-base wagon gate. They looked at each other and broke into tears.

To replace the sixteen-year legend who would play six more years until he was forty-three, the task fell to the beetle-browed kid from Texas A. & M., Wally Moon. Wally hit the first pitch opening day onto the right field roof for a home run against the Cubs.

A .304 hitter as a rookie, Moon would play five seasons in St. Louis and seven in Los Angeles, compiling a career batting average of .289. He hit twenty-four home runs for the Cardinals in 1957 and was especially effective in Los Angeles's surprising surge to a pennant in 1959. With an inside-out swing in the cozy-shaped Coliseum, the lefthanded batter looped nineteen homers to left and batted .302.

Even so, except in the pocket-sized football park, Moon wasn't quite the outfielder expected, either defensively or when throwing. Except when Bill Virdon played center field in 1955, with Musial returning to first base, the Cardinals had a fast outfield that couldn't throw. As a result, they put too many opposing runners on second base, not only setting up potential runs, but also negating the double-play opportunities that are available when the other side has a runner on first.

As mentioned, Moon figured with Jablonski in one of the episodes by which St. Louis fans, never warm to Stanky as a former bitter rival who had come into the home camp,

cooled even more. At one juncture of a tied game with Jablonski at bat, Moon was thrown out trying to steal home. The crowd came down hard on the dumb so-and-so manager.

Off work that day, I just KNEW that Stanky hadn't used a steal sign with Jabbo batting because he'd built so much faith in Jablonski as a clutch hitter and believed in Jabbo himself, too. Typically, as a manager who blistered his players privately yet defended them publicly, Stanky had told Moon that he'd take the rap.

By the time, after an open date, that I reached Moon in the clubhouse and convinced him that as a popular player he could stand the responsibility for his questionable-judgment move better than the beleaguered manager could, the damage had been done. To this day, even though I quoted Moon with the truth in the *Post-Dispatch*, some still think Stanky was the dummy. He was really Edgar Bergen, but Eddie was digging his own grave as if he were Edgar Allan Poe.

When the Cardinals played the Philadelphia Phillies in a dragged-out first game of a Sunday doubleheader, Stanky stalled through the early innings of the second game, hoping that it would be called previous to five innings because of a technicality that lights were not to be used in any Sunday night game begun after 6:30. (Earlier, former commissioner Happy Chandler had feuded with Fred Saigh, who then wanted to play Sunday night ball, now a practice in some cities).

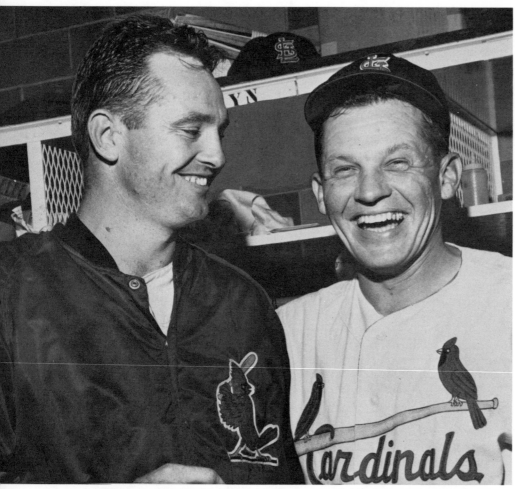

Hot Potato: Larry Jackson (left), a standout rookie in 1955 with Ken Boyer and Bill Virdon, was the best of the staff for several years even if he wasn't quite so outstanding as expected. Larry, later a sports writer and state legislator from Idaho, could beat the good clubs, as witness his smile here after a 1-0 victory over the Los Angeles Dodgers. Bob Nieman, outfielder pictured with him, broke into the big leagues with two successive home runs for the old St. Louis Browns (1951).

Good Start, Finish: Luis Arroyo, chubby, rosy-cheeked Puerto Rican, won his first five games as a starter with the Cardinals in 1955, then flattened out. But, coming up with a good screwball, Arroyo also developed relief pitching into a specialty at New York.

Embroiled in a time-consuming fight with Terry Moore, his former coach then managing the Phils, Stanky saw the game finally forfeited to the visitors when veteran umpire Ralph "Babe" Pinelli decided, logically, that Redbird reliever Cot Deal was throwing pitches wildly against the backstop as a delaying tactic. The crowd booed Stanky more than the forfeit. Oddly, they should have booed the umpire, too, because the 6:30 ban had been lifted and Pinelli didn't know it. Still, Stanky was suspended.

By 1955, Anheuser-Busch had decided it needed the skills of Dick Meyer more than the ball club did. Meyer recommended as an assistant-on-the-premises a former Knothole Gang member, Vaughan "Bing" Devine, long-time successful general manager of the Rochester farm club. Devine would play an important part in the Cardinals' future.

In late May, the youth-oriented Cardinals were two games under .500 (17-19) with kids Ken Boyer at third base, Wally Moon and Bill Virdon in the outfield and a new, smiling righthanded pitcher, Larry Jackson, who over the years with the Cardinals would baffle the Redbirds as well as the foe. A good hitter, even better fielder and best at picking off runners, the hot potato from Idaho could beat the good ball clubs better than the poor ones.

Redbird teams traditionally have had worse breaks from the barrier, but in a Sunday doubleheader at Cincinnati, angry at the ninth-inning loss of an opener, Stanky had stalked into the visitors' clubhouse and sought to sweep a cold-cut picnic off a traveling trunk. The yellow mayonnaise jar banked off the tan mustard and into the catsup, breaking all the jars. Stanky's cut hand was as red as the catsup.

I reported the mishap, which Stanky attempted to conceal, and I thought I did it sympathetically. But the camel had caved in from the last straw.

As some members of St. Louis detoured to Chicago by way of St. Louis for the funeral of the long-time trainer, Doc Weaver, the machinations were in motion. Doc Weaver had been ailing for some time and, wisely, the Cardinals had implored Doc's friend, gifted Bob Bauman, to stay with the Redbirds and not to follow the Browns to Baltimore.

When Weaver died, more than one tear was shed. A rookie left-handed starter who would win a relief reputation with the New York Yankees, Luis Arroyo, was forlorn. "Who now will play the man-do-leen for me?" asked the Puerto Rican sadly.

The sad day for Stanky came in the news that he had been replaced as manager by Harry Walker, a long-time Redbird organization man and hitting instructor who had the same weakness I have: Ask us what time it is, and we'll tell you how to make a watch.

Gussie Busch had liked Stanky very much and only reluctantly followed suggestions that he had gone about as far as he could go. Even so, Gussie permitted a most unusual press conference out at Grant's Farm. Stanky presided, even cheerfully, at ceremonies introducing "The Hat" to succeed "The Brat."

Privately, afterward, over a Budweiser, Stanky let down his laugh-clown-laugh exterior. Softly, he said: ". . .and I would have managed this club next year for nothing."

A good manager, better than his record, but he wasn't THAT good!

14

My Man Stan

The journey up the yellow-brick road to the Wizard of Pennant Odds for the Cardinals took more zigs than a knuckleball thrown against the wind or more zags than Anheuser-Busch's early changes of direction.

At first, as mentioned, Gussie Busch had sought quickly to buy talent. Trouble was, at a time the reserve clause was as binding as an old slave-era's collar harness, the Big Eagle simply couldn't outbid the other side. And when he mentioned a half-million dollars to Brooklyn for first baseman Gil Hodges and even a not-so-cool million for Willie Mays (The sum would be tripled or better now), the Giants' Horace Stoneham chuckled as the Dodgers' Walter O'Malley had.

Stopgap purchases, as noted, had been less than satisfactory. Walter Shannon, who teamed with Joe Mathes to run the farm system then, recommended "forced feeding," hurrying up young talent on the grounds that premature stride into the majors might hasten a player's polishing.

Consequently, the ball club Harry Walker inherited from Eddie Stanky in late May, 1955, was young. It changed, further, as Walker, who like other big-league managers gone back to the minors for a spell, encouraged bringing up players from Triple-A who were just that—Triple-A.

The 1955 Cardinals finished a forlorn seventh,68-86, even though they hit a club record of 143 home runs (33, Stan Musial; 23, Rip Repulski; 19, Wally Moon; 18, Ken Boyer; 17, Bill Virdon; 11, Red Schoendienst).

(A year before, Stanky had asked club publicist Jim Toomey to chart exactly how many times the home club and visitors hit the right-field screen. He was convinced it would be to the Cardinals' advantage to take down the barrier because the Redbirds then had a 2-to-1 edge. But when the thirty-foot high barrier was removed, increasing both sides' advantages, results were negligible. The screen originally put up in 1930 went up again in '56 to stay.)

By then, a result of the new organization's zig-zag course, the Cardinals had taken a new direction. Busch had listened intently when, seeking the best general manager available, he had been told by Taylor Spink of *The Sporting News* that the man was Frank Lane of the Chicago White Sox.

Lane, hired, came in determined, first, to bring his own manager. Walker, naively, had used much of 1955 as a testing ground, even holding morning practices after night games, a take-off to an earlier day in baseball. Lane brought in Fred Hutchinson.

Hutchinson, a former schoolboy wonder, came from the Seattle Pacific Coast League team in his home town. Previously, manager for two and a half years at Detroit, where he'd brought Al Kaline into the lineup as an eighteen-year-old outfielder, Hutch was a hard-nosed, handsome former pitcher who breathed competitive fire. When angry, he had an uncontrollable temper. A ladies' favorite and a man's man, the curly-haired thirty-seven-year-old wasn't the smartest manager, but he probably was the most respected.

Taking over in 1958 as *Post-Dispatch* sports editor, I had learned from him that if you couldn't subdue the white heat of anger at a given moment, you could pop the nearest light bulb, as Hutch would do, or shot-put a heavy wire-service printer roll, as I did, without taking out the anger on any individual. You'd blow off steam rather than a gasket. Everyone would get the message, and no one's personal psyche would be unnecessarily or unfairly bruised.

If Lane had stopped with Hutch, unfortunately dead eight years later of cancer, the Cardinals might have developed a championship ball club sooner.

It wasn't bad, really, to stabilize the Cardinals as Lane did, "vulcanize" them, as he put it—by adding a couple of seasoned gaffers. One was

the one-time Brownie hurler who had become a free-drinking bullpen marvel with the Boston Red Sox, Ellis Kinder. And it was good to have back as a reserve catcher and coach the time-expanded, hard-hitting Walker Cooper.

Lane and Hutchinson brought back former Cardinals as coaches, a pleasant sentimental gesture. Terry Moore and Johnny Hopp came, and former Browns' lefthander, Al "Boots" Hollingsworth. But in the same unpredictable swoop, Lane insisted on removing the traditional twin redbird-on-bat insignia, the club's uniform trademark. He substituted a scrolled "Cardinals." Many growled.

Under Hutchinson's gifted leadership, achieved after hard nights spent crunching ice as he wore down Canadian Club and his coaches, the Cardinals had an ex-

Ruffled Redbirds: Fred Hutchinson (left) and the man who hired him, Frank Lane, could use the most colorful (harumph!) language. Hutch actually could get more angry than Frantic Frank, the wheeler-dealer, but they were a compatible pair from the time both joined the Cardinals in 1956. Lane showed good judgment. He never got the manager mad enough to fight.

Proud Pop: Walker Cooper (right), gimpy-kneed and overweight at 42, but still a good hitter, came back to the Cardinals in 1956. With him came his lovely daughter, Sara Ann Cooper, Miss Missouri.

The Blazer: Don Blasingame, taking over second base and lovely Sara Cooper as his wife, posed with photographs of three great Cardinal second basemen whose giant photos, used for the first St. Louis baseball writers' dinner in 1958, hung at old Busch Stadium (Sportsman's Park).

citing spring training in 1956. They led the major leagues with a 21-11 record, and they opened just as brightly. They were first with 13-7 when "Trader Frank" Lane couldn't resist living up to his nickname.

First, "Frantic Frank" dealt shortstop Alex Grammas to Cincinnati and Solly Hemus to Philadelphia, putting shortstop in the hands of a rookie, Don Blasingame. "The Blazer," quick and agile, was a second baseman, not a shortstop, it soon developed, and he moved across the bag as a result of a later lineup change. Subsequently, he had a long line of duty in Japan.

Not, however, before he married Walker Cooper's lovely Miss Missouri daughter, Sara. Aware that Busch bred for bloodlines to acquire the best horses, Walker Cooper acknowledged that the big boss might one day have an interest in a boy who would have major-league background on both sides of the family.

"Trouble is," said Cooper, who had slowed with age, weight and balky knees, "he'll run like me and hit like Blasingame."

Lane was a good fellow, truly. If you divided and then subtracted Frank's frantic profanity in the pressbox, where he liked to sit on the roof nearby, squinting like a sun-worshipper who didn't see well and listening to the radio, he was an engaging personality. Ball players had to learn that Frank really didn't mean it when he'd say as an athlete swung and missed: "Oh, how can the ball stand it." Or, as they muffed a play: "Hang a lantern on the ball."

Married, even though his wife probably didn't know it, Lane lived for baseball, traveling always with a radio at his ear and a stack of newspaper sports sections under his

arm. A former Cincinnati "park rat," as he put it humorously, he was a fitness faddist, a former crack Big Ten basketball and football official, who worked the coldest days with muscular arms bared. Frank didn't look his age, whatever it was. He got no kicks from champagne, either, but only out of those blasted baseball deals.

His logic escaped me. For instance, he dealt for Herman Wehmeier, a big Cincinnati right-hander who had been one of the Cardinals' kissing cousins, 0-and-14 against them. And, needing a short-stop, he traded Hemus to Philadelphia for infielder Bobby Morgan. I pointed out that Brooklyn had found he really wasn't a big-league shortstop. Said Lane, defensively:

"Well, yeah, but he played more than 120 games for the Phillies last year at SECOND BASE."

Why beat a dead horse? Or, rather, one who would follow the sun into Mexico each winter as he roamed far and wide, scouting for other clubs? Lane actually was a different and better general manager after Busch blew a whistle on him.

The pull-in-the-reins edict came just after a blow to the farm system when Bill Virdon, who had been the second straight Redbird player (Moon) to be named Rookie of the Year, was dealt to Pittsburgh for Bobby Del Greco. The spectacled Virdon, later a successful manager, immediately blossomed into a .319 hitter with the Pirates. Even when he leveled off at bat for them, he patrolled deep center at Forbes Field with a skill that helped win the 1960 pennant and world championship.

"V" For Victory: Bill Virdon, a brilliant defensive center fielder who hit enough and proved at Pittsburgh, New York and Houston that he could manage, too, was dealt from the Cardinals in a trade that looked bad—and was!

Del Greco, who had impressed Hutchinson in the minors, had hit two homers one day at Pittsburgh with Lane in the stands. Bobby really made only one impression in the majors. Next to the last night of the 1956 season, as faltering Milwaukee faded, Del Greco fielded sensationally against the Braves to help Wehmeier beat Warren Spahn, 2-1, in an extra-inning game that cost a pennant won by Brooklyn. Opening day the next season, Del Greco dropped the first fly ball hit to him by the Braves, and miffed Milwaukee players scalded him with their caustic comments.

The bell-ringer for Busch was the multiple-player deal at the trading deadline by which Lane sent Red Schoendienst and others to New York for Alvin Dark and others. Loss of the popular Schoendienst brought an outburst of protests in St. Louis. Also, Lane summarily threw rookie outfielder Jackie Brandt into the deal because, as he put it, "The Giants wouldn't make the trade, otherwise."

To men in the Cardinals' farm system, Brandt represented a fast, strong-armed outfielder as well as a potential hitter, the kind who would shore up an outfield that lacked balance. Actually, though he played eleven seasons in the majors, Jackie really didn't make it big. Not at all what I'm sure the scouts or I, as an outside observer, anticipated. Still, his potential before loss in '56 was devastating.

Just as the departure of Schoendienst teed off the folks on both sides of the Mississippi and elsewhere in the Redbirds' area of influence, Busch was burned up at a report that Lane was preparing to deal Stan Musial to Philadelphia for Robin Roberts. Roberts was a good pitcher, indeed v-e-r-y good, but he'd been overworked in six consecutive twenty-plus seasons. And Musial, though tailing down the previous two seasons to .310, still hit twenty-seven homers, drove in 109 runs—and was a middlin' team's gate magnet.

Busch issued a statement. There would be NO deal for Musial. Lane was told that hereafter there would be no trades without first clearing them with Dick Meyer and, therefore, Gussie himself.

In effect, Lane lost for any future general manager the *carte blanche* temporarily accorded him. With top-brass approval, he dealt wisely and well for 1957 after a fourth-place rundown to 76-78. For instance, wide-sweeping curve ball righthander Sam Jones came from Chicago for Tom Poholsky. Philadelphia's booed RBI man, Del Ennis, was obtained for Rip Repulski.

Further, Lane got a jolt to his pride when at the jocular pre-season party thrown by the Knights of the Cauliflower Ear, Busch concluded in gravel-voiced gratitude to his fellow Knights:

". . .And if the Cardinals don't win this year or next, Frank Lane will be out on his bleep."

Lane, indignant in a hell-bent-for-Florida training trip the next day, drove his sporty car, vroom-vroom, with the top down. Unfortunately, he wound up in Florida with a face full of temporary Bell's palsy. A lengthy telegram to Busch urging that the least Gussie could do

was to extend his contract beyond 1958 did not succeed.

The Cardinals almost did, though, by gosh. Their pitching perked up behind the top-level work of two 15-9 pitchers, Larry Jackson and a twenty-one-year-old kid, Lindy McDaniel. Jones was 12-9 and Stan Musial rebounded at bat with a tremendous .351 season.

Actually, in a solid five-club race, the Cardinals led past the All-Star game in St. Louis. The Yankees' Casey Stengel allowed as how he and his Yankee teammates might be back in October. Everything went well until a break came in August. Jackson, winning for a team that couldn't seem to lose, dropped a game when personal hex Harry Anderson of Philadelphia hit a home run in the ninth inning.

The Cardinals lost nine games in a row, six to the lowly Chicago Cubs who appeared under St. Louisan Bob Scheffing to have a pair of pitching nuggets in two rookies, Dick Drott and Moe Drabowsky. Each beat the Cardinals twice. While the Redbirds and three other clubs sagged simultaneously, Milwaukee surged to ten straight victories, including three over the Cardinals. The Braves had put the final piece in their jigsaw when they'd given the Giants a package of players for the second baseman manager Fred Haney desperately wanted—Red Schoendienst.

Before the season ended, the Cardinals took a second run at the far-in-front team. As the Redbirds arrived in Milwaukee, manager Hutchinson cleverly posted a lineup in

Dark Bright: Alvin Dark, a former brilliant football player, was a bandy-legged shortstop who was a hit-and-run devotee and, later, a successful manager.

RBI Man: Del Ennis, heckled by his home-town crowd in Philadelphia, came over to the Cardinals in a profitable trade that sent Rip Repulski to the Phillies and drove in 105 runs in 1957.

which he listed rinky-dink non-players. He told his players to get lost for the night, including the McDaniel boys.

"At least," Hutch told the 4-H brothers, "you can get double-thick malted milks."

The McDaniels, shepherded by Wilmer Mizell, Hal Smith and especially Alvin Dark, the bandy-legged former Giants' shortstop, were special favorites of an 87-67 ball club that deserved Frank Lane's accolade for "magnificent effort."

The club tried upstairs, too. The Cardinals had peeled off sizable bonuses. They'd given $50,000 each to players. Among them was Dick "Ducky" Schofield, the versatile Springfield, Illinois, infielder who would last a lengthy career, even though most of it was spent on a bench.

Under bonus restrictions at the time, any player given more than $6000 would have to stay frozen on a major-league roster for two years. To ease the short, stocky Schofield's concern about lack of height, Eddie Stanky had held a measuring contest in the clubhouse among his shorter people—himself, Slaughter, Joe Presko, Solly Hemus, prize-hitter Harry "Peanuts" Lowrey and the kid, Schofield.

Afterward, Stanky said, surprised, "Next to me, the shortest player was Slaughter. How come you writers never describe Eno as 'little'?"

In 1957 the younger of the tall McDaniels was a greater surprise than his brother Lindy who had prompted Musial to nudge a writer one night in the clubhouse after the elder McDaniel had gone nine innings to win.

"Repeat that one, Lindy," Stan urged.

McDaniel smiled. "I said," he noted, "that if you don't walk anybody or throw a home-run ball, it's going to take a lot of singles to beat you."

Yes, out of the mouths of babes. . .

In June, after school was out, eighteen-year-old Von McDaniel, with a peaches-and-cream complexion, came grinning into St. Louis from a farm south of Hollis, Oklahoma, signed for the same fifty G's brother Lindy had received in 1955. He'd sit on the bench with that pimply-faced kid signed out of Beaumont High School, Bob Miller,

Pinchy: An apt nickname hung on Harry "Peanuts" Lowrey when the slick, golf-playing athlete turned out to be a masterful pinch-hitter for the Cardinals in the 1950s, even though he hopped up and down in the batter's box as if he had been given a hotfoot.

another pitcher who looked so much smaller and younger.

But on a swing through the East, with the Cardinals trailing Philadelphia, manager Hutchinson, himself a big-league pitcher before he was twenty, impulsively had the kid warm up in relief. The teen-ager went four scoreless innings.

Three days later at Brooklyn, with the Cardinals again behind, Hutch had McDaniel warm up. Just as suddenly, the Cards went in front. Surely, the manager would switch to a more mature pitcher; but, no, again impulsively, Hutchinson stuck with the lad who had been pitching a week before on a red-clay skinned school infield close by the Texas border.

When Von toed the Ebbets Field rubber in the seventh, nursing a one-run lead against a team that had broken so many St. Louis hearts with late-inning rallies, he was positively superb. But, suddenly, in the ninth, crafty Pee Wee Reese beat out a bunt. Dark hurried in from shortstop as free-swinging, Hall of Fame-bound Duke Snider stepped in to hit.

Mainly, Alvin wanted to be sure McDaniel knew how to pitch to him. "Do you know who this is, Von?" Dark began.

"Sure," was the solemn reply—"Mr. Snider!"

Mr. Snider grounded out and the following Friday night at St. Louis, when Hutchinson tried to conceal the fact that McDaniel would start, hoping not to ruffle the kid, the manager couldn't fool anyone. The park was packed as McDaniel hooked up in a duel with a young lefthander, Danny McDevitt. He led into the sixth inning, when the Dodgers filled the bases with none out. The crowd groaned—what a shameful demise to a storybook game!

But—wait!—the lanky, stiff-backed lad with the precision control and the sharp slider he kept down around the knees wasn't through or even aroused. Elmer Valo hit sharply back to McDaniel. Von calmly started a double play by way of the plate, and then he fielded a ground ball off Gino Cimoli's bat for a ho-hum ending. Later, though he would tail off to 7-and-5, he would pitch a one-hit shutout against Pittsburgh.

The Cinderella season ended for the Cardinals at Milwaukee, after a magnificent thirteen-of-seventeen

surge had narrowed the lead at one point. In late August, Musial, protecting Moon on a hit-and-run play, swung so hard trying to pull a high, outside pitch that he suffered a hairline fracture of the right shoulder, tearing heavy muscles.

It looked as if he'd be out for the season, but sixteen days later, he convinced Hutchinson he could play. He pinch-hit safely, then returned to first base and, though unable to swing powerfully, he punched the ball safely time and again.

A critical game was lost at Cin-

Just Like Me'n Paul: That's what Dizzy Dean (center), then an overstuffed national baseball telecaster, said when he put his arms around the McDaniel brothers, Lindy, 21, and Von, just 18. That was 1957, the year the McDaniels almost helped pitch the Cardinals to a pennant.

cinnati when Jerry Lynch homered off Herm Wehmeier in the ninth, and Roy McMillan's first home run of the season beat Wehmeier in the tenth. When Milwaukee clinched in late September with an eleventh-inning homer by young Henry Aaron off Billy Muffett, a chunky Redbird relief standout that season, Fred Hutchinson called Musial aside and shook hands with him.

The Man had hiked his average eleven points while playing injured. "Take off the rest of the way, Stan," said Hutch. "I'd like to look at some kids, and the way you've been hitting, hurt, the rest of these guys couldn't catch you in the batting race if they tried all winter."

Musial, batting .351 with twenty-nine homers in only 134 games, had driven in 102 of the 171 runners Toomey's figures showed he had found in scoring position. And with only forty-three hits to go for 3000, a figure last reached by Paul Waner at Boston sixteen years earlier, he began the 1958 season as if—

"As if," he said with his crooked smile, "I might get hit in the can by a cab."

He didn't, but only because he was even quicker with a bat than on his feet. Just poking the ball, as he'd done after his 1957 injury, Musial was hitting .484 at Chicago in early May. He mentioned casually to coach Terry Moore that he wished he could walk four times the next day to save the big one for St. Louis, where a capacity crowd was expected. Moore mentioned it to Hutchinson.

Hutch called in the St. Louis press and said, "I'm not going to snow you. I could tell you tomorrow that Stan wasn't playing because he had a belly ache, but, hell, I'm just not going to use him—unless I need him—when 30,000 can see him instead of 6000 here (Wrigley Field)."

Next day, with Sam Jones trailing in the sixth, one on and one out, Hutchinson needed The Man. He beckoned to the bullpen. Stan came up to face another Pole, Moe Drabowsky. With a "2 and 2" count, Moe threw a curve ball away. Stan leaned into it and knew instantly, he said, that the long fly ball to left field was between Walt Moryn and the foul line. Number 3000, like number one, was a run-scoring double.

As umpire Frank Dascoli fielded the throw-in, a mob scene followed. Hutch trotted out to shake Stan's hand and to tell him that he wished Musial could have done it in St. Louis, but—.

Maybe rattled, Hutchinson forgot and took out Musial for a pinch-runner. The story had a happy ending, anyway. The Cardinals won, 5-3. Musial, en route to the clubhouse, kissed a pretty blonde next to the Cardinals' dugout and was asked if he knew her. Grinning, Stan said:

"I'd better."

Wife Lil, of course, had joined many close friends for a two-day trip to St. Louis after a premature party by partner Biggie Garagnani at their restaurant. The train trip was the last ever taken by the Cardinals at a time when the move by Brooklyn and New York (Giants) to Los Angeles and San Francisco had made the airplane mandatory. The memorable ride was like a political barnstorming tour. At stops at Springfield and Clinton, Illinois,

crowds waited for Musial to come out and say a few words. Proudly, Sam Jones hugged a magnum of champagne Musial had bought him. Harry Caray presented Stan with special 3000-hit cuff links. The Illinois Central chef whipped up a special cake for the twilight ride home.

The triumphant trip ended late, near midnight, but Union Station was packed as it used to be for the Christmas holidays. Musial made a big hit with the kids. "No school tomorrow," he giggled.

He made a big hit the next night, too. First time up with that full house there, he hit the first pitch onto the roof for a home run. But then, leveling off, obviously tired and distracted, he dipped to .337.

The Cardinals also sagged. Lindy McDaniel faltered and had to be shipped out. Worse, the bubble burst for Von McDaniel. Privately, Hutchinson had been guarded, fearful that the so-called second time around might be troublesome.

In my opinion, the boy was victimized (1) by getting out of shape for the first time in his young, active harvesting-playing farm life as he sat in a college classroom all winter and then (2) he didn't have the maturity to understand the temporary debilitating effect steamy Florida weather would have on the body and arm in spring training. When Von McDaniel reached that dull, heavy-armed moment, he didn't know it or understand it. The harder he tried to throw, the more he wrapped his right arm behind his head. He lost coordination, control and a baseball future. The phenom of '57 was the flop of '58. He pitched only two more major league innings.

3000!: Stan Musial, pinch-batting, reached out and slashed a wide-sweeping curve ball off Chicago's Moe Drabowsky on May 13, 1958, at Wrigley Field. The Man became the first player wtih 3000 hits since Paul Waner, 16 years earlier. The catcher is Sammy Taylor and umpire Augie Donatelli.

Three of a Brilliant Kind: Stan Musial poses with Tris Speaker (left) and Paul Waner when the Cardinals invited all living 3000-hit players to St. Louis for a celebration at which the ball club gave Stan an expensive silver-goblet punch-bowl set with each season's hits engraved on it. Two other living 3000-hit players, naturally Hall of Famers, too, couldn't make it. Napoleon Lajoie was too feeble and Ty Cobb regretfully was ill at the time.

Class of the Clan: The baseball-playing Boyers were a most interesting family. The best, the one on whom Bing Devine correctly based his own term as general manager, was Ken Boyer. A converted pitcher who played one good season in center field (1957) for the Cardinals, Boyer was a great third baseman and good hitter.

The sixth-place tie with Chicago was the finish for Fred Hutchinson. "The Big Bear," as he was called by Joe Garagiola, who had joined Caray and Jack Buck on the Cardinals' broadcast, took that glowering look over to Cincinnati to win a pennant (1961) for Bill DeWitt. As Garagiola cracked, Hutch was happy, only his face didn't know it.

Hutchinson helped the new general manager, Bing Devine, as "Der Bingle" generously would admit over the years. Devine had become GM after the 1957 season when Lane, presumably still stung by Busch's win-or-else ukase, had gone over to Cleveland, where he distinguished himself further by dispatching to Kansas City a young outfielder—Roger Maris.

Devine, forty, a former baseball player and basketball star at Washington University, had a prison pallor and, a bit like Hutch, he smiled more inwardly. As a Knothole Gang graduate, he had been such a dedicated Cardinal fan—Mom and Pop, too—that the Devines' idea of a summer vacation was to get into the family car and to follow the Redbirds around the league in the Gas House Gang era, stopping where the ball club did. "Watty" Watkins, the right fielder, had been especially nice to the quiet, skinny blond kid.

Devine didn't live on personal feelings, however. He'd tried out with the Browns in 1938 as a minor-league infielder. In '39 the English major, who spoke almost as complexly as I write, got his chance in the Cardinals' front office as an assistant to the P.R. man, Ed Staples. Ultimately, before and after World War II service as a Navy officer, he ran minor-league ball clubs at Decatur, Illinois; Fresno, California and Columbus, Georgia. Just before beginning the dress-rehearsal six seasons at Rochester, he was the

Cardinals' tub-thumper the one year Bob Hannegan was president.

As business manager in 1940 at Johnson City, Tennessee, the Appalachian League town where he would meet and marry lovely Mary Anderson, Devine played second base a time or two when rapid roster changes left the ball club shorthanded. He quipped that he was such a weak hitter he would get the "take" sign on a "3 and 2" delivery.

With the Cardinals, where he became fast friends with young shortstop Marty Marion, Devine pitched batting practice. Once, he was knocked off the hill, a shin painfully damaged, because batting champion Joe Medwick liked devilishly to take potshots at pitchers. But, forgiving if not forgetting, Devine later hired Medwick as the Cardinals' minor-league hitting instructor.

When Devine went to the winter meetings after the 1957 season, he hitched part of his future to an idea. The Cardinals had used third baseman Ken Boyer in center field much of the 1957 season in which Boyer had fielded well but hit only .265. Lane had been thwarted in a bid to deal the player to Pittsburgh.

Devine decided he could build with Boyer, acknowledging that Philadelphia had made "a very fair" offer. The Phils would give their placehitting batting leader, center fielder Richie Ashburn, and return lefthander Harvey Haddix.

"I'm sticking with Boyer," said Devine. "I'll bank what little reputation I've got that he's going to be a star—and at third base."

In that downbeat '58 season,

the strapping third baseman hit .307 with twenty-three home runs and ninety RBIs, the springboard to a career as the Cardinals' best all-round third baseman and to his 1964 season as Most Valuable Player of the world champions.

At Colorado Springs, too, Devine and Hutchinson sparred numerous hours with two articulate Cincinnati trade masters, Gabe Paul and Birdie Tebbetts. Ultimately, Hutch urged the unusual deal of three pitchers for two outfielders. Four of these left no mark in the game, but one twenty-year-old outfielder the Cardinals obtained, Curt Flood, became a great center fielder and, eventually, a steady .300 hitter.

Before the 1959 season, Devine swung another deal that was a stepping stone toward the end of the

A Master at Work: Curt Flood, a masterful center fielder as well as a swift hitter who became a good one, had an extraordinary ability to paint, as evidenced in this striking likeness of Dr. Martin Luther King, Jr.

Future vs. Present: Making the deal by which he gave up pitcher Sam Jones (right) for first baseman Bill White, general manager Bing Devine banked on the future and was right. Jones almost helped the Giants to a pennant in 1959; White was a centerpiece of the Cardinals' world championship in 1964. Note that Bill here is using a fielder's glove, working the outfield for a time.

yellow-brick road. He sent right-hander Sam Jones to the Giants for lefthanded-hitting first baseman Bill White.

Devine had rehired the former manager Busch liked, Eddie Stanky, at a post for which the sharp instructor was best suited—player development. On special assignment, Stanky had agreed that White would be a good one.

When Devine went home after making the deal, his wife and four attractive daughters sat silent at the dinner table, toothpicks in their mouths, an amusing dissent against the Jones deal. "Sad Sam" always pitched with a toothpick in his mouth.

Devine's view was that if the Cardinals couldn't win the pennant, he didn't care who did. Jones almost pitched the Giants to a pennant, blown late. For the Cardinals in a 71-83 seventh-place season, enlivened by Joe Cunningham's .345, newcomer White hit promisingly, .302 with twelve homers and seventy-two RBIs in 138 games. (Once, he tied a record with fourteen hits in two successive doubleheaders.)

But the ball club, short of pitching, had too many first basemen in 1959—Cunningham, White, George Crowe and the aging Stan Musial. As outfielders, Cunningham and White were pretty good first basemen. A deal with the Dodgers to improve the outfield defensively,Wally Moon for Gino Cimoli, served only to put Moon in the money.

For a new manager, Solly Hemus, Musial created a problem, and Solly didn't handle it well.

When dealt to Philadelphia, Hemus had written a bread-and-butter note that pleased Busch. Personally, sounded out by Dick Meyer at lunch one day and given a few names to consider, I gave Hemus a most favorable grade, aware, naturally, that his biggest problem was lack of managerial experience. But, aware of his hustle and his apprenticeship under Stanky, I honestly thought the "Mighty Mouse" could be "The Brat" (with a better sense of humor).

For one, Ken Boyer, who always thought Stanky and Los Angeles's Walter Alston were the most knowledgeable managers for whom he played, said he believed Hemus had done well with the men who actually played for him. But I thought he battled the umpires unnecessarily, drawing down their wrath with cutting asides, such as to a hefty ump, "Hey, get off there, you're tilting the infield."

Mainly, though, I questioned Hemus's handling of Musial. To me, the Mouse will go down as the manager who had at least this experience: By playing twenty-four games in 1959, most of them pinch-batting, thirty-five-year-old Solly was the last player-manager in the National League.

When Musial batted only .255 in 115 games, it was natural to assume that, virtually thirty-nine, The Man suddenly might have caved in to athletic age. But Stan protested quietly with two points of legitimate dissent.

One, from management on down, the conclusion had been that if Stan played less in spring training—and he seldom had not played in deference, in part, to camp-game spectators—he would not tire as he had in 1958.

That wearisome season had ended in Japan, where Stan had hit well but not for distance. At a press conference, a writer wondered what he did other than play baseball, and Stan said he was in the restaurant business.

"Ah-so, Musial-san," said the Nipponese newspaperman, "are you then a waiter?"

In 1959, Musial's second conclusion, based on the belief that he really hadn't conditioned himself properly by playing less, was that his reflexes weren't gone. How could he tell? "Because," said Musial, "they're not throwing the fast ball by me."

Early in 1960 then, Musial began an intensive training program under Walter "Doc" Eberhardt, long-time St. Louis University physical-education teacher. Doc's triple "S" (strength-stamina-suppleness) methods have been used ever since at the Billikens' gymnasium and at camp.

Musial looked pretty good and hit the same in spring training, but he got off almost as slowly as the Cardinals, who lost the first game ever played at San Francisco's Candlestick Park, 3-1. Two years earlier, when big-league ball went West, Stan the Man had broken in with "4 for 4" at Frisco and had been "4 for 4" his first game at Los Angeles' Coliseum.

By late May, with the Cardinals down in seventh place, Musial batting .260, Hemus told Stan to be ready to play the second game of a doubleheader at Chicago. When the Cardinals won in the first game for their first road victory, Hemus played a silly hunch. He stuck to the same righthanded lineup even though righthander Don Cardwell was pitching the second game for the Cubs. Cardwell handed the Cards their first no-hit defeat since 1919.

In late May, Devine swung a deal that would prove another positive stride toward the gleaming green championship. He gave up lefthander Vinegar Bend Mizell to Pittsburgh for a converted shortstop Devine felt could be a good second baseman. His name was Julian Javier. If "Hoolie" had ever hit righthanders nearly as well as he batted against lefthanders—and he helped curb the club's old southpaw weakness—he'd have been a Hall of Fame ball player.

To Devine—and this IS provocative!—Javier was so good with a glove, ground-covering, throwing, pivoting and high-tailing it for pop flies, that Der Bingle classified the Dominican as better afield than even Frank Frisch, Red Schoendienst or Rogers Hornsby.

In the long run, Javier would help St. Louis considerably, but, for the moment, Pittsburgh chased its first pennant since 1927. When the Pirates came to St. Louis, manager Danny Murtaugh asked me, "What's the matter with the Polack?"

Musial, benched "indefinitely" as Hemus told a New York writer, had been called down to Grant's Farm, where he listened much but said little as both club president Gussie Busch and vice-president Dick Meyer tried to break it gently that the manager sought to go with a younger club.

"Whatever you want is all right with me, though I think I can still help the ball club," said Musial, hurt mostly because he felt he hadn't had a fair chance. He appreciated, though, he would explain later, that Busch had even gone beyond the $91,000 Stan had reached as salary

Forward, March: Again looking beyond the end of his slender nose, Bing Devine dealt colorful lefthander Wilmer "Vinegar Bend" Mizell (right) to the Pittsburgh Pirates in 1960, mindful he might help the Pirates win. They did. The rebuilding Cardinals got from the Bucs' top farm a shortstop they moved to second base. The Dominican Republic's Julian Javier (pronounced "Hoolian Havier") became defensively outstanding and a good hitter against long-time lefthanded nemesis pitching.

terms with Devine in 1959 to tear up the contract and order one for $100,000.

Still, he was interested when I approached him with the gist of a conversation with Murtaugh, who couldn't and wouldn't tamper, but who said that, yes, indeed, he would be most interested if Musial were available. Would Stan be interested?

"Yes," Stan said. "I never thought I'd say this, but yes."

A few days later, the Pirates' general manager, Joe L. Brown, phoned me. Off the record, he insisted, this was his view:

"If Stan were available, we'd grab him in a second. As Danny said, we couldn't give up a young star for him, but I don't want to do this to Bing Devine. To offer too little would be unfair to Bing because the public, I'm sure, would be behind Stan. It wouldn't be fair to Devine."

Consequently, no moment of embarrassing truth ever was reached.

In late June, after a medley relay of left fielders (Leon Wagner, Ellis Burton, Walt Moryn, John Glenn and the injured one who had done it before he was hurt, Bob Nieman), Hemus put Musial in left field at Philadelphia. He'd spent a month on the bench during which his batting average had shrunk to .238.

Musial hit so hard the next three weeks, twenty for forty-one, that by the first All-Star game to which he was invited rather than elected, his average was .300. Said Hemus, gratefully, "Musial has delivered the most key hits the last few weeks that I've seen any player get in years."

Celebrating, Stan hit his sixth All-Star home run, two more than any other major league player into the 1980s. It was hit off former

teammate Gerry Staley of the White Sox into the upper stands of New York's Yankee Stadium. The visit was Musial's first to the Stadium since the 1943 World Series.

Musial lit a fire under the Cardinals, too. His .275 average was deceptive, because he hit for distance and with timing, too, as witness seventeen home runs and sixty-three RBIs in 116 games, of which he started only eighty-eight.

The big winner that year was Ernie Broglio, 21-9, aided by the greatest single-season relief performance I've ever witnessed by a member of the Cardinals. (Uh-huh, even better than Al Hrabosky's.) Lindy McDaniel, having added an overhanded forkball that fell off the plate as savagely as Bruce Sutter's · later, not only was 12-and-4 with twenty-six saves. His earned-run average, 2.09, was good and would have been greater except for two starts in which he was hit.

Most astonishingly, in 116 innings, he gave up just eighty-five hits. He walked only twenty-four batters and struck out 105. Lindy McDaniel would pitch fifteen years more in the majors and quit at age forty in 1975 when he still could post a 5-and-1 record. He was often A-1, but never so over-powering as in 1960.

The Cardinals finished a strong third, 86-68, but not before scaring the Jolly Roger out of the Pirates, particularly when Musial beat them three times with home runs in a week's time in late August. He beat Bob Friend in the ninth, 3-1, Roy Face the next night in the ninth, 5-4, and Friend again in the fourteenth inning, 3-2. Not even Stan's old friends in Donora were talking to him then.

In 1961, Solly Hemus's team got off so slowly that at the fourth of July milestone, general manager Bing Devine made a decision. With the team treading water in fifth place, 33-41, he would change horses in midstream. Just after Bill White homered three times in a game at Los Angeles, Devine made the move. He promoted coach Johnny Keane, a long-time organization manager who had been Hemus's field foreman at Houston in the Texas League and had finally agreed to coach.

Unkindly, Hemus suggested that Keane had been disloyal, falsely maligning the former seminary student from South St. Louis. As a player, Keane, a wiry little infielder, might have made it to the majors, but in the minors the Irishman suffered a career-crippling blow. He was hit so severely with a pitch that he had hovered between life and death.

As new manager, Keane made two moves. He re-installed the dusky greyhound, Curt Flood, as his center fielder—hit or not—and took Larry Jackson out of the bullpen. Jackson's jaw had been broken in spring training when he was hit by Duke Snider's broken bat. When "Jax" could pitch, Hemus had kept him in relief.

The revisions helped. Jackson came around, and Flood began his transformation into a fielder who could hit, batting .322. By contrast, as the Cardinals finished fifth with 47-33 under the new manager, Musial felt bad that his .288 average of fifteen homers and seventy RBIs in 123 games hadn't been more productive.

So Stan was surprised, pleasantly, when Keane told him closing day at Philadelphia, "Stan, I think you

What's That Smell? A cigar? No, a pennant. Johnny Keane, nearing the 1964 pennant in a dramatic four-way finish, spars with the press in his clubhouse office.

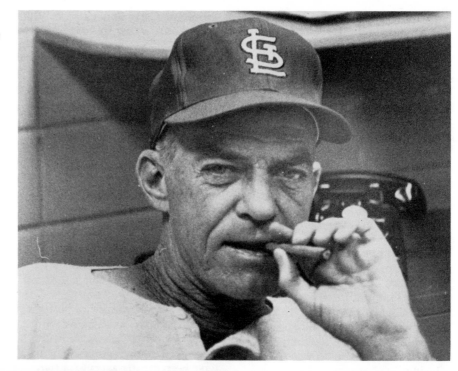

Return of an Old Pro: One of baseball's best hustling ball players, Orestes ''Minnie'' Minoso (third from left), had been acquired to give the Cardinals righthanded pop and some of his special get-up-and-go, but Minnie was seriously hurt in May, 1962. Although outfielder-catcher Gene Oliver, shortstop Julio Gotay and third baseman Ken Boyer welcome him back, Minnie played only 39 games. He was a St. Louis washout.

could have played more, not less. Get yourself in the best possible shape and IF next year is your last year, let's make it a great one.''

Devine decided that age needn't be a factor. He dealt for a colorful, hustling old Chicago White Sox star, Orestes ''Minnie'' Minoso, but early in the going Minnie ran into that unyielding green left-field concrete at Sportsman's Park, suffering crippling injuries. Short on relief pitching, too, the Cardinals finished sixth in a new ten-team league even though their 84-78 record was a good one.

The National League had added Houston and returned a franchise to New York (Mets), increasing the schedule to 162 games. Musial, frankly, said he felt the expansion had added some pitchers who made batting more comfortable for the competent. It did, too, result in roster reshuffles as the new clubs got some live bodies.

One of the Cardinals' losses was that pitcher who had seemed so young and immature beside Von McDaniel back there in 1957. That one-time pimply-faced kid, Bob Miller, lasted seventeen seasons through 1974 until he was thirty-five years old. He'd changed uniforms fourteen times and nervously plucked the upper left sleeve of each one with his pitching hand.

In July, when Musial was hitting a robust .347, Keane asked tub-thumper Jim Toomey to calculate how much Stan would have to play to qualify for the batting title (502 plate appearances). Just a little speed-up, Toomey figured. So Keane stepped up The Man's pace, hopeful he might win an eighth batting title.

Actually, at nearly forty-two, old No. ''6'' had a brilliant season, batting .330, hitting nineteen homers and driving in eighty-two runs. He started 116 games. Pinch-hitting, he was extraordinary, reaching base fourteen of nineteen times, hitting .615. And the old lefthanded, foul-line-to-foul-line batsman hit .325 against righthanders, .345 against lefthanders. However, Los Angeles' Tommy Davis won the batting title.

The Dodgers looked as if they'd win the expanded pennant, too, especially in the final week. The second-place Giants had just survived a three-run homer by Musial in the ninth for their second straight when Horace Stoneham, the clubowner who liked to sit up with a cold toddy and a warm baseball companion, invited Musial and roommate Red Schoendienst for an annual social visit.

''I'd ask you to take it easy on us tomorrow, Stan,'' said Stoneham, ''but the last time I did was at your restaurant, and the next day (1954) you hit five home runs against us!''

''Yeah, Horace, don't ask,'' chuckled Musial. The episode was funny to The Man, but not to his host. The next afternoon Stan got his last ''5 for 5'', and Gene Oliver hit a three-run homer as the Cardinals dealt San Francisco's wavering pennant hope a 7-4 blow.

Los Angeles then was only one victory away from at least a title tie with four to play as the Cardinals flew down the coast that evening. The Dodgers had lost to newcomer Houston. They still needed one more. They never got it and, in fact, would not even have reached a playoff blown to the Giants if San Francisco hadn't lost once more.

The Cardinals were superlative against their old foes. First, Jackson won a ten-inning game, 3-2. Then Ernie Broglio approached his 1960 skill in a 2-0 triumph over Don Drysdale on a fly ball dropped by giant Frank Howard.

The Cardinals won a final game, 1-0, on Gene Oliver's critical eighth-inning home run off lefty Johnny Podres's change-up. The damaging defeat for the Dodgers had an interesting St. Louis postscript.

St. Louis's shutout pitcher that day was a herky-jerky southpaw veteran, master of changing speeds and slow curves, Curt Simmons. The one-time Philadelphia Whiz Kid, cut loose by the Phillies, had been picked up by Devine two years before, sight unseen. When rain kept the Chicago Cubs' Lou Boudreau from taking a pre-game look at Simmons and the Cardinals' Solly Hemus, too, Devine had a hunch.

Der Bingle, driving as he liked to do often while he pieced together the pros-and-cons of his pros, stopped at a Maryland filling station, put in a credit-card call to Simmons and came to terms with him.

As a Redbird, Simmons did handsomely against all, especially Henry Aaron. Curt said, graphically, that ''trying to sneak a fast ball past Hank is like trying to sneak the dawn past a rooster.'' So he'd merely show Aaron the wasted fast one and then get him regularly with those dew-drop-in slow curves. Frustrated, ''Hammerin' Hank'' stepped right up into one drooping hook and hit it onto the right-field roof. But he was declared out. He had stepped on home plate.

In beating the Dodgers twice the final week of the 1962 season, Simmons was out there in rotation in place of a rangy righthander who had led the club in earned-run average his second full season. In batting practice, scheduled to face L.A. in St. Louis before the last swing West, he'd broken an ankle bone, oddly, when his spikes caught at the plate. Baseball fans and the major leagues would hear much more from him: Bob Gibson!

For Musial, who had hit five homers in a doubleheader, won an All-Star game (1955) with a tremendous home run at Milwaukee and grabbed batting titles and Most Valuable Player awards, there was just one more goal—to go out with a winner!

It had been a l-o-n-g time since Stan came out of the Navy in 1946, reporting directly to camp late in spring training, giggling as he shook hands happily with old teammates and left a false thumb in each startled guy's hand.

The 1963 Cardinals almost enabled a storybook player to go out with a storybook finish. The infield was literally the National League's All-Star infield that year—Bill White, Julian Javier, Dick Groat and Ken Boyer—and Tim McCarver was a take-charge leader in his first full season as catcher. Ernie Broglio (18-8) and Bob Gibson (18-9) had virtually matching records; Curt Simmons was 15-9 and Ray Sadecki was a helpful 10-10.

A Key Move: Acquisition of Dick Groat filled the Cardinals' needs at shortstop, where they got a good hitter and steady if not far-cruising shortstop. Groat, an All-America basketball player at Duke, had gone directly into the big leagues at Pittsburgh and was the National League's Most Valuable Player in 1960.

Devine and Keane felt they needed a shortstop and an outfielder. They wove an intricate three-club deal by which the Cardinals would give up two good hands, Larry Jackson and Lindy McDaniel, but they'd get Groat, the National League's MVP in 1960, from Pittsburgh to play shortstop and the Cubs' lanky George Altman for the outfield.

The effort almost was crabbed by Branch Rickey. B. R. had come back as a senior consultant past eighty. Somebody was always recommending someone to Gussie Busch. Bob Cobb, who ran Hollywood's Brown Derby restaurants and had run that city's Triple-A ball club, suggested hiring the old man for whom Cobb had the Rickey-cult admiration. A good idea.

At first, Rickey recognized his limitations, but then he began to remember Bing Devine as he had known him earlier, a front-office kid who posted those thirty daily organization standings on the office blackboard when the Mahatma headed the herd. No, by Judas Priest, Rickey didn't want Groat because he was sure young Julio Gotay would be topflight as an all-round shortstop. Poor Julio, who must have led the league in Rolaids, Tums or whatever the Caribbean country kids chew when their bellies flutter under pressure, never was the answer—anywhere. F-i-n-a-l-l-y, the Groat deal was completed.

Altman, unfortunately, didn't hit in St. Louis as he had in Chicago, but Groat batted a brisk .319 and fielded with judgment and reliability if not range. The Cardinals still were far back in mid-August when Musial, after conferring with Devine, said he thought he'd call it a career at nearly forty-three.

Gussie Busch couldn't make the press conference announcement at his Bauernhof, the German-atmosphere play area of Grant's Farm. On a muggy, rainy day, they let me make his apologies, his regrets and the big announcement. Musial, wet from emotion as well as the weather, said in part:

". . .I'd like to go out with a winner. Our 1942 club was farther back. . ."

The Cardinals came on like the champions of old. Seven games out, they began to win. For this old baseball writer, who remembered a musical good luck piece played down the stretch in 1942 and to turn about the '46 season, KMOX's Bob Hyland did what his father, Dr. Robert F. Hyland, had done the second time around. Thwarted, young Hyland did the typical. He got the grand Poo-Bah of nutty novelty music, Spike Jones, to cut a copy of "Pass the Biscuits, Mirandy" from Jones's own private gold record. Mirandy passed the biscuits and victories. Ten in a row. Defeat. Nine in a row.

Nineteen of twenty and suddenly the Dodgers, nosed out by San Francisco the previous year, were only a game ahead as they came to a town that had World Series atmosphere.

The series was one of the best I have ever seen. The Cardinals played very well, but the Dodgers were superlative. In the opener Musial, who had been hitting pretty stoutly in the stretch, unloaded a game-tying home run off Johnny Podres in the seventh inning. It was Stan's 475th and last. With the 1-1 deadlock, it darn near tore down the house.

Curt Flood, of all people, misjudged a fly to help the Dodgers to a run, and after Ernie Broglio went out for a pinch-hitter, the Dodgers

got to the able little reliever Bobby Shantz for two runs and a 3-1 victory. Ron Perranoski saved it.

A scintillating star overnight after long apprenticeship, Sandy Koufax was 25-and-5 that year. He held the Cardinals hitless the next night until Musial singled in the seventh inning. By then the Dodgers had snapped a twenty-eight inning scoreless streak for Simmons to win, 4-0.

Musial got two more hits the next inning as Gibson seemed en route to victory, but a home run in a big ninth by a new kid virtually passing through, Dick Nen, a late-season call-up from Oklahoma City, tied the score. Southpaw bullpen ace Ron Perranoski gave up a leadoff triple to Groat in the twelfth, but he turned back the Cardinals. The Dodgers swept the series in the thirteenth, 6-5.

By then, Musial was a grandfather. Earlier, daughter-in-law Sharon had delivered Dick's first child, son Jeffrey Stanton Musial, as Stan and Lil sat up much of the night sipping coffee. That night at an old-timers' game, Terry Moore and Joe Medwick had teased The Man:

"Hey, you belong over with us."

"Next year," he said, smiling, and "Old Gramps" grinned even more as he teed off first up for a two-run homer, a fitting celebration of a big-league playing grandpa.

With the pennant lost despite ninety-three victories, the most by the Cardinals since 1949, the last go-around included season-ending ceremonies on the day when Musial would play his final game before a packed house and live home television. If only Stan the Man could go out head high. . .

See Ya, Pal: Which is one of the ways Gussie Busch would say it. Here, Gussie presents to Stan Musial on The Man's final day in uniform (Sept. 29, 1963) a likeness drawn by Amadee Wohlschlaeger of the St. Louis Post-Dispatch. *St. Louis baseball writers had used this sketch, called The Man-and-the-Boy, in their drive for a statue outside Busch Memorial Stadium, then in construction. As you can see, what the writers envisioned and what happened were two entirely different hunks of bronze.*

After ceremonies that included a parade, speeches and the display of a mockup of Amadee Wohlschlaeger's "The Boy-and-The Man" design for a statue which baseball writers hoped to erect at the new stadium, Musial went up and took a called third strike. Cincinnati's pitcher, twenty-three game winner Jim Maloney, was a fast-firing righthander who needed that one to make certain the Reds might finish as high as third and not drop as low as fifth.

As Musial took over the ball used on Strike Three for presentation to Hall of Fame director Sid Keener, former *St. Louis Star-Times* sports editor, trainer Bob Bauman growled uncommonly at Musial, "Bear down, boy."

The psychology paid off. Loping to left field, The Man nodded. To hell with the fol-de-rol. He had to concentrate.

Next time up, he singled. Third time up he singled, breaking a scoreless tie. Now, manager Johnny Keane decided it was time to end on the head-high note. He sent out a pinch-runner.

At first, some booed. Then, almost to a man, woman or child, they began to applaud and cheer. Cincy manager Fred Hutchinson said to his freckled, rusty-haired second baseman, rookie Pete Rose:

"Now you can say you played against one of the best, kid. . ."

It was a good time to say good-bye.

Farewell to a Happy Habit: Stan Musial swings the last time and grounds a single off Jim Maloney, Cincinnati's 23-game winner, in his last time at bat in the major leagues.

15

A Keane Time

Just past the pivotal trading deadline in 1964, Bing Devine and the Cardinals' assistant general manager, Art Routzong, sat in the visiting club's box at steamy Houston's Colt Stadium, a stopgap forerunner of the Astrodome. A new Redbird on the wing had just made his debut with the ball club and, pinch-hitting, had struck out feebly.

Seated nearby, a Houston fan guffawed and jeered. "Who," he sneered loudly, "could have made that deal?"

Devine, rising to leave with the game's end, looked at Routzong and said, sardonically, "Yeah, Art, who COULD have made that deal?"

Der Bingle had, of course. He'd dealt a prominent St. Louis pitcher, Ernie Broglio, to Chicago for a little-known young outfielder, Lou Brock, as key men in a multiple-player deal. Much of the St. Louis press and public hadn't liked it. Typically of managers, like a kid

with a new toy, Johnny Keane had rushed Brock into action. Pitcher Jack Spring had looked like winter in the summer and Brock, as mentioned, had fanned.

To give up Broglio, a twenty-eight-year-old pitcher who had won twenty-one and eighteen games over two of the last four years, was about as popular as the bubonic plague, considering, especially, that Brock, at twenty-five, hadn't hit or fielded well in two full seasons with the Cubs.

But Keane and Devine needed a good left fielder more than a pitcher at that point. Ray Sadecki, with whom Keane had feuded and then set forth in rotation, was having the season of his career and that big, wide-shouldered, narrow-hipped righthander, Bob Gibson, had become a potential star. Curt Simmons was a reliable guy, and a Toronto electrical engineer who would go into medicine, Ron

Taylor, showed class, too.

The prime need was for someone to fill Stan Musial's shoes in left field. St. Louis's handsome Charley James, the former University of Missouri halfback, hadn't been quite the answer. "Chopdown" Charley, so-so as an outfielder, had leveled off his average, not his tomahawk swing.

As the team that scared the bejabbers out of L.A., which had waltzed through the Yankees four straight in the 1963 World Series, the Cardinals were floundering worse than the defending world champions.

At Los Angeles in mid-June, a crisis developed. Over Dick Groat's period with the Cardinals, the management had given the former Duke University basketball All-American personal hit-and-run privilege. Like Alvin Dark, he handled the bat adroitly for the hit and run. Like Dark, too, he over-used the instrument at times, putting a teammate in motion and hitting behind him. Now, when Dick did it in a losing game against the Dodgers, the play malfunctioned and base-runner Tim McCarver was thrown out. Keane said simply that hereafter he (the manager) would order the hit-and-run when he wanted it. Groat sulked.

At the time Devine was maneuvering toward an outfielder. As the plane left Los Angeles for Houston, he slid into the seat next to Keane and said, "I can make the Chicago deal."

The Kid and the Comeback: Two winning lefthanders for the Cardinals as they emerged at long last as strong pennant contenders were Ray Sadecki, a 20-game winner who had to win his way out of manager Johnny Keane's doghouse, and an old pro, Curt Simmons, signed as a free agent by Bing Devine. Ultimately, Sadecki became author of a change-up almost as refined as Simmons's slick let-up.

Pleasant Paisano: Everybody liked good-natured, long-jawed Ernie Broglio of the duck-tailed haircut and propensity for late hours and late victories often saved by Lindy McDaniel in relief. When the Cards traded him to the Cubs for Lou Brock in 1964, Ernie crowed, "I'm glad to join a winning team."

Keane looked straight ahead. "Make it," he said.

So Broglio left. The lantern-jawed big guy with the duck-tail haircut grinned to a St. Louis reporter and said, "Good, now I've got my evenings to myself."

The pitcher, "Bright-Lights" Broglio, who spent more time in the arms of Bacchus than Morpheus, arrived triumphantly in day-game Chicago and rubbed sulphur in the molasses.

"It's good," said "Earnshaw," as Solly Hemus had called him, "to be with a WINNER." Ouch, Chicago hadn't had a winning ball club and was headed for eighth place.

Brock came into St. Louis quietly and sat at the end of a bench. I wished him well, walked away and Keane beckoned. "Let him alone," the manager asked. "I've told him there would be no pressure on him."

The Cardinals, fifth behind San Francisco, seven and a half games out on the trading deadline, began to pick up with the fleet feet of the left field Mercury who could hit a baseball frightfully far at times. It's no wonder that, watching the magnificent body the Cubs had been attracted to him.

Arkansas-born, reared in Monroe, Louisiana, by a mother who had a sizable family, Lou got his feel for baseball when his fourth-grade teacher proved "a positive person," as Brock would put it. Lou threw a spit ball at a girl in his classroom, missed and hit the teacher. "Teach" sent him to the library to research four ball players: Joe DiMaggio, Stan Musial, Don Newcombe and Jackie Robinson.

His love affair with baseball began.

At Southern University in Baton Rouge, where he majored in mathematics for three and a half years, the Cubs presented him with a bit of arithmetic he couldn't resist. They gave him a $30,000 bonus-salary combination after he starred for the United States in the 1959 Pan-American games.

At the time married to high school sweetheart Katie Hay, a dietitian, Lou practiced what Katie preached. As a nibbler, he stuck to carrot sticks, fruits and other wholesome food for snacks rather than junk stuff.

Released from the tension at Chicago and from the sun-and-wind hazards of Wrigley Field, he began to hit and run in St. Louis. Living up to his later estimation as a better-educated Pepper Martin, said Brock:

"I like dirty-suit players, hard-nosed guys like Mike Schmidt, Ken Reitz and others. You can have those guys who get up and carefully dust themselves off."

The Cardinals began to perk up with Brock, not brilliantly, but an unfunny thing happened on the way to a pennant that, as a result, would be—for some of us, anyway—bittersweet. Bing Devine was fired.

After Dick Groat lost his self-anointed right to play hit-and-run, the articulate, sensitive shortstop began to groan and moan to many ears, including those of Milwaukee's great third baseman, Eddie Mathews, a friend of Elizabeth Busch, later his wife.

A Barrel of Fun and Hits: Two laughing guys of the game, Stan Musial and his illustrious left-field successor, Lou Brock, giggle it up when Stan the Man was general manager in 1967, but it wasn't so funny in '64 when Brock was just beginning his quest for 3000 hits, too.

Star Bright: Dick Groat wasn't jumping for joy, but he might have in 1963, the year the entire Cardinals' infield—(from the left) Julian Javier, Bill White, Ken Boyer and Groat—were All-Star game starters.

Innocently, Liz told her father one day what Eddie told her of Dick's complaints. Gussie put great faith in loyalty, which customarily he returned in kind. By the time he got around to hearing about it and asking about it, Bing Devine and Johnny Keane thought it was long solved, satisfactorily.

At New York for a series immediately after Johnny Callison of the league-leading Philadelphia Phillies had homered in the ninth to win the All-Star game at Shea Stadium, the Cardinals moved into the park to conclude the first half of the season.

Bing Devine was putting together the last pieces of the puzzle.

He brought up native St. Louisan Mike Shannon, a jet-haired home-town Irishman who had a bit of Li'l Abner's rugged handsomeness. Shannon, signed away from unrelated Dan Devine at more than $65,000 when Dan'l thought he had a championship quarterback at the University of Missouri, had struggled up the ranks. He could battle the boards for fly balls, he could throw powerfully and, though he could look hopelessly suckered at bat at times, he had a knack of making critical contact when it counted most.

Shannon filled the outfield, and a well-seasoned righthander, George "Barney" Schultz, called up by Bing Devine, brought along a knuckle

Moon Man: An early nickname of gabby, gifted, aggressive Mike Shannon, the home-town Irishman who played right field and then third base on championship Cardinal ball clubs, didn't last. Black Mike really wasn't all "spaced out." He was just rehearsing for the day when, after a serious rare disease ended his career prematurely, he could step in behind a microphone for KMOX Radio on the Cardinals' play-by-play broadcasts.

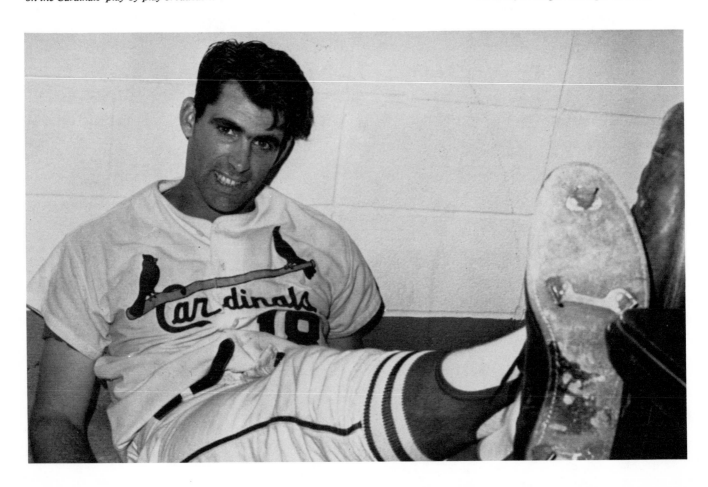

ball, experience, an unflappable nature and the kind of fortunate twist of fate a good fella deserves. He got hot at the right time.

So from a subpar 40-41 at the halfway point, the Cardinals began to move up. By August 17, though still nine games behind Gene Mauch's front-running Phillies, they were 63-55.

Suddenly, Devine was out. Routzong, too.

Back there at the midway oasis in New York, just before a bat-weakened mononucleosis convalescent, Frank Thomas, wrapped a ninth-inning home run around the leftfield foulpole to beat Curt Simmons, Dick Groat had cleansed

himself. Manfully, Dick got up in front of the visiting troops at Shea Stadium and apologized for having second-guessed the manager.

So, heck, for Devine and Keane, it was over. Besides, Branch Rickey knew the rift had been repaired the right way. But Busch didn't know. When Liz told him and he met next with Keane and Devine—after all, the Big Eagle then was running the brewery, too—he wondered if the general manager and manager didn't have something to tell him? They were puzzled. Come now, men, wasn't there something they didn't want AB of A-B to know?

No, honestly, they thought they didn't. Busch thought they were hiding the Groat matter from him. Reliable right-hand man Dick Meyer was hospitalized at the time, unable to provide the soothing effect he had on the old man. Annoyed that Devine continued to show faith in Routzong, a long-time organization man the chief thought talked too much about playing personnel when he was essentially the nuts-and-bolts business manager, Gussie got up his Dutch. Bing was bounced.

The Cardinal players were stunned. At the suggestion of Rickey, who had become patronizing at best to that former "office boy," Devine, Busch brought in from Denver a big general manager who had been out of baseball two and a half years. Bob Howsam had lost his shirt when he backed Rickey's ill-fated Continental League venture, a third major-league contrivance. The proposed bid, for which Howsam had expanded the ball park, fizzled. It did, though, bring Houston into the National League and New York again, too. The third league puffed away in one of Rickey's many cigars. B. R. began merely to chew them on a doctor's advice.

Howsam, largely at Cincinnati, would prove to be a competent general manager and ultimately president of the Reds. At St. Louis, encouraged to deal, he later would make a couple of advantageous trades, too. But he had less to do with the Cardinals' success in 1964 than the fans in the stands or less, certainly, than Busch himself. Gussie, after all, had spent time, money, patience—and impatience.

Storybook Style: George "Barney" Schultz, who toiled a long time, mostly in the minors, got his big-league chance, and his knuckleball helped the Cardinals dance crazily down the stretch in 1964. Barney later became a Redbird pitching coach and ultimately took his good nature and fuzzy lingo to Japan.

With no further changes, the Cardinals began to move, winning more frequently. Still, they were six and a half games behind Philadelphia with twelve to play when the frustrated Phils came into St. Louis for a late September series. Now the Cardinals were like the Dodgers of 1963, the seasoned stretch contenders. They knocked off the Phils three in a row.

Even so, Philadelphia still seemed comfortably, if not securely, in front. St. Louis, Cincinnati and even fourth-place San Francisco had a fractional chance. But the Phillies were gripped in a ten-game losing streak and, critically, the Reds lost an extra-inning battle to Pittsburgh at home. Ironically, Cincy was beaten on a surprise squeeze-play bunt by rookie catcher Jerry May. Not only had May never squeezed in a run before, but, also, Bill DeWitt, operating the Reds, had ordered interim manager Dick Sisler to cease and desist using the archaic offensive gesture.

With three games left the Cardinals were a game in front. They could win if they could knock off the Mutts. . .er, Mets. . .who were about forty games behind with a 51-108 record. But Casey Stengel's mongrels were, as the old geezer said, amazin'.

The Thin Man: Dal Maxvill weighed only 155 pounds and looked as if a strong wind would blow him farther than his light bat could hit a ball, but Maxie, the Washington University electrical engineer from Granite City, Ill., electrified Redbird fans with sure-handedness they hadn't seen at shortstop since Marty Marion. First, he starred in a World Series—at second base.

First night, lefty Alvin Jackson won a 1-0 jewel from Bob Gibson. Next day, as the Mets tattooed twenty-game winner Ray Sadecki, 15-5, the race was closer than one clock second to another. If, in fact, San Francisco hadn't lost that day, four clubs would have gone into the last day with a chance. The Cards and Reds were tied, the Phillies only one game behind.

For the showdown, Keane went with Curt Simmons. Unfortunately Julian Javier was out and infield reserve Dal Maxvill, essentially a shortstop, played second base.

The scoreboard showed hopefully that Philadelphia, breaking that ten-game losing streak too late for itself and too soon for Cincinnati, was on the way to a lusty 10-0 rout. If only the Cardinals could win. . .

Simmons wasn't sharp, but the Cardinals' bats boomed. Curt Flood hit a home run as part of a .311 season. Bill White, finishing like a whirlwind the second half to drive in 102 runs with a .303 average, hit his twenty-first. Ken Boyer, whose twenty-four homers and 119 league-leading RBIs would win him the MVP award, had a couple of hits. So, too, did Brock, a sizzling .348 hitter with twelve homers and thirty-three stolen bases in 103 games since he was acquired for—what's his name?—Ernie Broglio.

To save the game, manager Keane went to the man who would become his top stopper and the Cardinals'—Bob Gibson. And then old Barney Schultz, thirty-eight, came in out of the bullpen. The close race for the pennant, St. Louis's first in eighteen long years, ended when—kerplop!—Tim McCarver, the twenty-two-year-old kid from Memphis, latched onto a pop foul. A pennant! Forty-and-41 the first half of the season, 53-28 the second half.

After the ninety-three-victory season, exactly the same by which the Cardinals finished second in Stan Musial's last year, the Redbirds' senior vice-president summed it up with a superstar's seldom-matched lack of conceit.

Said Musial, saluting Brock, "The Cardinals couldn't have won with me in left field."

Throughout that World Series and two more which followed in the 1960s, Lou Brock and Bob Gibson were a priceless pair.

Frankly, as one who watched the Yankees whip the National League too many times in Series play, I thought the New York ball club nudged home in front in 1964 by Yogi Berra, the gifted goblin of the Hill, was a shell of the past. Still, for the Cardinals to gain the rare distinction of becoming the one NL club to win more Series head to head against the Yankees, three out of five, the '64 set was exciting.

The Yankees lost a game and a key casualty in the opener, a game in which Mike Shannon blasted a 420-foot home run with one on in the sixth inning, tying Whitey Ford, and McCarver doubled to rout the Bombers' money-game southpaw. Off another lefthander, Al Downing, little Carl Warwick delivered his first of three pinch hits, and Curt Flood tripled.

Ford, beaten 9-5, would not return for the Series, which was tied a day later when New York right-hander Mel Stottlemyre won in a disputed situation over Bob Gibson. With the score tied in the sixth, 1-1, umpire Bill McKinley ruled, over valiant argument, that Joe Pepitone had been hit by an inside breaking ball, a turning point that led to an 8-3 Yankee triumph and a reminder of Fred Hutchinson's reprisal one time to the same American League arbiter:

"They shot the wrong McKinley. . ."

The Series shifted to New York, where Curt Simmons dueled even into the ninth with Jim Bouton, the New York righthander who would win greater fame as a clubhouse-confidential author. Simmons drove in the run that tied the score, but he went out in the ninth for Schultz, who had worked three scoreless innings to save Ray Sadecki in the opener.

Barney threw one knuckle ball too many. The clock struck twelve for the Cinderella of the mound. Mickey Mantle hit it a majestic mile into the upper right field stands for a 2-1 victory. The homer, "The Switcher's" sixteenth, broke Babe Ruth's previous Series record of fifteen.

The home run is a devastating instrument. A day later, Al Downing rode an early three-run lead off Sadecki into the sixth inning when the Cardinals filled the bases. Captain Ken Boyer, the player Bing Devine had refused to trade seven autumns earlier because Bing banked his little reputation then on the third baseman's potential, jerked a pitch into the left field stands.

The grand-slam homer held up as a 4-3 victory when Roger Craig, a philosophical professional who had suffered dismally through two disastrous seasons with the Mets, teamed with Taylor for eight-plus innings of pluperfect relief pitching.

A day later the all-round athletic ability of Gibson, who a modern-era critic, Frank Frisch, thought would have made one heckuva good shortstop, saved a game won by the timely bat of batterymate McCarver.

With Gibby leading into the ninth against Stottlemyre, 2-0, an error by Groat gave Mantle a life. Next up, Pepitone hit a hot smash from which the former Harlem Globetrotter couldn't recoil fast enough. The ball hit the righthanded pitcher on his right hip, as he followed through emphatically. It squirted toward third with the rapidly-reacting Gibson in hot pursuit.

Gibby's outstanding effort was accompanied by a great throw and a similar call. Although a putout seemed highly unlikely, American League umpire Al Smith delayed his call, then flashed an out signal. The Yankees beefed, but instant replay showed Smith was right-on. So Tom Tresh's homer, which would have won the game except for the great fielding play, merely tied it.

Ordinarily, you figured in this kind of situation the Yankees would win, anyway, but McCarver, a .478 batter, came up in the tenth and hit a three-run homer off Pete Mikkelsen.

Oomph: As Dizzy Dean used to say, "Show me a pitcher who winds up in good fielding position and I'll show you a guy who ain't following through." Dean, like Bob Gibson (here), relied on cat-like dexterity to recover in time to field batted balls.

That one, 5-2, won the Series for St. Louis.

After the Yankees roughed up Simmons back in St. Louis to tie the Series, 8-3, the day of decision saw the Cardinals muscle Stottlemyre early to give Gibson a 6-0 lead. Included were home runs by Brock, a .300 hitter in his first World Series, and three hits by Boyer, including his second home run.

Ultimately, as a result of Mickey Mantle's three-run shot, the Yankees got back into the ball game. In the ninth inning, traumatic for the home folks, Ken Boyer's younger brother, Clete, homered. So did Phil Linz.

Sure, Gibson was laboring and the Yankees' batter was their classy second baseman, Bobby Richardson, who already had set a Series record with thirteen hits. On deck was the decided home-run threat, Roger Maris. Seated quietly on the Cardinals' bench, where now and then he would resort to his old shin-kicking soccer experiences, manager Keane came to a decision he repeated later:

"Win or lose I go all the way with Gibson."

Gibby reached back for the lit-tle extra that was left. Richardson popped up to Maxvill, the silhouette shadow who had played second base in injured Javier's place and, as Red Schoendienst had predicted to Keane, Maxie played it well.

For the first time since 1946, the Cardinals were world champions.

They set a record in 1965. They fell farther than they had in 1931, dropping to seventh with 80-81. And they did it under another manager, Red Schoendienst. Johnny Keane had dropped a bombshell on Busch the day after the World Series.

The *Post-Dispatch* had an unforgettable Page One that day, October 15, 1964. Nikita Khrushchev had been dumped as high potentate of the Soviet Union. The Red Chinese had exploded their first A-bomb. The Yankees had fired pennant-winning Yogi Berra in his one season as manager. And Keane, expected to accept formally a new term as manager of the Cardinals, had walked away.

A Swashbuckler: Tim McCarver, the bonus kid from Memphis who turned down top college football scholarships from Notre Dame and Tennessee, was a winning ball player with a winning smile. He was most formidable tagging out runners and a good timely hitter, batting more triples than most catchers. McCarver became a Philadelphia play-by-play broadcaster and got into games at the end of the 1980 season to give him a rare distinction of having his name in big-league boxscores over four decades.

Some who were knowledgeable will insist cynically that Keane knew Berra would be fired and that he would be hired, which would amount to palpable tampering by the Yankees. Fact or fiction, it is true that Keane was extremely unhappy that friend Bing Devine had been fired. He was also displeased that Busch had had a handshake agreement with Leo Durocher to succeed Keane as manager unless, of course, the impossible happened, which it did. Additionally, obviously aware of a contemplated managerial change, the new general manager, Bob Howsam, had ignored a field foreman accustomed to daily powwows with the GM.

So Keane stepped down in St. Louis and four days later was named manager of the Yankees. At the time, aware that Pittsburgh had an interest in him when he quit St. Louis, I wrote that I thought he should have taken the upcoming Pirates rather than the fading Yankees. Harry Walker had two lusty ninety-plus third-place seasons with the Pirates. Keane finished a subpar sixth at New York in 1965. He lost sixteen of his first twenty games in '66 and was canned.

Within a year he was dead of a heart attack at only fifty-five.

He S-c-o-r-e-s: As KMOX's hockey artist, Dan Kelly, might put it, that's what Johnny Keane looks as if he's doing here at New York's Polo Grounds, kicking the ball bag in disgust, probably over an umpire's decision. A miffed Keane quit as Cardinals' manager to go with the Yankees and died all too soon.

16

A New Nest for El Birdos

Like Spanish-speaking Jose Carioca and other lovable birds of a feather from Walt Disney's talented, animated pen, the Redbirds went Latin in the late 1960s: Caribbean and downtown.

"El Birdos" found a new nest. Befitting one of the most beautiful stadiums anywhere, they played with championship class in 1967 and '68. They were, in truth, close to the caliber, all round, of the 1931 and '42 champions. And they did it under one of their best players ever, Red Schoendienst. The selection of the long popular Schoendienst as manager was a natural public-relations choice after Johnny Keane's egg-on-the-face exit.

Rejected by the Braves after a brief comeback from his tubercular surgery, Red had turned down a chance to play regularly with the American League's new Los Angeles (Anaheim) Angels for his old boss,

Fred Haney. He chose to stay in St. Louis, his adopted home, as a reserve. He became, first, a top-grade pinch-hitter, then a coach early in 1963, the same season his long-time road roommate, Stan Musial retired.

Red's first St. Louis team (1965) skidded on a Brazilian banana to seventh with an 80-81 record, despite Bob Gibson's first twenty-game season. Gibby had missed that number a season earlier when he got into a squabble with an umpire and was thrown out before a game went five innings.

Actually, Gibson was almost a man alone on the mound in '65. His twenty complete games were equal to the total of the ENTIRE St. Louis starting staff.

To bolster the Cardinals' vulnerable bullpen, which general manager Bob Howsam did by acquiring veteran lefthander Hal

Beautiful Servant: If you'll forgive the Chris Von der Ahe German, that's what "Schoendienst" supposedly means. Red was just that, even when he'd shown a post-career profile helped by a favorite product, Budweiser. If he seems sour in this first of 12 seasons as Cardinal manager, you'd be unhappy, too, if the lowly Mets had just scored 14 runs with the help of five Redbird errors.

Woodeshick from Houston, Howsam paid dearly. He gave up Mike Cuellar, who, shipped to Baltimore, would become a consistent twenty-game winner with pennant-winning ball clubs for the Orioles. Howsam also threw in a righthander who would win a reputation in more ways than one.

Ron Taylor, at the time a graduate in electrical engineering from the University of Toronto, was dealt to the New York Mets to help the 1969 world champions there as he had the '64 Cardinals. More important, the conscientious Canadian turned to medicine, worked his way through school in the off-seasons and became a doctor. He was team physician when big-league baseball came to Toronto with the expanded Blue Jays.

Before the 1966 season, during which the Cardinals finished sixth in the ten-team league despite an 83-79 record and another twenty-game season for Gibson, there were changes that did not improve the ball club. The left side of the infield had faltered in '65. So Howsam sent Ken Boyer to New York for third baseman Charley Smith and pitcher Al Jackson. The *Post-Dispatch* managing editor then, Art Bertelson, didn't like the way I mentioned that Smith played third base like a plumber, dugout language for incompetence, but Smith WAS a plumber and he did play third base as if he had a wrench in his left hand.

Sent to Philadelphia was shortstop Dick Groat, who also had dipped. Bill White was shipped to Philadelphia as well, but he resented the implication by Howsam that he was older than his listed age, thirty-two. White had held up in '65 by hitting twenty-four home runs in a .289 season. In Philly, despite an Achilles heel, torn twice, Bill won a home,

physically, and a radio future with the Phillies and then the New York Yankees.

Another player dispatched in that deal also had a radio and television future as a baseball commentator and a reputation as a stand-up comic, Bob Uecker. With the Cardinals, "Ueck," was a strong-throwing, good defensive catcher whose light bat kept him on the bench mostly behind Tim McCarver. He would win national attention behind a mike third only to Joe Garagiola and Dizzy Dean among ex-Cardinals.

With the Cardinals, he also lost a game that would have defied Uecker's deadpan humor, demonstrated so ably in his impersonation of "Krueger, the U-boat commander" with a delightful German accent. If only Ueck would tell about the game against the Giants when, score tied in the tenth inning, bases loaded for San Francisco, Alvin Dark grounded sharply to Javier at second base.

Playing halfway, ready to go for an inning-ending double play or to the plate if necessary, Javier juggled the ball an instant and, recognizing he couldn't risk losing the DP, he fired belt high to the plate. The ball almost hit the plate umpire in the navel because Uecker had left home to go down and back up first base. The winning run, of course, scored.

Afterward, bumping into Tom Sheehan, the Giants' florid-faced super-scout, I allowed that, man and boy, I'd been watching the Cardinals for forty years and had never seen that play.

"No," boomed Sheehan in his big bass, "and, man and boy, I'll bet you've never seen many catchers, either, whose last name begins with the letter 'U.' "

Things really weren't all funny in 1966. For one, Alex Johnson, a husky righthanded-hitting outfielder obtained by Howsam after two seasons, proved quickly that he had great God-given gifts, like brother Ron, a University of Michigan back who starred for the New York football Giants before injuries. But Alex didn't have Ron's attitude. Except for Rogers Hornsby—maybe!—he was the fastest big man I ever saw skimming down to first base, but he played outfield as if he were trying to work a crossword puzzle at the same time. Although he would recover to have two solid seasons at bat with Howsam at Cincinnati (.312, .315) and one at California (.329), because of his indifferent attitude this good athlete missed a chance to be great.

A much better deal in 1966 would pay off handsomely the next couple of seasons. On a red-letter day in May, the Cardinals' last at old Sportsman's Park, a trade was made with the Giants. Privately—and I'm afraid I broke an old friend's confidence by using this in an effort to get Howsam to move—I quoted Bing Devine, then with the Mets. Bing said, yes, that if he needed a righthanded hitter as much as the Cardinals did, he would give lefty Ray Sadecki for Orlando Cepeda.

The pouting "Baby Bull," gimpy with a troublesome knee and not eager to give up first base to Willie McCovey and move to the outfield, hadn't made life easy for SanFran manager Herman Franks. The Chicago Cubs had muffed a big chance to get a straightaway power hitter—Cepeda would have hit fifty homers in smaller Wrigley Field—when Leo Durocher also tried to lure another Giants' player in exchange for southpaw Dick Ellsworth.

Cha-Cha: San Francisco's Baby Bull, Orlando Cepeda, encouraged by late Dr. I. C. Middleman and with trainer Bob Bauman's tireless help, built a gimpy knee to the point that he was the National League's Most Valuable Player in 1967—and a good glove man at first base, too.

"U" For Humorous: Bob Uecker, a strong-armed catcher who couldn't hit much, led the Cardinals with deadpanned laughs on the path to a pennant and en route to his own reputation as a baseball color man and as a stand-up (or sit-down) comic on radio, television and the Knife-and-Fork League.

Heck, I knew you didn't mess with Horace Stoneham, a square man who didn't like anyone to take advantage of him. Cepeda for Sadecki would do nicely. Finally, Dick Meyer urged Howsam to go ahead with the business. The Cardinals' team doctor, I. C. Middleman, a capable replacement for the late Dr. Robert F. Hyland, examined Cepeda in the clubhouse and suggested that if Orlando would be willing to work hard under the sharp surveillance of trainer Bob Bauman, he'd be okay.

The deal was made and Cepeda hit a club-leading .303 with seventeen home runs, en route to bigger things.

Howsam had tried a bit of Branch Rickey's old flim-flam of getting some extra talent, too, but, fortunately, he'd gone back to the one-on-one. Rickey was gone now, retired a year and dead only a few months, and I felt bad for any part I had in his dismissal.

Back in October, 1964, I'd written a story that before the long-awaited pennant, just about the time of Devine's dismissal, Rickey had written a memo to Gussie in which he proposed that by mid-August, if the Cardinals hadn't improved, he would return Mike Shannon and Barney Schultz to the minors. Even more negative to the future AND present, he would bench Javier at second base in favor of a Tulsa catcher, Ed Pacheco, he envisioned as a second baseman.

Rickey—"Branch Richelieu," as I'd labeled him in a bit of nasty reaction to his behind-the-scenes' whispering advice to Busch—was fired as senior consultant.

A newsman—honest, fellas!—can have a heart even if judgment and job must come first. I didn't like to hurt the old man (B. R.) and it's no fun, either, to jab Busch here or there as I have done and will do. I didn't respect Mr. Rickey because I didn't feel you could always believe him, but I admired his baseball contributions. I did respect Busch, but I wasn't awed by him.

One of the many things for which St. Louis was indebted to Busch happened in 1966. After all, that year the Cardinals staggered out of the Grand and Dodier ballpark. Whipped by the Giants, 10-5, with home-run slugger Willie Mays appropriately blasting the last long one there, they moved May 12 into the stadium jewel downtown.

Mike Shannon got the Cardinals' first hit there. Atlanta's Felipe Alou, best all-round of the three baseball brothers, hit two home runs as if the new park would be easy for long-ball hitters. Happily, the Cardinals won in twelve innings, 4-3. Lou Brock's single scored Curt Flood with the run that put reliever Don Dennis over young, indestructible Phil Niekro.

For the beautifully designed stadium located in the formerly run-down area south of the heart of downtown, St. Louis owed old newspaper suggestions augmented by the blood-and-guts idea of Charley Farris. An urban renewal program under the aegis of Civic Center Redevelopment Corporation would create the tax-relief complex if—

If, that is, St. Louis capital would show enough interest to put up $20,000,000 to qualify for a $33,000,000 loan from Equitable Life Assurance Society. Included were a 400-room riverfront motel, four garages with daily downtown potential and the centerpiece—the stadium.

An office building and other facilities could follow under the CCRC tent, but—first!—the ball-park for baseball and for the football Cardinals, who had come from Chicago with a promise of a larger, better place to play.

The vital need was for a dramatic kickoff to raise the $20,000,000 here, because wise business men knew, essentially, that if they could keep the stadium itself from being a financial white elephant, it would take additional subsidies. Bankers Jim Hickok and Preston Estep, co-chairmen, went to the public benefactor, the Big Eagle.

You bet your sweet life, to use one of Gussie's favorite expressions, the squire of Grant's Farm wanted new stadium. From the brewery, CCRC wanted a whopping $5,000,000. The brewery's board of directors balked. A million would do.

No, five.

But, Gussie, we've already spent $2,500,000 to spruce up the old stadium and, furthermore—

August Anheuser Busch, Jr., put down his filtered cigarette and pounded a polished table for emphasis.

"No, dammit, no," he said. "Five million."

So Civic Center got Anheuser-Busch's inspirational leadoff contribution and thirty staggering years of ballpark concessions and parking fees. May Department Stores, flagshipped by Famous-Barr, came up with $2,500,000. The amounts ranged down. My alma mater, the *Post-Dispatch*, contributed $100,000. Even the St. Louis baseball writers coughed up $1000. But loss of ancillary concessions rights by the brewery was even more gracious than the five mil.

Good Show, Gussie: To sign in tandem for 1955 his two top stars and road room- mates, Stan Musial and Red Schoendienst, Busch brings along to his brewery office the long-time Redbird secretary, Mary Murphy, who helped type ALL of Musial's major league contracts. She lent Red $5, too, for meals his first day in town 13 years earlier. Standing center is Busch's long-time stand-up man, executive vice-president, one-time ball- club general manager and ultimately brewery president, Richard A. Meyer.

That's Right, You're Wrong: Branch Rickey had a point when he tried to persuade veteran infielder Julian Javier to switch-hit because he batted poorly against righthanded pitching, but B. R. was full of Boston baked beans when he recommended that Javier be benched. Here, the great bespectacled second baseman makes a diving stop against Elston Howard for a fancy force play in the 1967 World Series with the Red Sox.

If it hadn't been for Busch, there would have been no stadium. The Gateway Arch, which had topped out shortly before, would have been a ghost along the levee of river packets, steamer travel, excursion and showboats.

These were salad seasons for Busch, who was becoming a senior citizen, with the feet of his own little people racing through his French Renaissance mansion down there where the stags clanged antlers for winners' rights in mating season. The brewery was going well and—right then!—the ball club even better. Curiosity would bring out 1,712,980 in 1966 and, as the Red-birds flapped their wings as if they were eagles, too, winning ball clubs produced the Redbirds' record of 2,090,245 in 1967 and a robust 2,011,177 in '68.

Funny thing, that pennant in 1967. It just seemed to happen. Opening night, Bob Gibson shut out Hall of Fame rival Juan Marichal of the San Francisco Giants. The Cards won a whopping 101 games out of 161, winning the pennant by ten and a half games over the same Giants, even though no St. Louis pitcher won more than sixteen games!

A rookie retread, Dick Hughes, bespectacled twenty-nine-year-old

Fleeting Fame: Dick Hughes, bespectacled, dry-witted Arkansan, had one touch of genius for the Cardinals, a 16-6 record and 2.67 earned-run average in 1967, but he failed in the World Series and quickly was gone as a scout because of arm trouble.

Sentimental Journeyman: When a guy wants to call Larry Jaster just a "journeyman" pitcher, which he really was, he's got to remember that everybody might believe that except Los Angeles. In 1966, winning 11 games, the lefthander pitched five shutouts, all of them against the Dodgers.

righthander, was tops with 16-6. Nelson Briles, a twenty-three-year-old kid who looked like a face-lifted bulldog, came out of the bullpen when Bob Gibson was hurt after the All-Star break and won nine in a row. He was 14-5. The lean lefty, Steve Carlton, just twenty-two, was 14-9. Gibson, 13-7 when he keeled over still trying to pitch with an ankle broken by a line smash off Roberto Clemente's bat, was the nominal staff leader for whom Schoendienst had earmarked a date with destiny in October.

The trick of winning pennants, obviously, is to get as many pitchers over .500 as possible. Ray Washburn was 10-7, coming back from a torn shoulder muscle that kept him from achieving true greatness. Al Jackson lefthanded his way to 9-4, and Larry Jaster was 9-7. It wasn't the same as in 1966 when, fabulously, tying a big-league record set by Grover Cleveland Alexander, Jaster shut out one club (the Dodgers) five times; but it helped. So did witty Ron Willis's 6-5. Even Joe Hoerner, .500 at 4-and-4, contributed also because he was part and parcel of the loose, free-wheeling attitude of the ball club.

Hoerner was so helpful that one night down in Atlanta, when a bus driver ducked off for a smoke or whatever, just about the time the winning gang was ready for a heigh-ho ride back to their hotel, Joe jumped behind the wheel and ricocheted the bus downtown. He probably set a record for thrills as well as for the number of backseat drivers.

In that period, Curt Flood, the center field star, led in team hitting with .335. Lou Brock hit twenty-one homers and Javier, having the kind of year Branch Rickey had in mind when B. R. urged him futilely to switch-hit, batted .281 and homered fourteen times. Workhorse Mc-Carver hit fourteen homers and batted .295, a figure that earned him runnerup recognition as MVP.

Actually, except for steady, surehanded Dal Maxvill at short-stop, the lowest-hitting regulars were the prime figures in a position switch that solidified the club. Between them, a new third baseman and an old right fielder conducted themselves professionally and formed a firm friendship—Mike Shannon and Roger Maris.

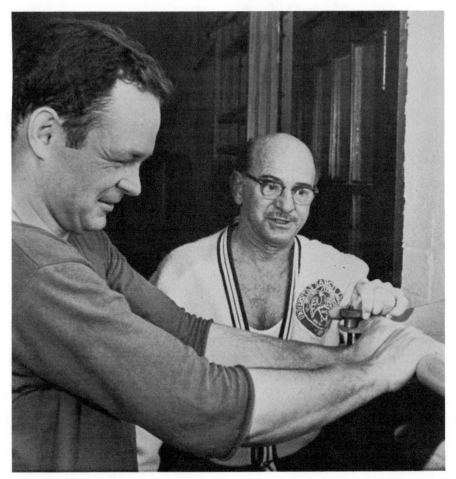

Sideshow: Joe Hoerner (left), sidewheeling lefthander whose career once was jeopardized by a heart problem, was a portside pixy who later went into travel-agency business with Dal Maxvill. Relief pitcher Hoerner here gets wrist-strengthening tortures from Walter C. "Doc" Eberhardt, long-time St. Louis University physical-education professor who has tended to Redbirds' winter-and-spring fitness ever since Stan Musial's comeback.

Peace, It's Wonderful: Roger Maris, who found himself misunderstood and his relationships with the press, too, en route to his single-season career record of 61 home runs with the New York Yankees, came to the Cardinals in 1967. As relaxed as shown here, the smart right fielder hit timely if not hard, because of a damaged hand.

A Spitting Image: Joe Schultz, former Browns' catcher who looked so much like his father, a former outfielder of the same name with the Cardinals and farm director at Pittsburgh, too, was the coach who made "El Birdos" a byword. He also worked diligent Mike Shannon into a third baseman, then left for an ill-fated stay as Seattle manager. Ultimately, a hip ailment curtailed coaching at Detroit.

In one of Howsam's last deals before hopping over to Cincinnati, the Cardinals had obtained Maris from the New York Yankees for cash and Charley Smith. A former home-run king, twice winner of the American League's Most Valuable Player award, Maris had soured under the pressure of his record sixty-one home runs in 1961. He had hurt a hand, too, but he knew how to make the plays. He found a new home, happiness and, thanks to Gussie Busch, a secure future with the Anheuser-Busch distributorship for Gainesville-Ocala in Florida.

Maris in right field batted .261 and drove in fifty-five runs in 125 games. At third base was the right fielder, Shannon. In early autumn Schoendienst and especially coach Joe Schultz had been working out the future broadcaster. They had to use Fairground Park because old Busch Stadium had been donated generously by Busch to the publisher of the *Globe-Democrat*, Richard H. Amberg, for establishment of the Herbert Hoover Boys' Club.

By spring training, Schoendienst and the new general manager, Stan Musial, concluded that the "Moon Man," as the guys called Shannon because they thought the gregarious guy was spaced out, could make the vital move. He could. Although batting only .245, he hit twelve homers and batted in seventy-seven runs in 130 games.

As general manager, Musial had good fortune in a job for which, I, honestly, didn't think he was qualified. I knew he'd become a fast student at reading the Garagnanis' restaurant-and-hotel financial books, but the technicalities of a GM's job, including the long, regular hours, just didn't jibe with my analysis of "Stan the Man." I didn't know that whenever he encountered a problem he couldn't

comprehend, he'd pick up the phone and call an old friend, Bing Devine, who had become president of the Mets.

With magnificent Musial good fortune, Stan had to make only one roster move through the heart of the season, obtaining righthander Jack Lamabe from the Mets when Gibson was hurt and Briles stepped up from the bullpen.

A major factor in the pennant breeze was Orlando Cepeda at first base. "Cha-Cha" hit the way he had in his savage peak at San Francisco, where he, not Mays, had been the Bay area's early hero. He batted .325, hit twenty-five home runs and drove in 111 runs. The Baby Bull became the National League's only unanimous choice for their Most Valuable Player until Philly's Mike Schmidt in 1980.

Cepeda had worked hard with a weighted boot to build up his knee. He was a good-natured, good-looking guy who could run and field, too. His only weakness was that he could hold everything except a buck. With his chop-chop chatter and the stereo he carried everywhere except into the shower, he was the life of the party. Inferentially, the Puerto Rican was perpetrator of the ungrammatical, Spanish-bastardized nickname first chortled with glee by Joe Schultz: "El Birdos!"

Nice Nellie: Nelson Kelley Briles, a bilingual bulldog they all called "Nellie," came out of the bullpen when Bob Gibson was hurt in 1967. He won eight straight games and one in the World Series, too.

17

Gibby
& the
Go·Go Guy

Hereafter, especially for their performances up to and throughout the rousing seasons of 1967 and '68, then into the baseball record books, Bob Gibson and Lou Brock would run and finish as a championship thoroughbred entry: 1 and 1-A.

In this case, they were numbers "45" and "20," both since retired as done previously only with Stan Musial's "6" and Dizzy Dean's "17."

In 1967 the gifted El Birdos, a ball club of strong pitching and defense and adequate speed and offense, beat back a mid-season challenge by Leo Durocher's Chicago Cubs and won going away.

In September, Gibson came back from his broken leg and tuned up, proving he was ready. That was all Schoendienst wanted to know. In the World Series, it was almost all Gibson and Brock.

Gibson, who had clinched the pennant September 18, won the Series opener October 4 at Boston,

2-1. The Red Sox had suffered a bad break of fortune. Their top pitcher, Jim Lonborg, had been needed the final game of the regular season. Against Gibson, they used Jose Santiago. Not bad, Santiago pitched well and homered for Boston's only run.

Brock went "4 for 4," stole two bases and scored both Cards' runs, driven in by Roger Maris, who showed the old pro's touch. Rog twice cuffed the ball on the right side with the infield back.

Next day, facing Dick Hughes, Carl Yastrzemski, truly tremendous that best of his career's seasons as a daily Merriwell at Fenway, homered twice. Lonborg allowed only an eighth-inning double by Julian Javier in a 5-0 work of pitching art.

Back in St. Louis, there was excitement and a mix-up. Busch Memorial Stadium, which "held the heat very well," as Casey Stengel quipped at the steaming 1966 All-Star game, was really hot—and they'd oversold it. Adroitly, the Cardinals shoehorned in a few extra thousand by using folding chairs in the wide aisles.

The 54,575 in attendance, the same count for each day in town, were treated to a good ball game. Mike Shannon, an excellent October competitor, homered, and bulldog Nelson Briles hung on to win, 5-2. When Gibson came back to beat Santiago again, this time 6-0, it seemed that the Cardinals held a commanding World Series lead.

Again, however, Lonborg was masterful in the get-away game in St. Louis. He pitched a three-hitter, marred only by Maris's home run. Kid Carlton pitched well, but lost, 3-1.

Back at Boston, with the Cardinals using a Series record total of eight pitchers after Hughes again failed, 8-4, the Series was tied. As before, there would be—to quote the pressbox poets—no tomorrow.

Climbing aboard the bus the final morning out there at Quincy, Massachusetts, where the Cardinals were housed, I was aghast to learn that Gibson was sullen, surly, almost steaming. In the mess of an overcrowded breakfast room, the starting pitcher had been shut out. His only belated service had been a piece of burned toast, which he spurned, equally burned.

As one who had nursed an ulcer and fed a fast-emptying stomach, I envisioned the worst: A tired hungry Gibson giving out near the wire. Since I had worked in Boston and was familiar with the area, I had the bus drop me at a cafeteria. I rushed in and ordered two ham-and-egg sandwiches to go, then grabbed a cab to Fenway Park.

Lonborg, trying to go with two days' rest, finally gave out. Gibson hammered a home run, Dal Maxvill a triple and Javier a conclusive three-run homer. Brock, in addition, stole three bases to give him a single Series record of seven to go with his .414 average.

Gibson, splendid, threw a three-hitter in the 7-2 final. He finished with three record-tying victories in which he yielded just fourteen hits and one earned run in twenty-seven innings, walking only five batters and striking out twenty-six.

The king of the hill was awarded the Series-decisive automobile by *Sport* magazine. Graciously, Bob Hyland of KMOX told Brock to take his pick of a car, too, at the radio station's expense.

Even though Gibson had eaten only one of my sandwiches before the game—he washed down the other one with champagne and a grin afterward—I congratulated myself. I figured Gibby had gone seven innings, and that my egg had sustained him in the eighth and the ham in the ninth.

Silly boy. Early the next season, I talked with him before a hot May game on a Sunday afternoon against Cincinnati. Casually, he mentioned he'd left early the night before after the pre-game infield exercise he took whenever he wasn't pitching. He had gone over to his hotel, had a glass of wine and a Caesar salad and had gone to bed.

Only a Caesar salad? But, then, when had he had his full meal Saturday? Oh, only a sandwich around mid-day. And this morning? Just prune juice and a cup of coffee.

Hey, wait a minute, really nothing, then, except a salad and prune juice since that single sandwich twenty-four hours ago? Right? Right!

Indeed, and all Gibson did that Sunday afternoon when he'd had virtually nothing except a competitive heart in his innards was to strike out fifteen Reds in the broad daylight. So there went my World Series recollections, shot to hell.

In 1968, Robert Gibson, nicknamed "Hoot" because of the old silent screen cowboy, was positively overwhelming. He did it for a new general manager, too, because after the death of partner Biggie Garagnani, Stan Musial realized he ought to spend more time with the restaurant-hotel combination and less at the nine-to-five job.

Besides, the GM really was more than a day-time job. Stan mentioned Bing Devine, who had helped him so unselfishly but by now was president of the Mets. Dick Meyer, a Devine man, was delighted. How would Gussie Busch take it?

The story is, of course, that Gussie remembered a beautiful standup letter of mild criticism he'd received in high praise accorded Der Bingle. It had come off the pen of Devine's oldest daughter, Joanne, at the time of his dismissal in 1964. A great story and, sure, I believe it. But I know, too, that Alfred Fleishman, the public relations wizard and semanticist who had been the city's director of recreation when he was only a kid (twenty-seven), was a guardian of Gussie's faith, a champion of Busch's image.

So Der Bingle was back, and it's worth mentioning here that he never had any contract trouble with Gibson, because, as a result of their mutual respect and Busch's appreciation of the pitcher's worth, Gibby got top dollar before free agency blew the lid off Pandora's box and the bank vault.

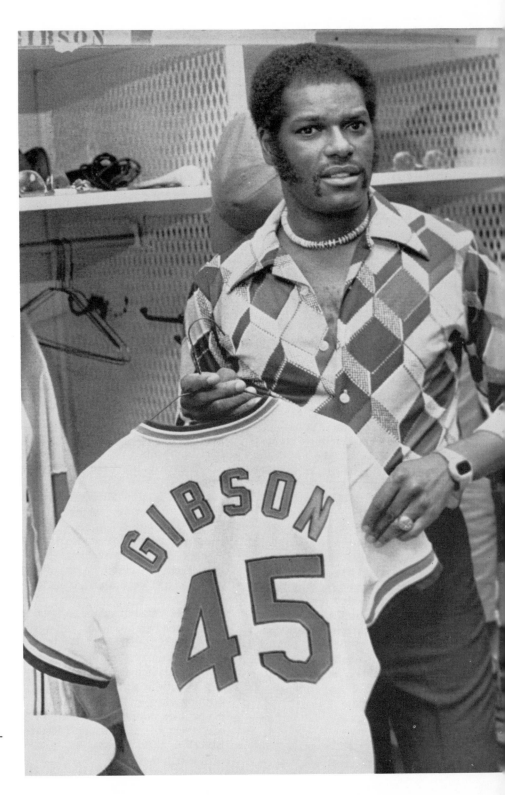

Gibby the Great: Bob Gibson, not smiling here when he hangs up No. "45," the uniform he made famous for the Cardinals from 1959 through 1975, was the Redbirds' winningest pitcher ever (251). He also set World Series records for most consecutive victories and strikeouts and one year (1968) had the lowest earned-run average (1.12) ever posted by a 300-inning pitcher.

In 1968, Gibby was worth his weight in gold-leafed Budweiser labels. He made a positive joke of the game. He was 22-9 as the Cardinals romped home in front with a 97-65 record, but, heck, that was really only the tip of the iceberg; thirteen of his victories were shutouts.

There's more. In thirty-four starts he finished twenty-eight times. He pitched 305 innings, allowing only 198 hits. He walked sixty-two batters and struck out 268. He won fifteen games in a row. Over one period of ninety innings, he allowed just two earned runs. His 1.12 earned-run average was the lowest ever recorded by a pitcher who worked 300 or more innings.

In the "Year of the Pitcher," as it became known, Gibson was THE pitcher, but the primary ink went to an engaging guy named Denny McLain with Detroit, the majors' first thirty-game winner (31-6) since Dizzy Dean of the 1934 Gas House Gang.

Just before the World Series, the Dodgers' former pitching superstar, Sandy Koufax, talked about Gibson. Sandy knew part of the story and, if he didn't, he could have learned the rest from the *Post-Dispatch*'s Dave Lipman and Ed Wilks, who combined for G. P. Putnam's Sons to write *Bob Gibson, Pitching Ace.*

Gibby was mentally tough, having been brought up the hard way. Fatherless, he grew up in an Omaha ghetto, his ear bitten by a rat when he was a baby. He'd suffered rickets. He was asthmatic. He'd battled pneumonia and won because an older brother had promised him a baseball glove if he lived.

He had been a switch-hitter catcher and shortstop on a school-age team and had grown so fast in high school that he needed a doctor's permission to compete in sports because of a heart murmur. He'd been the first black to play basketball for Creighton University, so agile that he could almost put his elbow on the rim of a basket. Gibson was so competitive, in fact, that when he came back to work out against the Bluejays' varsity, he'd outleaped and outwrestled a kid who would win a reputation as a rebounder and become a pro basketball coach, Paul Silas.

Koufax knew that Gibson, as he himself did, also pitched with an arthritic elbow that needed cold applications after he pitched. "But you don't hear about it because he doesn't talk about it," said Sandy, pausing. "If he (Gibby) goes against McLain, Gibson will eat him up."

Once again, in a World Series it was Gibson and Brock.

In the Series opener at St. Louis, Shannon, another good man in an October clutch, singled home the first run off McLain in the fourth inning, and Javier singled in two more. Brock homered to make it 4-0.

Gibson, meanwhile, though pitching in bright, clear weather, was whistling that fast ball which must have made it look as if No. "45" were firing a .45. His slider darted across the outside corner as if making a sharp left-hand turn to first base. Strike out...strike out...strike out...

By the ninth inning, with the scoreboard message center keeping watch-and-word behind his back and the crowd roaring, McCarver rushed out to tell Gibson that he had tied Koufax's Series strikeout record of fifteen.

"Get back there, dammit," Gibby snarled.

Strike three...strike three...A new record—seventeen. I don't believe I've ever had a greater athletic thrill.

The Tigers, however, broke St. Louis's proud record of never having lost a seven-game World Series and—at the finish, darn it—I sensed it.

Briles was beaten by a pudgy lefthander, Mickey Lolich, 8-1. With Brock running amuck, the Cardinals clobbered the Tigers in the third game, 7-3, aided by McCarver's home run.

A twin rain delay in the fourth game might have taken something away from Gibson, who that day achieved his World Series record of seven consecutive complete-game victories, even though rain delayed the start thirty-five minutes and caused a seventy-four minute wait in the third inning. Gibby hit a home run and breezed, 10-1.

The Series was decided in the fifth game. What could have been a Cardinal clambake, a short-snorter Series, wound up disastrously. With Brock's leadoff double, the Cardinals got away quickly against Lolich. By the fifth, however, when Brock doubled again, Julian Javier delivered a single to left on which Brock was retired at the plate on a tremendous throw by Willie Horton.

If Brock had slid, the argument was, he would have scored. Lou's rejoinder was that catcher Bill Freehan's foot had him blocked off. Frankly, I believe he could have slid, but to second-guess Brock would be the height of ingratitude. All the man did was to bat .464 with a record-tying thirteen hits and steal seven more bases to tie his own Series mark. He scored six and drove in five of the Cardinals' twenty-seven runs.

Probably the Tigers deserved the best because, for one thing, to get veteran outfielder Al Kaline, a future Hall of Famer who had been injured, into the Series, manager Mayo Smith boldly moved center fielder Mickey Stanley to shortstop and got away with it. For another, Kaline, given his one Series chance, made it golden. He batted .379 with eleven hits and eight RBIs.

Still, the Cardinals might have won in five if—

When a bullpen-battered Detroit batted in the seventh, Smith let Lolich bat because he didn't want to go to his secondary men. From left field, Brock glanced over and saw the unexpected that was visible from pressbox heights. Right fielder Ron Davis was playing the right-handed-hitting opposing pitcher much too deep. Brock hollered to Curt Flood, who relayed the word to Davis. Too late.

Lolich hit a high, short fly—"a can of corn," the old saying goes—but the ball fell in for a gift one-out single. When lefty Joe Hoerner replaced Nelson Briles, Dick McAuliffe bad-hopped a single over Javier's head. The inning well could and should have been over, but a walk to Stanley loaded the bases and Kaline's clutch single put Detroit ahead.

The Tigers' ultimate 5-3 victory set up a 13-1 merry-go-round in which Detroit scored ten times in the third inning off Ray Washburn and associates. That took it down to game No. 7 and, on KSD(K)-TV that day at noon with old boss Roy Stockton and Jay Randolph, I had a funny feeling that maybe we'd extended the rubber band once too often.

Snap! In the decisive seventh game, though the Cardinals had run wild with eleven stolen bases, the Redbirds seemed to get overconfident. In the sixth Brock singled and took a gosh-awfully long lead. Ultimately, Lolich picked him off, and when Lou flew toward second base, first baseman Norm Cash made an excellent, on-target low throw to retire him. In the same inning Flood also got on base and was picked off.

The game, therefore, was scoreless in the Tigers' seventh. With two out, Detroit got unexpected action. Cash looped a single to right. Horton grounded one between third and short for a base hit. Still, all was well when Gibson got Northrup—it seemed—on a sharp line drive almost directly to Flood in center field.

But, losing the ball, Curt took a couple of steps in, then tried to backtrack. As he pivoted, he slipped off stride to his right and then turned back too late. The ball cleared his head, glanced off the wall and—astonishingly!—the great Gibson trailed, 2-0.

Another run came in that inning and one in the ninth, too, an inning in which Shannon spoiled Lolich's bid for a shutout in his third victory, 4-1. But if there had been no misplay, Lolich and Gibson might have pitched out there until the snows fell.

Afterward, Flood, defensively, declined to discuss the misjudged play. Gibson, though he could needle with a championship rapier, knew when to be gentle. The pitcher shrugged. "He," Gibby said of Flood, "has saved many a ball game for me."

In the morgue-like clubhouse, came an announcement that most observers greeted as a sure-thing for the Cardinals in their bid for a pennant in 1969, the first year the National League would go to twelve clubs as a result of new franchises awarded Montreal and San Diego.

As the Cardinals hurried to dress for a plane trip to Japan, it was announced that St. Louis had acquired right fielder Vada Pinson from Cincinnati, to replace Roger Maris, who was retiring. For Pinson, they would give up relief pitcher Wayne Granger and young outfielder-first baseman Bobby Tolan.

Virtually everybody approved the trade. I certainly agreed that Pinson would add experience, but I didn't have the same feeling about him I'd had earlier. At one time I thought Pinson had 3000-hit potential, but he had seemed to lose something when Frank Robinson was dealt to Baltimore. Moreover, with passing years, I thought he'd been less effective defensively.

Still, I'm sure that if he hadn't broken a bone in his leg in a .255 season with St. Louis, he would have helped more. By contrast, the rangy Granger and swift Tolan, a lefthanded hitter who hung in their tough against lefthanders, reached stardom down by the O-hi-o.

I believe Stan Musial had something when he said, "I won't deal with Howsam because he took too many of our guys with him, and they know the Cardinals' personnel better than we know his."

The bubble burst in more directions than one. Not only did the Cardinals drop back to fourth in the new six-club Eastern Division, winning 87 games and losing 75, but Gussie Busch also lost his grand feeling of paternal *gemütlichkeit*.

Busch had been proud to put together the first $1,000,000 payroll in big-league history. By 1980 it was a whopping, free-agent inflated $5,000,000. Why, back in 1967, for instance, he'd paid Roger Maris more ($75,000) than the entire front nine of Frank Frisch's Gas House Gang had received in the 1934 Depression. He loved to put on picnics and parties for his players, too, but now one of his favorites, Curt Flood, had rebelled.

Over the years, Busch hadn't stuck his nose, figuratively, into the manager's dugout often, but, once, he had suggested that Flood be given more of a chance. Curt had, and he'd hit as well as fielded. The club had helped Flood through personal scrapes, too, and he'd given Busch a delightful portrait. Gussie liked it so much that he asked Curt to paint other members of the family, too, at $250 a pop.

Now, however, after dropping from .335 to a club-leading .301 in 1968, the Year of the Pitcher, Flood was quoted as saying he wanted $100,000 (from $72,000). I winced when I read that the player had added: ". . .And I don't mean $99,999.99, either."

Gosh, you don't wave a red flag in a bull's face or challenge a beer baron like Busch, either. Ultimately, Curt would settle for $90,000, a good raise before free agency and inflation sent salaries berserk. But the damage was done. For Busch, the fun had become a funny business. Come to think of it, business that wasn't so funny.

Faded With Vada: When the Cardinals announced after the 1968 World Series that they acquired Vada Pinson to replace retiring Roger Maris in right field, everybody awarded the Cardinals the 1969 pennant, post haste, but they forgot to notify the New York Mets—or Pinson. The former Reds' hitting star was handicapped by a broken leg bone. He was also overrated afield.

Another change in 1969 was at first base. In spring training Devine dealt Orlando Cepeda to Atlanta, where the Milwaukee Braves' transplanted star, Joe Torre, was having contract trouble with Paul Richards. In 1968, Cepeda had dipped down to .248 with the Cardinals. He and the ball club had been bothered constantly by his creditors. Some had become so bold that they even had invaded the runway behind the dugout to badger the man-child between innings.

Torre was extremely serviceable. As a kid he had been twitted as "fat" by older brother Frank, later Braves' first baseman and then vice-president of Rawlings Sporting Goods in St. Louis. Cutting down over the years, Joe had reached a new peak of lean, articulate talent.

In an historic deal—historic, certainly, because it led to Curt Flood's challenge against the legality of the reserve clause—the Cardinals sent Flood and Tim McCarver to Philadelphia as St. Louis's key men in a deal for which the other side's natural attraction was Richie Allen. Curt refused to go.

How would Allen, the tempestuous, two-fisted drinking athlete, often considered undisciplined, perform in St. Louis? Fine! Richie and synthetic turf came at the same time, and both made a good impression. Given a rousing welcome opening night, Allen appreciated the good will and was a good fella. He played first base usually, moved to third now and then and also butchered up the outfield a bit.

At bat, he brought the big ballpark to its knees. Out the entire final month with a pulled hamstring, Allen played only 122 games, but the righthanded power hitter pounded thirty-four home runs and drove in

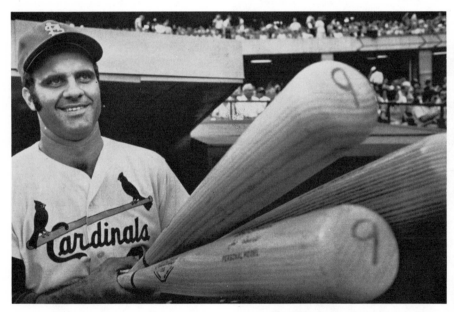

A Profit From a Prophet: Personable, knowledgeable Joe Torre always struck observers as a likely manager, which he became, but not before the versatile athlete, once teased as "too fat" by older brother Frank, a big leaguer, put in seven solid seasons with the Cardinals. Obtained by Bing Devine for Orlando Cepeda, he caught pretty well, played third base acceptably and did even better at first.

Own Worst Enemy: Probably that would be the best way to describe Richie Allen, the homer-hitting iconoclast who came to the Cardinals in the Curt Flood-Tim McCarver deal. Although a notorious loner, chided about his undisciplined life style, Allen was hot in only 122 games with the Cardinals. He drove in 101 runs and hit a Busch Memorial Stadium record of 34 home runs.

101 runs. Offensively, he was more effective than his .279 average, but he hurt his St. Louis future in September by skipping many treatments for his injured leg.

Still, full of giggle water as the Cardinals made their final trip into old Connie Mack Stadium, where he had played with the Phillies, a wobbly Allen insisted on playing. His wife even phoned Red Schoendienst and asked the manager not to play him. Red concurred, but Richie was so persuasive that Red shrugged his shoulders and put him in the lineup.

Loaded, Allen singled, walked and homered before Schoendienst got him out of there in Richie's frothy farewell to Philly and to the Cardinals.

Devine dealt him that winter to Los Angeles for an over-rated ball player, Ted Sizemore, whose biggest asset was taking pitches when batting behind Lou Brock. Two years later, bouncing over to the Chicago White Sox, Allen won the American League's Most Valuable Player award. He hit thirty-seven homers, drove in 113 runs and batted .308.

When major-league baseball sought more offense by lowering the pitching mound and increasing the strike zone after Gibson and associates made run-scoring as difficult as hockey or soccer scores, Gibby beefed about the injustice to the pitchers. H'mm, in 1970 he posted a 23-and-7 record. Torre, catching more often than he played third base, hit twenty-one homers, drove in a hundred runs and batted .325. Reliably, Brock was .304 with fifty-one solen bases.

A blow, naturally, was the loss through illness of Mike Shannon. His career was halted to avoid threat to his life. Another blow to the Cardinals was Steve Carlton's dip from 17-11 to 10-19 and Mike Torrez's drop from 10-4 to 8-10. The Car-

dinals held fourth place, but they dropped eleven victories to 76-86.

The Cardinals made a strong pennant bid in 1971, a result of solid seasons. Joe Torre, resembling a Rogers Hornsby or Joe Medwick of old, trimmed down his weight even more and upped his average to .363, winning a batting title and Most Valuable Player award. Torre, playing third base, certainly didn't get a leg hit out of 230 as he belted twenty-four homers and drove in 137.

Lou Brock got 200 hits, batting .313 with sixty-four stolen bases.

Matty Alou, acquired from Pittsburgh for Nelson Briles and pinch-hitting specialist Vic Davalillo, showed old base-reaching skill and even more RBI strength, batting .315 and driving in seventy-four runs.

As the first of the stars of the 1970s, Ted Simmons came in to make his first full season a memorable one. He hit .304 with seventy-seven RBIs. The switch-hitting first draft choice of 1967 from suburban Detroit had turned down a football scholarship at the University of Michigan to opt for the majors. Orginally, "Simba" didn't hit well enough righthanded to suit himself,

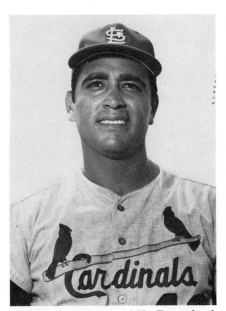

One That Got Away: Mike Torrez, handsome righthander was 10-and-4 in his first full season with the Cardinals, 1969, but then, beset and upset by marital problems later solved, he fell off to 8-10 and was dealt to develop more fully as a pitcher elsewhere.

A Family Plan: Mateo "Matty" Alou, middle of the three ball-playing Alou brothers from the Dominican Republic (Felipe and Jesus), came over to the Cardinals and hit .315 and .314 as a high-salaried player. Then he was unloaded to pennant-bound Oakland. In St. Louis, Matty once hit a ground-ball home run, a grass-cutting ground smash that went through to the center-field wall for an inside-the-park base-emptier.

Simba Behind Bars: Ted Simmons, one of the Cardinals' top switch-hitters ever and baseball's, too, takes time out in spring training to meet a young person's request for his autograph. The catcher traded to Milwaukee was called Simba because for a time his hair grew so long that it resembled a lion's mane.

but he threw a football lefthanded to build up the upper arm from the righthanded batting stance. Early in his career he showed the determination that made him an All-Star standout.

To Red Schoendienst, a manager who had played with pre-war hard-nosed characters, there never had been one who could shake off a foul to the shanks as unflinchingly as Simmons, the solid son of a harness-horse trainer. If the bear his wife Maryanne saw stalk up behind him as Simba nibbled on a fish during a post-season camping trip hadn't been scared away by her screams, there might have been one helluva fight or one surprised bear.

If the Cardinals had had a second Steve Carlton or, in fact, if twenty-two-year-old Jerry Reuss just had had previous experience in 1971, the Cardinals might have made it. The two tall lefthanders showed much with more to come. Steve was 20-and-9, Reuss 14-14.

At a time Flood was challenging the reserve clause, souring Busch as the Cardinals were required to give up Willie Montanez and a first-round draft choice because Curt wouldn't report to Philadelphia, the young talent wanted handsome salary hikes. The Cardinals, despite a fourteen-victory climb to ninety, had dropped in attendance a bit for the third straight year (to 1,604,671). Eventually, as is obvious from salaries paid in the late 1970s and into the 80s to the likes of Simmons,

Keith Hernandez, Garry Templeton, George Hendrick, Bobby Bonds and Bob Forsch, Gussie could shift fiscal gears. But in the early '70s, the grand geezer of Grant's Farm was as immovable as a Clydesdale with a mule's disposition.

Consequently, when Carlton, Reuss and Simmons held out, Busch directed general manager Bing Devine to do the best he could to get him some new, more grateful faces with whom to deal. As a result, Carlton went to Philadelphia for Rick Wise and Reuss to Houston for Scipio Spinks. (Spinks might have made it if he hadn't been hurt.)

Fortunately, in Simmons's case, the kid employed a new tactic. He just didn't sign, a circumstance that eventually, tested elsewhere, would create the free-agent status. Courts ruled that the contract stipulation holding a player for "one more year" meant exactly what it said. Not Sunday, Monday or always, just one more season.

Ultimately, as Simmons kept his mouth shut other than to say lightly that it was "a matter of principal, not principle," Dick Meyer was able to effect a Missouri compromise, a two-year agreement by which, in effect, Busch got what he wanted the first year and Simmons got even more the second.

The Redbirds, then, saved one but lost two in a moment of top-level pique. As I'm sure Busch must recognize whenever he narrows those blue eyes and reflects in the haze of his trophy room, at least a couple or more division titles or pennants or better got away because Carlton wore Philadelphia raiment and Reuss another club's colors. Big Steve was a twenty-seven-game winner the first year he left here and was still No. 1 into the 1980s. Reuss, though not quite so spectacular, was also a big winner into the '80s when the Cardinals were short of pitching, especially of able lefthanders.

In 1972 the Cardinals fell back again to fourth, 75-81. Brock and Simmons held up, Alou batted well for average but not for production, and only Bob Gibson, 19-11, was a pitcher above .500. Wise was exactly even, 16-16, and young, hungry Reggie Cleveland wasn't quite there, 14-15. A loss was that Torre dropped considerably to .289.

In the words of the Cole Porter song, Joe was just "too hot not to cool down." He stayed in the same lower neighborhood in 1973, which came close to becoming one of the most magnificent moments in the history of the Cardinals. If only Bob Gibson hadn't been hurt. . .

By now, he was twice (1968 and '70) winner of the National League Cy Young award as top pitcher. He had won the MVP (1968) and he'd set a National League strikeout record (1972). Finally, too, though he believed he'd never do it, he'd joined Ray Washburn as a Redbird pitcher who had thrown a no-hit game.

Temper, Temper, Boss: You know, it just doesn't pay to get up some mornings, especially angry, as Gussie Busch was when, miffed at salary holdouts, he urged trades that sent away Steve Carlton (left) and Jerry Reuss. Carlton became the National League's top pitcher at Philadelphia and Reuss still was a winner at Los Angeles in 1980, eight years after he was traded.

They Also Starred: Reggie Smith (left) might have been a bit brittle and his salary-delayed contract terms troublesome his third year with the Cardinals (1976), but he was a .300 hitter, a good runner and better outfielder. He was traded to L.A. for a ham sandwich and disgruntled Joe Ferguson. Al Hrabosky, wearing his Fu Manchu mustache, but a smile instead of a scowl, was a super reliever in '75 and '76.

Whitewash by Washburn: Ray Washburn, deprived by injury of becoming perhaps one of the Cardinals' best pitchers ever, had a big moment in September, 1968, the day after the pennant-winning Redbirds had been held hitless by the San Francisco Giants. The Giants laughed. Hah! Next afternoon, as shown here, Washburn no-hit SanFran. Washburn had five straight low-hit victories at the start of the 1963 season before he suffered torn shoulder muscles. His patience and efforts of Dr. Stan London and trainer Bob Bauman brought him back—partway.

Washburn had done it in September, 1968, at San Francisco, back to back with the Giants' Gaylord Perry as the Cardinals gamboled to their pennant. Gibson did it at Pittsburgh's Three Rivers Stadium on August 14, 1971.

When big No. "45" took aim and fired Strike Three past the Pirates' twin sluggers, Dave Parker and Willie Stargell, the Cardinals' broadcaster, witty and urbane Jack Buck, a sentimental Irishman who knew the Gibson few of the fans did, broke down in his emotional play-by-play.

In '73, it was time to weep for the Cardinals, *in toto*, as they got off to their worst start ever, losing twenty of the first twenty-five games. But from those ashes of defeat, the Redbirds rose like a phoenix to a point where, unbelievably, they were in first place in early August, eleven games over .500, five games in front.

If Gibson hadn't been hurt, tearing ligaments as he slid back into first base in a game at New York, chances are the Cardinals would have won at least a division for the most incredible comeback in the history of a club noted for comeback tradition.

Instead, in defeat, Gibson imprinted his importance even more than in victory. Without their stopper, the club blew the cork and the division. Down the stretch, both Rick Wise and Reggie Cleveland backed away from victory. With the Cardinals slumping horribly and second-place Pittsburgh shy about taking advantage of it, Yogi Berra's third-place New York Mets came on to win with a ridiculously mediocre 82-79 record. Yet the Mets even upset the Cincinnati Reds and carried the Oakland A's to a seventh game of the World Series.

Devine, almost bitterly, dealt Wise and outfielder Bernie Carbo to Boston after the season for a much-needed power-hitting outfielder, Reggie Smith, and then sent Cleveland to the same club later in the same inter-league trading period for pitchers Lynn McGlothen, John Curtis and Mike Garman.

Smith, a muscular, good-looking outfielder, a power hitter from either side of the plate with ability to catch the ball and to throw it, had had some misunderstanding with Boston management and the press. He came to St. Louis anticipating trouble, but he encountered good will that brought two good seasons.

Reggie could seem brittle at times, but he still produced. In 1974 he had twenty-three homers, a hundred RBIs and a .309 average in 143 games. A year later he played eight fewer games but still got nineteen homers and seventy-six RBIs when batting .302.

Fine points of contract arrangements with the Cardinals in 1976 struck a late snag, and at the trading deadline, he was shipped to Los Angeles for, essentially, catcher-outfielder Joe Ferguson. The deal stank. Ferguson, who had about as much chance of beating out Simmons as the current sideshow character, Fredbird, didn't want to play the outfield for which he wasn't well-equipped either. Busch Memorial Stadium seemed to forestall him completely. He went to Houston in 1977. (Yes, Mr. Rickey, an addition by subtraction.)

In 1974 the Cardinals made a respectable bid for the division that had slipped away the previous year. Trouble was, Gibson, at thirty-eight, couldn't quite overcome the effects of that knee surgery. Although he'd come back surprisingly to pitch well enough to beat Steve Carlton—no easy feat for the Cardinals—the final

weekend in 1973, he had not pushed good winter conditioning at home.

For the Cardinals in 1974, Lynn McGlothen, obtained by Bing Devine as part of the Reggie Cleveland deal, came up with a splendid season, 16-12, and Al "Mad Hungarian" Hrabosky was fantastic in relief. The colorful lefthander, who gave the hitters the back of his uniform to cogitate and then the back of a bristling fast ball, was 8-1 and had nine saves.

As an all-round player who I, personally, thought would be even better, Bake McBride broke in extremely well. The lanky flash from Fulton became Rookie of the Year, batting .309, and he figured in one of the rarest of games.

The Fulton Flash: Once that description fit Fulton's Olympic sprint star of 1936, Helen Stephens, so it was just right for another mid-Missouri swiftie, Bake McBride, a good all-round outfielder short only a topflight throwing arm in St. Louis. The Baker helped put the icing on Philadelphia's wedding cake in 1980.

People's Choice: A fans' favorite, twice dealt by the Cardinals, was Ken Reitz, the hard-playing third baseman who ran so desperately s-l-o-w. Also, he didn't have enough power or consistency to go with his brilliant fielding skill. Home runs such as this, when he was greeted by Ted Simmons, were too infrequent from a third baseman.

Down the exciting stretch in September when every game was s-o-o important, Ken Reitz, the brilliant-fielding third-base tortoise, hit a game-tying ninth-inning home run. Thanks largely to a full game's scoreless relief by Claude Osteen, who would become their pitching coach, the Cardinals then settled down to an e-x-t-r-a inning duel with the Mets.

In the wee hours of the morning, with commissioner Bowie Kuhn bravely sticking it out, a tired McBride got on base. It was the twenty-fifth inning of the latest, longest game ever played, just an inning short of the famous Joe Oeschger-Leon Cadore marathon played between Boston and Brooklyn in 1920.

The Baker took a long lead, drew a throw and—lo!—the ball got away. As if propelled by an outboard motor, but more likely drawn by the strong magnet of that comfortable bed waiting for him at the New York Sheraton, McBride flashed around the bases to score.

Upstairs in the pressbox, Jack Buck phoned a hurry-up Star-of-the-Game standby, Reitz, the man who had kept the game alive, hours and innings ago. Buck proved himself the master of all situations. After an appropriate opening commercial, Jack brought the third baseman to the microphone located downstairs at Shea Stadium.

"And now," said Buck, "the star of the game, Ken Reitz. Congratulations, Ken—and good night!"

It was good night, really, for Bob Gibson, too. The great pitcher no longer could put his weight savagely on the left foot for his emphatic follow-through. He struggled to an 11-13 season. Even so, with the race in its final week in which a playoff with Pittsburgh could be achieved if the Cardinals and Pirates won their final games, the Redbirds led by a run in the eighth inning at Montreal, 2-1.

One on, two out, Mike Jorgensen was the batter, a pretty good lefthanded hitter. Some observers, such as Jack Buck, thought this was a propitious time to bring in Hrabosky. In retrospect, of course, I guess I'd have to agree. But, then, like Red Schoendienst, I never thought of taking out the big money man of the mound. Jorgy tagged him for a staggering two-run homer and an Expo victory, 3-2.

The blow that broke the Redbirds' back reminded me of a story Henry Aaron had told earlier. A young Atlanta player had tagged Gibson for a line drive that was caught. The kid came to the bench, grumbling, about that "lucky stiff."

Aaron, who said little, couldn't resist a comment. "Son," he said, "a couple of years ago you'd have been glad to get a loud foul off Gibson."

For Gussie Busch and his gang, the cruelest blow came a day later. The Cardinals were rained out at Montreal, but Pittsburgh would play Chicago. If the Pirates lost and the Cardinals could win a makeup game, there would be a division-title playoff at Pittsburgh.

Busch and his buddies had gathered in a private room at the Bevo Mill for a few drinks, a bite to eat, a little gin rummy and a telecast of the Pirates-Cubs' showdown. The Cubs got off to a whopping lead and even clung to a run's edge in the ninth when a low-breaking pitch by Rick Reuschel eluded catcher Steve Swisher for a passed ball. Pittsburgh went on to win the game—and the division. There WAS no tomorrow.

Tired and inwardly old, Busch addressed himself to Ben Kerner, former St. Louis Hawks' basketball owner and a personal friend who was on the Cardinals' board of directors. "Drive me home, Hawk," Gussie said quietly. All the way down the Gravois, the old man never said a word.

Gibson's career ended a year later, a sad 3-10 season for a giant of pride and contribution. In an impressive farewell in which Busch gave him a $30,000-plus land cruiser, Gibby said good-bye. He'd be gone, but never forgotten after a 251-174 record for a .591 won-and-lost percentage, seven victories in nine World Series starts, a seventeen-season career earned-run average of 2.91 and 3117 strikeouts in 3885 innings.

His election to the Hall of Fame in January, 1981, the first year he was eligible, was a fitting capstone of a truly unparalleled career.

—And then there was one. Back in 1974, the near-miss season that ended so agonizingly the wrong way, Lou Brock had achieved his finest hour or, rather, season. Hitting .306, he narrowly had missed his fourth 200-hit season, but, more important, he had climbed baseball's base-running Mt. Everest. He'd broken Maury Wills's twelve-year-old record for stolen bases.

The record came on September 10 against Philadelphia with a huge crowd on hand. Off the Phillies' Dick Ruthven, Brock reached base

and the audience chanted, "Go, go, go," which always sounded better than its chorused, "Lou, Lou, Lou." The "Lou" sounded too much like "boo."

With Reggie Smith using a stopwatch as always, figuring pitch-to-catch-to-second base at 3.5 seconds, about a split-second slower than Brock made it with his thirteen strides to baseball immortality, No. "20" with the taped injured hand slid in easily ahead of Bob Boone's throw to shortstop Larry Bowa: 105!

The Cardinals poured out of the dugout as if for a fist fight rather than a celebration. The game was halted fully ten minutes as dignified old Hall of Famer James "Cool Papa" Bell, the black champion of the Negro National League in stolen

bases, came out to make the presentation.

Brock's grateful reception, touching particularly the people with whom he lived most, meaning in the left-field bleachers, brought a roar of approval from the guys and gals for whom Busch had kept a one-buck price until inflation's skyrocket.

The shame of it, other than failure to win the division, was that even though Brock stole 118 bases in 1974, reaching base 255 times on hits and walks, he scored only 105 runs. In the language of the dugout, the lineup simply wasn't "picking him up" enough. Another shame: The Dodgers' Steve Garvey got the MVP award.

But Brock kept picking 'em up and laying 'em down. On August 29, 1977, at San Diego's stadium, get-

Lu-Lu: The grin tells it all after Lou Brock climbed the highest single-season mountain as a baseball base-stealer, accomplishing 105 against Philadelphia on Sept. 11, 1974, at St. Louis. Brock finished the season with 118, en route to a career high that broke Ty Cobb's 893.

ting his second steal of the night, Brock stole second in the seventh inning. It was the 893rd of his career, breaking a record Ty Cobb had set through a twenty-four-year big-league career that ended at age forty-two in 1928.

Brock, getting there in his sixteenth full season at age thirty-eight, still had goals to go. Essentially, though hoping to win one more, the prime target was to reach 3000 hits, the batter's equivalent of 300 pitching victories. But after three successive seasons hitting .300 or better, Brock dropped to .272 in 1977.

His base hits, always in a range from 190 to 200, had dipped to 163 in 1975, 150 in '76 and now 133, and his stolen bases, too, had skidded to thirty-five. Were there enough base hits left in Lou's Japanese-hollowed bat, enough fuel in the tank?

"I want 3000 hits not only because so few players have achieved it," he told me on a bus from St. Petersburg to Bradenton in the spring of 1978 for a game with a Japanese big-league team, "but to prove that I've been a hitter as well as a base-stealer."

Somehow, I think "True-Blue Lou" felt that he had been overlooked. For him as well as for Gibson, the Hall of Fame was an ultimate target.

When Brock dipped to sixty-six hits in only ninety-two games in

Move Over, Stan: Lou Brock gives the Cardinals two successive left fielders with 3000 hits, begging Charley James's pardon, when he seemed to swing easily, yet hit a torrid smash off Cubs' pitcher Dennis Lamp, Aug. 13, 1979.

1978, a season in which former teammate Ken Boyer succeeded Vern Rapp as manager, I felt, inwardly, that Lou had just two chances—little and none. I thought Boyer was whistling Dixie through a graveyard when he indicated that he would give Brock every chance in 1979. Oh, sure, but if Lou got hurt or if the hits came slowly again. . . After all, he was forty now.

Remarkably, Brock held up from start to finish. Given enough rest to stay as strong as possible, contenting himself with twenty-one stolen bases that brought his record total to 938, he played 120 games during which he got 123 hits. He hit .304, his eighth time over that magic mark, and finished his career with 3023 hits.

The big one came at 8:59 on a Monday night, August 13, 1979, as 46,161 erupted in joy at Busch Memorial Stadium. Chicago's Dennis Lamp had narrowly missed turning happiness into horror. He had low-bridged Brock, flooring him with a high-and-tight pitch that drew a gasp from the crowd. Near-miss disaster in a close call to triumph!

Brock always had wanted to "orchestrate my own exodus," as he put it, "and to leave in a blaze of glory." He even fantasized a hit up the middle, he recalled later, but he didn't figure that Lamp would get in the way. Still, considering what had happened to Lou, it was poetic justice plus an injury to the hurler's hand.

Literally, "King Louie of St. Looey" knocked the Chicago pitcher off the mound and out of the game with a torrid line drive that crunched off Lamp's hand and trickled over to third base, where, fielding it, Steve Ontiveros could have salt-peppered-and-eaten it. He had no chance to catch the flying feet that crossed first base and brought down the house as 3000-hit predecessor Stan Musial came on the field for an embrace.

Later, in a fitting sayonara to the star who crowned his own glory, retiring with royal grace, Gussie Busch, himself an old salt, presented Louis Clark Brock with a handsome boat in gratitude. Gussie then gave the happy athlete, who had brought so much joy to so many, what other Cardinal fans and most of the town would have liked to contribute, too: a hug!

Gussie's Gemütlichkeit: Impulsively, as Lou Brock announced his retirement as a player, beer baron-sportsman Gussie Busch gives him an affectionate hug. Later, the Cardinals' chief executive made it more effective with a handsome boat presented at a farewell for the King of St. Lou. Gesundheit, Louie!

18

Over the Rainbow...

A cliché born probably about the time Custer ran into too many Indians was dusted off after the Redbirds chirped into the 1980s, droop-feathered. The Godfather of Grant's Farm, Gussie Busch, got up his dander and a vibrant new man.

When I was knee-high to a line drive off Rogers Hornsby's bat, the bromide was—with good reason—that you "couldn't tell the players without a scorecard."

Back then when the Cardinals first flexed their muscles in the mid-1920s and for several years when I sat in the left-field wing of the old Sportsman's Park grandstand as a Knothole Gang member, the Cardinals played well but with deliberately conceived anonymity.

It was the time of the dime soft drink at the old orchard, as pressbox poets called it. A grilled hot dog, even more poetic if you hadn't lost your sense of smell, cost fifteen cents, an outrageous price then when

great newspapers sold for only two cents, street car rides were three cents for kids and seven for adults. You could watch Douglas Fairbanks, Sr., buckle his swash in silent films for ten cents. Lon Chaney, also the papa and not that bulky son, scared even the adults for two bits. And Tom Mix was paid an astonishing $10,000 a week as a movie cowboy who always got the villain, kissed his horse (Tony) and waved goodbye to the girl.

A ball player, if he got past $10,000 a year, was in the high-rent district, the only place in the ballpark where the cash customers even heard the starting lineup. The batting order was announced through a huge hand-carried megaphone for the benefit of the pressbox upstairs and only the center-cut trade close enough to hear announcer Jim Kelly's funereal bass. If you didn't sit right behind the plate, all you got was a chance to watch Kelly waddle down the foul lines to intone for the benefit of all—the half-buck bleachers and seventy-five cent pavilionites—merely each team's batteries.

In that era the last thing clubowners wanted to do other than pay high wages was to let the guys and gals know who'n heck was playing without the purchase of a five-cent scorecard. Baseball actually hasn't changed much, except that players swipe at fly balls one-handed with giant gloves. (Then, they slung pancake-flat smaller mitts onto the field near their playing positions between innings.) Uniforms, neat polyester rather than heavy flannel, fit now, almost too snugly. And they provide not only the numbers, but even the names of the players.

So the clubowners can't be accused now of the greed that well might be regarded as the players' sudden-wealth stance, because the ball club isn't so desperately eager to sell higher-priced scorecards as it was in that old nickel-scorecard era when uniforms were as blank as a scoreboard when Bob Gibson pitched. Equipment man Butch Yatkeman worked extra innings in 1981 to sew on proper names and numbers.

The reason now you"couldn't tell the players without a scorecard" or an industrious sewing-circle project was that Big Eagle Busch brought in with full authority an aggressive, glib guy they'd nicknamed the "White Rat" back home in New

Athens, Illinois. "The Rat" is so cocky he chased a cat.

Dorrel Norman Elvert "Whitey" Herzog was right down the eighty-one-year-old Busch's Bauernhof, the right partner for Gussie's game room in the mansion at Grant's Farm. He was good and funny, loud and opinionated, smart and aggressive. Busch, obviously impatient for one more pennant, with or without urging from sic-it-to-'em-chief shadows of publicly silent subalterns, went through three managers and into a third general manager before the 1980s were two seasons old!

The disappointing Cardinals really hadn't replaced Bob Gibson or Lou Brock and not Al Hrabosky, either, but Busch or the brewery, at least, was paying top inflated dollar to players now able to sign out under liberalized contract terms. Grand geezer Gussie simply wanted action.

First, Red Schoendienst, a hunting partner of whom Busch was very fond, left temporarily after a fifth-place finish of 72-90 in 1976. For once, general manager Bing Devine hadn't recommended retention of the Redhead, a record twelve-season manager of the Cardinals. Busch wanted a sterner man.

That's My Boy: Which is the way Gussie Busch (background) looks in high pleasure at the colorful, cocky antics of Whitey Herzog, whom he hired as manager in June, 1980.

210

Vern Took the Rap: Vern Rapp had a short, yet relatively not unimpressive stint, as manager of the Cardinals. He seemed to ease off his starchy approach to modern-day athletes at the start of his second season, but a slow playing-field start in 1978 and unwise comment hastened his departure. In this photo at a sports dinner, the Peter Pan of current players, Pete Rose, "Charley Hustle" of Cincinnati and Philadelphia, uses Rapp's back to sign an autograph. Also photographed, Vaughan P. "Bing" Devine, twice longtime Redbird general manager.

He got one in Vern Rapp, a Cleveland High School graduate who had been a catcher in the Cardinals' farm system. Vern had served a long time as a minor-league straw boss at Cincinnati for Bob Howsam, a spit-and-polish disciplinarian. Consequently when Gussie told Vern it was about time to say *Achtung* to the so-called spoiled brats, that was

right down Rapp's South St. Louis alley.

The Cardinals perked up to third place again in 1977. By then, Garry Templeton, a first-round amateur draft choice in 1974, had come in to play shortstop. To repeat, he is perhaps the best player ever developed in the Cardinals' original farm system (which was once the largest). If he can avoid the kinds of injuries that plagued him in 1980, preventing a third 200-hit season and record fourth successive leadership in triples, he could wind up in the Hall of Fame. Meanwhile, the poor kid who struck it rich will be cheered by many kids to whom he gave free seats in Templetown, a choice grandstand area almost parallel to The Wiz's defensive position.

Although in retrospect Rapp's single full season of 83-79, third place in the East, wasn't bad, the manager's relations with his players were strained. As the saying goes, it's easier to fire one man than twenty-five. Still, a factor in the decision to wrap up Rapp well could have been an injudiciuos remark.

Ted Simmons, though no longer a Cardinal, is not the "loser" Rapp tabbed him in an early 1978 confrontation. Simba, the sleepy-eyed, long-haired catcher who hit savagely, wasn't the best by far behind the plate—or the worst, either—but he wasn't a loser. He played hurt too often to endure that label.

The Wiz: My personal nickname for Garry Templeton, the sensational young shortstop. He well might be the best player developed in the Cardinals' far-flung farm system of 60-plus years and, barring injury or the unexpected, a probable Hall of Fame player. With him (left) is George Hendrick, a hard-hitting and solid outfielder.

Stung by Rapp, the hard-nosed Simmons, who is a soft touch for art's sake, was quiet and introspective after attending a piano recital with Jack Buck in Pittsburgh. The curious broadcaster ferreted the facts. Jack got his Irish dander up and aired publicly the cutting comment that helped cut out the commenter, the manager.

The Cardinals brought in Ken Boyer, the former third baseman who, at Devine's suggestion, had gone out of the organization to manage in the minors. Like Schoendienst, Ken was low key, if more articulate. Off to that sorry start in 1978, Boyer couldn't right the Redbirds. They finished fifth, 69-93.

Busch then fired teetotaling general manager Bing Devine, who had given up the presidency of the New York Mets in 1968 to replace Stan Musial, the championship GM he had helped tutor by telephone. Some suggest that Bing hadn't helped himself with the old man when he'd been offered an extensive, long-term contract by Montreal. He broke away from his year-at-a-time understanding with the brewery, obtaining a multi-season contract.

Thus, the Redbirds dropped their long-time general manager, a soft-spoken man who had the guts of a second-story burglar, if not a Whitey Herzog, as a trader. As one prejudiced in behalf of Der Bingle, whom I have known since we cranked out publicity releases for the Cardinals' thirty-club farm system in 1939, I can't drop Devine without this baseball epitaph:

Morally, ethically, Bing has high standing among baseball men who twice named him *The Sporting News'* major league Executive of the Year. He also helped many a baseball man get a job and, in addition, started others. One was the man who succeeded him before the

Bird of All Feathers: Ken Boyer, the former pitcher, center fielder and star third baseman, became captain, coach and—finally—manager of the Cardinals in early 1978. But when the ball club fell back, so did the most famous of the Missouri-born Boyers. Ken moved into the club's scouting and player development program.

Simba Roars: Ted Simmons, seven times a .300 hitter in the Cardinals' uniform and sent to Milwaukee in a provocative trade after the 1980 season, is restrained by Keith Hernandez as the catcher has it out with umpire Terry Tata. As always, the ump had the last word. Ted was thrown out of the game.

1979 season. At New York, he also first recognized the front-office potential as well as field talent of Whitey Herzog, who would have been his managerial nomination behind Schoendienst if Whitey then hadn't been skipper at Kansas City.

John Claiborne, plucked by Devine off the Washington University campus as a coach, worked himself up through the ranks with the Cardinals and, at Bing's suggestion, with the Oakland Athletics and then the Boston Red Sox. His credentials were good and his first season as St. Louis general manager, too.

Although Lou Brock was inspirational in Boyer's first full season with a classy .304 farewell, the club's most productive man in a promising third-place season of 86-76 was the young first baseman, Keith Hernandez. Although he might have lacked Stan Musial's team-man attitude or even earned Herzog's displeasure later by not hitting properly behind the runner on occasion, he was an extremely skilled craftsman. He fulfilled optimistic forecasts made by observers Bob Kennedy and Harry Walker about him. They were so optimistic that Devine defied practice and tradition to give a $30,000 bonus to a kid who had been drafted late and lightly.

Hernandez overcame the kiss of death—"another Stan Musial," they'd said—and hit a league-leading .344 in 1979, driving in 105 runs. His base-running might be timid at times, but he is spectacular with a glove. With almost Solomon-like wisdom, voting members of the Baseball Writers' Association of

H'mm, In or Out?: Actually, as shown here, John Claiborne (right) replaces Bing Devine as senior executive vice-president and general manager of the Cardinals at a ballpark press conference in September, 1978. Actually, the good-looking young guy is pretty sober-looking. Big Eagle Gussie Busch, actually listening intently, looks as if he's unhappy with his choice.

Fit to Be Tied: Keith Hernandez, Cardinals' collar-ad first baseman, meets at the New York baseball writers' dinner with Willie Stargell after the young Redbird and the old Pittsburgh Pirate shared the National League's Most Valuable Player award in 1979.

America declared a tie for the Most Valuable Player award. Keith shared the honor with Pittsburgh's well-liked dean, Wilver "Pops" Stargell.

Despite a bullpen weakness that would become even more glaring when Mark Littell went out with an injury, the outlook for Busch was fair and warmer for the 1980s. After all, Pete Vuckovich, a big Serbian, had pitched effectively in a 15-10 season. Rookie John Fulgham, called up in mid-season, posted a 10-6 record. Silvio Martinez, one of Devine's late acquisitions like out-fielder George Hendrick, not only had a 15-8 season; he had pitched a number of low-hit games, the kind Bob Gibson threw just before he stepped into pitching greatness.

Althought Bob Forsch, author of the Cardinals' first no-hit game at home in more than a half-century (Jesse Haines, 1924), had been off-form, he had suffered enough low-run defeats that Claiborne dealt from what he regarded as pitching depth.

John Denny was talented with a change-up and, rarely seen any longer, a good pickoff move. He took his temper and weak ankles to Cleveland along with a sizable, fast-moving outfielder who hit softly, Jerry Mumphrey. In return, the Redbirds apparently got what long had been needed, a righthanded-hitting outfielder with speed and power, Bobby Bonds.

If Bonds did only what was normal, that is, hit around .270 and maybe approximate his ability as one of the few ever able to hit thirty homers and to steal thirty bases a season— But he hurt his wrist and, perhaps older than his years, the thirty-four-year-old athlete was a bustout. Ultimately, Herzog couldn't give him away. Whitey released him.

Still, Claiborne's Labor Day dismissal in a disastrous fourth-place season of 74-88 despite six .300 hit-ters, was even more surprising than

the busting out of Boyer in June. After all, Herzog was available now, unemployed, and managers usually got hired only to be fired. But general managers? Would a wary GM now offer to trade the Clydesdales to avoid the guillotine?

Hopefully, not. In Claiborne's case, apparently, the handsome young man was hurt more by long-term, high-salaried contracts given to such spearcarriers as Darold Knowles, Bernie Carbo, Steve Swisher and Mike Phillips than by the ill-fated Bonds deal. And he'd looked presumably too far into the

The No-No Boys: First brothers ever to pitch major league no-hitters were the Cardinals' Bob Forsch (left) and Houston's Ken Forsch. The Redbird's effort in 1978 against Philadelphia at St. Louis was the first in St. Louis by a Cardinals' pitcher since Jesse Haines's at old Sportsman's Park in 1924.

club's future, if not his own, when he didn't take advantage of the Cubs' contractual dissatisfaction with the A-1 relief pitcher, Bruce Sutter. For Terry Kennedy, Leon Durham and say, Tommy Herr, no matter how promising they might be, Claiborne might have saved his job.

The GM job went to, of all people, the manager. In a throwback to the era of Branch Rickey, meaning young B.R. and not the old Mahatma, Busch tapped the manager who had done pretty well on the field here. (He'd won three division titles at Kansas City.) Whitey also helped himself, being witty, articulate and outspoken. One young Dutchman, who liked to kid that his small nearby home-town, New Athens, Illinois, had more saloons than grocery stores, knew himself and the older German well enough to tell the Big Eagle what he thought had to be done and not necessarily what most pleased the boss.

John Fulgham and Silvio Martinez had been hurt and would be wisely figured only as future question marks. Durable Pete Vuckovich ailed at times, too, and he or his agent itched to force the payroll higher. Even Ken Oberkfell, the big kid from the East Side who came on the club and ran Mike "Rocky" Tyson right off the team to Chicago by hitting .301 in 1979, was sidelined a good part of the season, requiring knee surgery.

Obie came back, wearing a brace, like an old Oriole, as they used to say when Cy Young was young and John McGraw, too. He would have fit another traditional expression of the Cardinals: lean (if not physically), hungry—and winners.

The final straw, of course, was the wrist-and-hand injuries that took the gifted Templeton out of the lineup twice. The Wiz or, as the boys back home called him, "Jump Steady," was the kind of leadoff whirlwind around whom Herzog wanted to build a lineup. Busch Memorial Stadium, a big park, needed speed and defense. How could Herzog do it with such a rally-clogging slowpoke on the bases as Ken Reitz?

You know, I honestly thought he planned early to trade matinee idol Hernandez, which would have been controversial. Still, it was provocative enough to deal Ted Simmons in a week even dizzier than the eye-popping past. Remember when Sam Breadon shocked everyone by dealing Rogers Hornsby for Frank Frisch and when Branch Rickey honestly told the Cubs' Phil Wrigley that Dizzy Dean was damaged goods in 1938? That deal got the Cards immediate help in two pitchers, Curt Davis and Clyde Shoun, and $185,000 of whopping-sized depression dollars.

Not even Bing Devine's Ernie Broglio-for-Lou Whosis (Brock) trade to Chicago at the dealing deadline in 1964 came close to what transpired as Herzog:

(1) Signed catcher Darrell Porter as a $700,000-a-year free-agent catcher from Kansas City; (2) dealt promising kid catcher Terry Kennedy, reserve infielder Mike Phillips, catcher Steve Swisher and young pitchers John Urrea, John Littlefield, Kim Seaman and Al Olmsted to San Diego for pitcher Rollie Fingers, first baseman-catcher Gene Tenace, pitcher Bob Shirley and minor-league catcher Bob Geren; (3) traded first baseman-outfielder Leon Durham, third baseman Ken Reitz and third baseman-outfielder Ty Waller to the

Chicago Cubs for pitcher Bruce Sutter, and (4) swapped catcher Ted Simmons and pitchers Vuckovich and Fingers to Milwaukee for outfielder Sixto Lezcano, pitchers Larry Sorensen and Dave LaPoint and outfielder Dave Green.

Phew! Then he rested.

Herzog, once a journeyman outfielder who spent eight years as an American Leaguer, coached briefly with Casey Stengel for the New York Mets before moving into the front office there and also launching a major league managerial career. He even speaks and gestures with many of Stengel's mannerisms, meaning colorfully.

But nothing up to improving the caliber of the Cardinals could be so colorful as the deals by which he sought to strengthen the Cardinals' woefully weak bullpen. Recently, Sutter had been the National League's best relief pitcher, maybe the best ever. He threw a split finger fast ball that looked like a fork ball held crookedly. Whitey was so smitten with Sutter that he didn't even keep Fingers, who had a longer reputation if one not quite so brilliant. Like Vuckovich, Rollie sought a heist-high salary or he'd go elsewhere in a year.

By dealing Reitz, Herzog planned to move Oberkfell to third base and use an even nimbler second baseman, Herr, hopeful he would hit enough. Although the left edge of the infield defense might lose something without Reitz, highly clever with a glove, the feeling was that Oberkfell would make the long throw powerfully.

Defense with speed, to repeat, are Herzog's main concerns, as they were Branch Rickey's. In Shirley, a lefthander, he had obtained a starting pitcher who might win more, hopefully, with a better club. The hope, too, was that Sorensen might offset Vuckovich. And even though Lezcano might hit closer in the National League to the .229 of a year ago than the .321 the previous season, his outfielding skills, running speed and throwing arm were expected to improve left field.

So with Green regarded, like the departed Durham, as a FUTURE star and LaPoint as probably a pitcher with great potential, the immediate question was this:

Would Porter, who battled back after overcoming an alcoholic-drug problem, hit and catch with the skilled and aggressive authority Herzog had known in the American League? In other words, would the rehabilitated lefthanded batter be good enough all-round to offset the switch-hitting ability of Simmons?

Simba asked to be traded rather than take the embarrassment of trying to play first base in the territory of Hernandez. A capable agent, typifying a new source of wonder, amazement and money in baseball, suggested that the Cardinals and Milwaukee make the move worth Ted's while with, oh, how about $750,000? After all, hadn't the Cardinals and Cubs kicked in $75,000 each to Reitz? Yeah, but Kenny really didn't want to leave St. Louis.

Whitey Herzog sounded more like Gussie Busch than Branch Rickey when Milwaukee asked him to cooperate financially for Simmons. The White Rat liked Simba, but not THAT much.

"Not one bleeping cent," said Herzog. Milwaukee picked up the check.

Obviously, now, no one has to chorus "Yes, Mr. Rickey," the order of the day when B. R. ran the

"O" for Oberkfell and Oriole: The "old Oriole" is a high tribute to a player who hung tough. That would fit Ken Oberkfell. Being hurt again early in 1982 affected his .300 batting style; but Obie, who earlier underwent knee surgery, moved to third base to make room for Tommy Herr, then won the second game of the playoff with Atlanta with a ninth-inning hit.

A Bearded Profit: Bruce Sutter, acquired by the Cardinals in Whitey Herzog's big bid for respectability, plugged the Redbirds' biggest leak in the beechwood dike—the bullpen. Sutter, featuring a split-fingered fast ball, led the National League in saves with twenty-five in 1981 and with thirty-nine in '82. A game-saver, too, in the championship series and World Series.

show, but the Redbirds still will have to rely on the streamlined version of Mr. Rickey's pet, the farm system. Or get from hyperthyroid Herzog the vigorous good fortune Bing Devine achieved in giving up pitcher Eric Rasmussen to San Diego in early 1978 for an outfielder, George Hendrick, whose bat speaks much more loudly for the Cardinals than "Silent George" did.

Hendrick and comrades came agonizingly close in 1981, a hyphenated season that was both good and frustrating. Breaking fast after a stumbling spring-training start (9-17), the Cards had a rousing April. They won eight in a row early, despite new catcher Darrell Porter's arm ailment. Second baseman Tommy Herr led the charge and Bruce Sutter saved game after game.

Unfortunately, a slump caught the Cardinals just before the June 11 player strike. The four division leaders then, including Philadelphia, were rewarded ersatz honors by Bowie Kuhn.

The Birdies, who were 30-20 the first half, led most of the second half, but they floundered after two cheek-for-jowl tests against Montreal, which finished one-half game ahead.

Would the near-miss ball club be able in 1982 to gain that long-elusive thirteenth pennant? The bookies bet they would not, favoring the Expos and the Phillies. They figured, after all, that Herzog had lost a potential Hall of Fame player.

Templeton, the National League's answer to Milwaukee's Robin Yount at shortstop, all-round, had become a pouting player whose personal problems crescendoed in a playing-field crisis. Tempy wanted out.

Herzog worked toward that goal, though his feet itched for golf

spikes, fishermen's boots, or hunting hikers. Eventually, Whitey convinced big boss Busch that he wanted to give up the general manager's job. His assistant, Joe McDonald, a one-time Brooklyn bat-boy and former general manager of the New York Mets, became GM.

First, though, Herzog dealt to sharpen even more the championship speed and defense that teamed with topflight relief pitching as the title mix in 1982.

Whitey slipped Philadelphia a mickey. After the Phillies obtained catcher Bo Diaz from Cleveland for outfielder Lonnie Smith, Herzog swapped pitchers Martinez and Sorensen to the Indians for Smith. The Phils were surprised. They wouldn't have wanted to trade with a division rival.

Next, Lezcano, unable to shake off a wrist injury suffered with the Brewers, was swapped to San Diego for pitcher Steve Mura. Mura, a steady loser with the lowly Padres, gave the Cardinals a mid-season lift in '82 before control problems confined him to the doghouse.

Uneventfully, it seemed then after an apparently ho-hum trade, Whitey swapped seldom-seen southpaw Bob Sykes to the Yankees for a minor-league kid the Yanks had passed over like cold mashed potatoes. His name was Willie McGee.

Finally, Herzog sent Templeton back to the West Coast, but not to the '81 champion L.A. Dodgers. He shipped Tempy to San Diego for Ozzie Smith.

Ozzie couldn't hit with Templeton, basically, but the young, slight, bearded genius with a glove was more

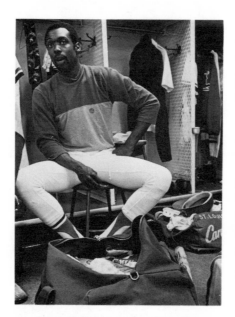

His Bat Speaks Louder: George Hendrick, rangy righthanded-hitting outfielder, still is a key performer. Hendrick, club's leading home-run hitter, made a key throw in seventh game of World Series and drove in deciding run. Silent George doesn't say much for publication, but he's a team man whose bat speaks for him, too.

Catalyst's Kid: Aptly, they called Lonnie Smith the offensive "catalyst" of the Cardinals, a result of his batting and base-running after Whitey Herzog pickpocketed him from Philadelphia in a three-way trade with Cleveland. Here, the rapid and relaxed Redbird left fielder has fun with two-year-old son Tramaine at the Cards' annual summer "game" with their youngsters.

spectacular afield and steadier, too. He became probably the Redbirds' finest-fielding shortstop ever, personable and a winner.

So the Cardinals had the Cough-Drop Kids, the unrelated Smiths. Lonnie and Ozzie combined with Sutter as the top three contributors to the Cardinals' cause in a year in which Herzog used his twenty-five-man team wisely and well.

Still, the outlook would have been as dark as Mudville the day mighty Casey struck out if it had been projected in April not only that the Cardinals would finish last in the majors in home runs but also that only Lonnie Smith would hit .300. Worse, two of the team's five pre-season pitching starters, Andy Rincon and John Martin, would both go

back to the bushes. Martin returned for only limited help.

Opening night at Houston, walloping Nolan Ryan, the strikeout king of no-hit fame, 14-3, Darrell Porter homered and the Cardinals hammered seven doubles. Although the Cardinals would make much use of "Whitey Ball"—the stolen base, the squeeze bunt, etc.—they hit plenty of "gappers," i.e., doubles and triples in the outfield slots.

The first-game winner, Bob Forsch, exceeded any season since his twenty-game year in 1977. Another pitcher, a big, muscular, bare-armed righthander obtained from Houston near the trading deadline a year earlier—Joaquin Andujar—lost his first start, a low-score defeat. The 1-0 game symbolized the big, tough Dominican's early-season efforts, but he went to a season even more im-

pressive than Forsch's 15-9.

Andujar finished 15-10, but, as Herzog said, with any luck he could have won about twenty-three. The flaming fast ball produced an earned-run average (2.47) second only to Montreal's Steve Rogers. Joaquin was unhittable down the stretch, winning his last seven starts and also three more in postseason play.

As a result, with husky young righthander John Stuper coming up to replace Rincon, proving himself a winner of big games rather than a big-game winner, the pitching question that had loomed large over the winter and larger in spring training faded in the magic mist of victory.

LaPoint, a lefthander obtained from Milwaukee in the big block-buster deal the year before, developed with the season, too. Like Stuper, he

Poetry in Motion: Ozzie Smith makes the cliche come alive with his grace at shortstop. The personable player obtained from San Diego for discontented Garry Templeton was both flashy and steady, sure-handed and spectacular. "Oz-zie" became a ballpark battle cry.

"S" for Superman, Superstars: Bruce Sutter (left) primarily put the Cardinals in the 1982 playoffs, and Darrell Porter kept them in the championship series and through the World Series. Porter, winning the Most Valuable Player award in both series, was given a sports car. The guy looks more like Clark Kent, i.e., Superman, than the actor (Christopher Reeve) who played the movie role.

218

pitched well in October limelight. Further, Dave Green, an outfielder pried previously from the Brewers, won his way onto the roster at St. Petersburg.

When the Cardinals opened their home season in an 11-7 loss to Pittsburgh, Lonnie Smith hit a grand-slam homer. The new man would prove a junior-grade Lou Brock at bat and on the bases, but the Cardinals had lost three straight. H'mm, same old pokey start.

But the Redbirds then ripped off twelve straight victories, the longest string since the Gas House Gang set the club record with fourteen in 1935. The Cards were not exactly in the catbird seat, but they meowed all season. They never trailed by more than three games and usually led the

National League East.

Fate, even when trying to frown on the Birdies, broke out laughing. Green, playing well as the fourth outfielder, was hurt in early May, pulling a hamstring muscle in a collision at first base. Herzog beckoned to Louisville for that kid acquired from the Yankees, McGee. Willie, a scared-rabbit switch-hitter, began to play like a more prominent player with the same first name (Mays).

The Cardinals were 14-7 in April, 17-11 in May and then dipped to 12-16 in June only because Sutter slumped briefly as the majors' A-1 game-saver. By then, Super Stuper, the boy journalist, had picked up Rincon's fallen baton.

Although essentially a win-one, lose-one ball club, the Cardinals took six in a row in July, a 15-10 month.

They were 17-12 in August, winning in the darndest ways. Why, they even got away with one when Glenn Brummer, built like a buffalo, stole home—with two out and two strikes on the batter!

Brummer, third-string catcher, helped when Gene Tenace, like forty-three-year-old Jim Kaat a title-wise old pro, was hurt after hitting hard early in Porter's struggling start. Broken bones sidelined Ken Oberkfell early, too. Soon and late, Tom Herr looked like the fife player in the Spirit of '76, but the trussed-up second baseman was a spirit of '82. Mustachioed Mike Ramsey proved a steady replacement for Herr when Tommy hurt the worst.

Surprisingly, Ramsey was picture perfect in Ozzie Smith's place in

A Turning Point: Good and bad, the moment when Dave Green pulled a hamstring muscle in a collision at first base in early May. Green, promising twenty-one-year-old outfielder from Nicaragua, hobbled off the field, aided by coaches Hal Lanier (8) and Chuck Hiller (4). With Green hurt, manager Herzog beckoned to Louisville for a "temporary" replacement who wasn't temporary—Willie McGee!

Willie the Winner: Willie McGee, almost bashful even in accepting manager Whitey Herzog's congratulations at the left, was an all-around asset as center fielder and in the '82 playoffs and Series, too. Here, behind the twenty-three-year-old rookie shaking hands with Herzog, are (from the left), coach Hub Kittle, catcher Darrell Porter, infielder Mike Ramsey, pitcher John Stuper, and offering a hand to Kittle, catcher Glenn Brummer.

September. Loss of Oz-zie was s-o-o critical because, as the field foreman put it, the shortstop had proved that if a guy prevented 100 runs, he didn't have to come close to knocking in 100.

Alarmingly, September 13 at Philadelphia, the Cardinals fell out of first place, shut out by nemesis Steve Carlton, 2-0. Would those near-miss moments of 1971, '73, '74, and '81 haunt them?

Next night, replacing Stuper in a white-knuckle duel, Sutter made THE pitch of the season. Bases loaded, one out, King Bruce, the "bearded profit," faced slugger Mike Schmidt. He induced the big guy to tap back to the box for a home-to-first double play.

The tense 2-0 triumph put the Cardinals back into the lead to stay. Although their bats were cold, their arms were hot. They ripped off eight straight victories, twelve out of fifteen, and their pitchers allowed only ten runs in a ten-day period. They pulled away rapidly. A five-game sweep at New York, where they had faltered a year before, set up the September showdown.

First, typically recoiling into a gun-slinger's follow-through and then cockily pointing a pistol-like finger at batters he conquered, Andujar beat favorite-cousin Montreal for the eleventh time in twelve decisions. Forsch followed there with a 1-0 victory. At home, Andujar turned back the Phillies for his sixth straight victory, 4-1.

A pennant was only flying-Mercury-feet away. On September 27 at Montreal, McGee hit an inside-the-park homer for three runs. Sutter came in with the heat on and retired hard-hitting Gary Carter on a grounder that put the Go-Go Guys six and a half up with only five to play. Unbeatable arithmetic. Then—and then only—they endured a losing

Bang! Bang! Joaquin Andujar, as color-ful as he is capable, has a habit of "shooting" down hitters with a cocked-finger pistol after blazing a third strike past them. "One tough Dominican," as Andujar likes to be called, is a pretty tough hombre, all right. He not only pitched bare-armed all summer, but even in the autumn chill of the World Series he wore no sweatshirt under his polyester uniform jersey.

The Great Dane: Dane Iorg (19), batting star of the World Series as the Cardinals' designated hitter, is greeted here by grinning Tommy Herr, the Cardinals' defensively brilliant second baseman, who ought to be wincing from all his injuries. Smiling at the extreme right is first-base standout Keith Hernandez.

streak as long as four games.

Atlanta—and the monsoons—paid an unusual visit to St. Louis for the city's first experience with the championship series. Rain washed out the opener with the Braves' veteran knuckleball artist, Phil Niekro, holding a fourth-inning lead, 1-0. A night later, pitching a three-hitter that was better and more significant than his no-hitter, Forsch put the Cards in front, 7-1.

Behind Stuper, Sutter, and associates in the second official game, the Cardinals won in the ninth, 4-3. With first base open, pitcher Gene Garber forgot the odds. Given a choice, he pitched to Oberkfell. Obie, batting .600 off the reliever, singled in the winning run.

So when McGee hit Rick Camp with a three-run triple and later homered in the third game, Andujar needed only a perfect seven-out aid by Sutter for a 6-2 wipeout at Atlanta to end the best-of-five series in three.

The World Series began with a letdown. Milwaukee third baseman Paul Molitor led the Redbirds' humiliation with a Series record five straight hits, two more than the Cardinals got all night off lefty Mike Caldwell. Score: 10-0.

The second game prospects were not good, either, when young Stuper trailed veteran Don Sutton into the sixth inning, 4-2. Porter, staking an MVP bid early, doubled in the tying runs. Giant reliever Pete Ladd walked in the winning run in the eighth. Redbirds 5, Brewers 4.

The Series moved to Sudsville for the first time since 1958 when the Braves lived there. In Game No. 3 the Brewers simply could not handle McGee. Shy-guy Willie homered twice off Vuckovich, then prevented two Milwaukee runs with a leaping

catch. But the 6-2 St. Louis victory was sobering. Andujar was carried off after he was hit on the right knee by Ted Simmons's hot shot in the seventh inning.

The Redbird outlook soon became as black as the crepe ribbons they wore on their uniform sleeves in tribute to the club's former third-base star, captain, coach, and manager, Ken Boyer, who had died of cancer in early September. They led the Braves in the seventh inning, 5-1. LaPoint dropped a throw at first base, opening the floodgates for six Milwaukee runs. To avoid their 7-5 loss, the Cards would have needed another Series grand-slam homer by Boyer.

Now the outlook became as dark as the inside of Porter's catcher's mitt. Yount had his second four-hit game of the Series, spearheading a staggering Caldwell's second Series victory over Forsch, 6-4.

Milwaukee needed just o-n-e more, but it rained on their parade back in St. Louis. After a two-and-a-half-hour delay, the Cardinals clobbered the Brewers, 13-1. Hernandez homered and drove in four runs. Porter homered also. Super-sub Dane Iorg, getting a National League taste of the American's designated-hitting delicacy, hit two doubles and a triple. The Great Dane batted .530 in five games.

Winning pitcher John Stuper introduced the visiting press to the "John Cosell Show," the clubhouse hijinks in which the rookie is the "broadcast" star over an empty bottle of Bud. Ramsey, Brummer, and Jeff Lahti are his funny foils. They could not stop 'em now, meaning the athletes' ad libs off the field or the ball players' brilliance on it.

Now the Redbirds fell back on their old seventh-game black magic by which they had won six of seven final games in World Series. Andujar, coming back off his knee injury,

led early over Vuckovich, 1-0, thanks partly to a clutch throw from right field by Hendrick, flagging down Yount in a scoring threat at third base. But Andujar gummed up a perfect bunt as part of a two-run first half of a long, exciting, and unforgettable sixth inning.

Here, the Cardinals gave 'em the old razzle-dazzle. Ozzie Smith singled with one out. The capacity crowd roared in anticipation. Lonnie Smith doubled over third base. The tying runs were on. Herzog began with rival manager Harvey Kuenn the kind of flim-flam at which the White Rat seldom loses.

Lefty Bob McClure relieved Vuckovich. Tenace batted for Oberkfell and walked, filling the bases. Hernandez, a late bloomer with eight RBIs in the last three games, singled to right-center, tying the score. Hendrick reached out and slashed a go-ahead single to right.

With chorused cries of "Bruce! Bruce!" filling the air, Sutter strode in, back erect. "No. 42" would wipe the suds off the Brewers. He did, 6-3, upholstered by two more runs.

Whitey's Go-Go Guys, beating the wizard of odds, had gone over the rainbow to find the world championship, the Cardinals' ninth. And amid the clamor of the foot-stomping song "Celebration," the 1982 good-luck version of the Gas House Gang's "We're in the Money" and the St. Louis Swifties' "Pass the Biscuits, Mirandy," Darrell Porter put it best. In a twangy Ozarks drawl, Porter, the man who got out of life's pits to become the World Series hero, yelled happily:

"Hoo-ee, I been to two county fairs and a goat roast—and I ain't never seen nothin' like this."

As Dizzy Dean would amen, "Me neither, podnuh."

The End of the Beginning: When Lonnie Smith (27) hit a grand-slam home run his first home game with the Cardinals, opening day, 1982 (April 10), the four-run smash didn't win the game, but it typified the resilience of the championship-bound Redbirds. From the left, the "other" Smith, unrelated Ozzie, behind him Orlando Sanchez, Keith Hernandez (37), and pinch-hitting handyman Steve Braun (26).

WHERE THEY FINISHED

Year	Position	Won	Lost	Pct.	Attendance	Manager
1900	5+	65	75	.464		Oliver Tebeau & Louis Heilbroner
1901	4	76	64	.543	379,988	Patsy Donovan
1902	6	56	78	.418	226,417	Patsy Donovan
1903	8	43	94	.314	263,538	Patsy Donovan
1904	5	75	79	.487	386,750	Charles "Kid" Nichols
1905	6	58	96	.377	292,800	Nichols, Jimmy Burke, Matthew Robison
1906	7	52	98	.347	283,770	John J. McCloskey
1907	8	52	101	.340	185,377	John J. McCloskey
1908	8	49	105	.318	205,129	John J. McCloskey
1909	7	54	98	.355	299,982	Roger Bresnahan
1910	7	63	90	.412	363,624	Roger Bresnahan
1911	5	75	74	.503	447,768	Roger Bresnahan
1912	6	63	90	.412	241,759	Roger Bresnahan
1913	8	51	99	.340	203,531	Miller Huggins
1914	3	81	72	.529	346,025	Miller Huggins
1915	6	72	81	.471	252,657	Miller Huggins
1916	7+	60	93	.392	224,308	Miller Huggins
1917	3	82	70	.539	301,948	Miller Huggins
1918	8	51	78	.395	110,596	Jack Hendricks
1919	7	54	83	.394	173,604	Branch Rickey
1920	5	75	79	.487	325,845	Branch Rickey
1921	3	87	66	.569	384,790	Branch Rickey
1922	3+	85	69	.552	536,343	Branch Rickey
1923	5	79	74	.516	338,548	Branch Rickey
1924	6	65	89	.422	272,884	Branch Rickey
1925	4	77	76	.503	405,297	Rickey & Rogers Hornsby
1926	1*	89	65	.578	81,575	Rogers Hornsby
1927	2	92	61	.601	763,615	Bob O'Farrell
1928	1	95	59	.617	778,147	Bill McKechnie
1929	4	78	74	.513	410,921	McKechnie & Billy Southworth
1930	1	92	62	.597	519,647	Gabby Street
1931	1*	101	53	.656	623,960	Gabby Street
1932	6+	72	82	.468	290,370	Gabby Street
1933	5	82	71	.536	268,404	Street & Frank Frisch
1934	1*	95	58	.621	334,863	Frank Frisch
1935	2	96	58	.623	517,805	Frank Frisch
1936	2+	87	67	.565	457,925	Frank Frisch
1937	4	81	73	.526	443,039	Frank Frisch
1938	6	71	80	.470	295,229	Frisch & Mike Gonzales
1939	2	92	61	.601	410,778	Ray Blades
1940	3	84	69	.549	331,899	Blades, Gonzales & Billy Southworth
1941	2	97	56	.634	642,496	Billy Southworth
1942	1*	106	48	.688	571,626	Billy Southworth
1943	1	105	49	.682	535,014	Billy Southworth
1944	1*	105	49	.682	486,751	Billy Southworth
1945	2	95	59	.617	594,180	Billy Southworth
1946	1*	98	58	.628	1,062,553	Eddie Dyer
1947	2	89	65	.578	1,248,013	Eddie Dyer
1948	2	85	69	.552	1,111,454	Eddie Dyer
1949	2	96	58	.623	1,430,676	Eddie Dyer
1950	5	78	75	.519	1,093,199	Eddie Dyer
1951	3	81	73	.526	1,013,429	Marty Marion
1952	3	88	66	.571	913,313	Eddie Stanky
1953	3+	83	71	.539	880,242	Eddie Stanky
1954	6	72	82	.468	1,039,698	Eddie Stanky